MW01180776

Speeches of War and Peace

Speeches of War and Peace

Larry Buttrose

For: Jane Blanks, the Carringtonians,
Eamon D'Arcy, Dwight David, Ruth Deleon,
Barbara Drake, Michael Duggan, Wendy Frost,
Leonie Hellmers, Peter Huck, Stephen Measday,
Marco Moretti, Louise O'Halloran, Creed O'Hanlon,
Merce Redon, Mark Trevorrow and John Webber –
friends in every meaning of the word.

Contents

Acknowledgements

My sincere thanks to Cheryl Tornquist for her skilled and resourceful research. Thanks also to Liz Lewis and Fernando Barrenechea, Robbie Park, my agent Rick Raftos, Fiona Schultz, Diane Jardine and all at New Holland Publishers—and my darling Belle, who kindly listened.

Introduction

The hour of departure has arrived and we go our ways; I to die, and you to live. Which is better? Only God knows. – *Socrates, Ancient Greek Philosopher (470–399BCE)*

According to Plato's *Apology*, Socrates spoke these words as he was sentenced to death after being convicted of both refusing to recognize the gods of the state and corrupting the young people of Athens. Socrates was a philosopher of the streets, who went barefoot and humbly clad among the people, asking simple yet fundamental questions about life and the way in which humankind chooses to live it.

As the death sentence was passed in court, and the people cried out in disbelief, Socrates spoke out, thus: 'You can assure yourselves of this … if you put me to death, you will not be doing greater injury to me than yourselves.'

Socrates was pointing to the futility of violence as a means of resolving disputes and answering questions. Since then, it is a theme that has been repeatedly taken up and debated by the many commentators who have challenged authority—with ideas rather than with weapons.

The words of Socrates would be echoed almost exactly two millennia later by another philosopher, the Italian Giordano Bruno (1548–1600). Found guilty by the Inquisition and ordered by the Pope to be burned alive at the stake, Bruno proclaimed: 'Perhaps you, my judges, pronounce this sentence against me with greater fear than I receive it.' In so doing, he made plain his belief that the Catholic Church was reacting with violence bred by fear and, as in the case of Socrates, it was a fear of ideas.

Around the same time that Socrates lived, another philosopher, Buddha (Prince Siddartha Gautama, c.563–483BCE), was articulating ideas in India that also showed his opposition to violence. Buddha believed that the world and all its allurements were the source of human woe, and that humankind could not find contentment while it sought fulfilment through worldly things. Instead, it would be rendered unhappy through disappointment and conflict.

Five centuries later, in Roman-occupied Palestine, a young man called Jeshua ben Joseph, or Jesus Christ (c.6BCE–c.30CE) as we know him today, preached the virtues of non-violence to his followers, urging them to turn the other cheek rather than fight, and even to show compassion for their adversaries—to 'love thine enemy'.

But such voices were few and far between. Much of the ancient history of humanity (as is the case in modern history), is written in blood in the accounts of battles and sieges, military victories and defeats. Some readers complain that all conventional history is portrayed as little more than a series of wars and battles and the dates upon which they were fought.

Accounts of ancient conflicts, real and legendary, have come down to us in the pages of literature, from the Bible to the *Bhagavad Gita*, from the hieroglyphs of the Ancient Egyptians to Homer's great Greek epic poem, the *Iliad*.

In the *Iliad*, Homer, writing in the 8th or 9th century BCE, revealed how love for one woman, Helen, led to the launching of a fleet against Troy, thereby sealing the fate of both the city and its people.

As the Elizabethan dramatist Christopher Marlowe (1564–93) wrote centuries later in *Doctor Faustus*:

Was this the face that launch'd a thousand ships
And burnt the topless towers of Ilium?
Sweet Helen, make me immortal with a kiss.

But the men of legend who rowed their ships toward Troy and raised their swords against it had never beheld Helen of Troy's face. They had only heard about Troy—and more tellingly, its riches—through the power of words. Therefore, arguably, it was not Helen's face that launched those one thousand ships: it was the spoken word.

At the Council of Clermont in France in the year 1095, Pope Urban II (1042–99) uttered a rallying cry that rang to the very ends of Christendom. It was a call to arms, to war, and initiated the First Crusade against Islam. The words that he spoke at that Council are worth revisiting now:

'You must hasten to carry aid to your brethren dwelling in the East, who need your help for which they have often entreated. For the Turks, a Persian people, have attacked them, as many of you already know, and have advanced as far into Roman territory as that part of the Mediterranean which is called the Arm of Saint George. They have seized more and more lands of the Christians, have already defeated them in seven times as many battles, killed or captured many people, have destroyed churches and have devastated the kingdom of God... Oh what a disgrace if a race so despicable, degenerate, and enslaved by demons should thus overcome a people endowed with faith in Almighty God and resplendent in the name of Christ! Oh what reproaches will be charged against you by the Lord Himself if you have not helped those who are counted like yourselves of the Christian faith! Let those... who are accustomed to wantonly wage private war against the faithful march upon the infidels in a war which should be begun now and be finished in victory. Let those who have long been robbers now be soldiers of Christ. Let those who once fought against brothers and relatives now rightfully fight against the barbarians. Let those who have been hirelings for a few pieces of silver now attain eternal reward.'

As we see in this speech, it is not only Muslims who have spoken of holy war, and it is not only presidents who have sent men to fight and die in the distant battlefields of the East. For most of human history, down to the present day, the speeches of leaders have invoked some higher purpose—be it a god or a set of beliefs—to spur men to leave behind their loved ones and home and hearth to march off to war.

For the most part such flights of oratory have simply masked the usual reasons for armed conflict: the gaining of territory, resources or economic advantage. Some of those who went to war may have recognized this, just as some of the soldiers dispatched to invade Iraq in 2003 would have known that any higher purpose was most probably political nonsense, and that the war was really about oil and strategic advantage.

Men march off anyway, often because the oratory of their leaders has convinced them to do so. It acts in the same way on their families and friends, who further encourage them to go and fight. Thus, do they answer the call of what they feel is their duty. But this is also the case with the oratory of leaders of a different kind—the thinkers, humanists, religious leaders and others, who argue the case against warfare. They, too, have been able to invoke a higher purpose: they exhort followers to acts of social disobedience and non-violent opposition to authority, which those individuals would not have undertaken without the persuasive oratorical power of their leaders.

The Indian nationalist movement of the first half of the 20th century and the American Civil Rights Movement of the 1960s were galvanised by the words of Mahatma Gandhi (1869–1958) and Jawaharlal Nehru (1889–1964) in India, and Dr Martin Luther King, Jr (1929–1968), in the United States respectively. Those movements would, invariably, have occurred anyway, but the passion of those three men, as expressed in the speeches that they made, ensured that both movements had the necessary impetus to take effective and successful action when they did—through essentially non-violent means.

Unfortunately, though, war has always been more active in the human imagination than peace. We use terms like victory, glory and valour in connection with it. Peace, by contrast, is defined by the absence of war. When we think of peace, we might think of our homes, families, friends. Artists attempting to depict peace and its benefits have often created images of orderly towns and flourishing gardens, neat factories and trading vessels plying the sea lanes, but such depictions have historically found far less resonance with the general populace than images of war, of heroic figures in the thick of battle with sword and spear, gun and grenade in hand.

Peace has no drama and the human mind would, for some reason, seem to be drawn to drama, and to its engine, conflict. How much more difficult is it then for speakers to promote the virtues of peace over the glory of war, no matter what ghastly truths that glory masks?

Part of the challenge for the thinkers and orators of non-violent change and the global peace movement was to try to make peace and non-violence sexy. If the psychoanalyst Sigmund Freud (1856–1939) is to be credited, eros, the love urge, and thanatos, the destructive urge, are tightly interwoven, the yin and yang of the unconscious.

One of the most noted orators of the 20th century, US President John F. Kennedy (1917–63), recognized the dilemma between war and peace. Establishing a Peace Corps was one of the first acts of Kennedy's presidency and, in doing so, he drew upon the lexicon of war to mobilize young people to a global campaign for peace by attacking—at least in theory—the root cause of war, that is poverty.

Signing Executive Order 10924, which established the Peace Corps on 1 March 1961, Kennedy stated:

'Life in the Peace Corps will not be easy. There will be no salary, and allowances will be at a level sufficient only to maintain health and meet basic needs... But every American who joins the Peace Corps... will know that he or she is participating in the great common task of bringing to man that decent way of life which is the foundation of freedom and a condition of peace.'

Kennedy's speech to the US Congress on that same day specifically recognized that the meeting of basic needs of the peoples of developing nations was crucial to the security of the international community as a whole. He said:

'Throughout the world the people of the newly developing nations are struggling for economic and social progress which reflects their deepest desires. Our own freedom, and the future of freedom around the world, depend, in a very real sense, on their ability to build growing and independent nations where men can live in dignity, liberated from the bonds of hunger, ignorance and poverty.'

The corollary to Kennedy's statement is that if the world's underprivileged had improved living conditions, they would be far less likely to wage war, conduct guerrilla insurgencies or commit acts of terror. Warfare, after all, is, in the end, a very extreme way of arguing over something: usually land or resources—or, according to the legend of Troy, the love for a beautiful woman.

Although Kennedy's own life was cut short in 1963 by a murderous volley of bullets, his vision has lived on. Since 1961, nearly 200,000 young people have volunteered for the Peace Corps, serving in nearly 140 countries around the world. The last few years have seen a resurgence in volunteers on university campuses, and the Peace Corps will soon celebrate its 50th anniversary. And, no matter what political position one takes, nor how cynically people might view the outcome and the enterprise as a whole, the Peace Corps remains a fitting memorial to a man who, at the very least, articulated a strong desire for peace.

In this book you will read how national leaders have urged their citizenry to resolve disputes through acts of 'glorious' violence, and how thinkers have called upon their followers to do so by reason, debate and non-violent dissent. The oratory that speakers of all hues have used to rouse ordinary men and women to fight foes, or to struggle for peaceful change, is recorded in the pages that follow. I have drawn them from a wide variety of speakers, some of them inspirational, such as Martin Luther King, Jr, and Nelson Mandela (1918–) some of them insidious and brutal, such as the political leadership of Nazi Germany. Whatever their utterance, one ignores the documents of history at peril.

Given the time-scale and breadth of this book, and the number of speakers included, nearly all of the speeches have been edited, although some shorter ones, such as the 'Gettysburg Address', spoken by Abraham Lincoln (1809–65), are published in full.

I hope the reader finds this book rewarding, challenging and insightful.

– Larry Buttrose

Revolution and Civil War

The dawn of the Enlightenment in the 17th century set history onto a hitherto unknown course. The Earth was no longer at the centre of the universe, and God no longer central to the human concerns of many nations. Instead, it would be reason and science that would rule the world, with human intelligence the key player in the next act of its history.

The days of kings and dukes were numbered too: in their place would rise the entrepreneurial class, the bourgeoisie, and the nation-states we see marked on today's world map. The British monarchy fell, replaced at the apex of power by the assembly of the people, the Parliament. Soon, the American colonies clamoured in revolt against their masters on the far side of the Atlantic, and intoxicated with new notions of human equality and liberty, they fashioned a new republic.

The failing monarchy of France was also for the chopping block as Revolution swept the nation, and the surviving members of the aristocracy fled abroad. But the Revolution soon degenerated into the Reign of Terror as its leaders quarrelled and killed, and within a little more than a decade a new self-styled emperor would rule France, Napoleon Bonaparte.

In the decades to come, new nations would be forged from the duchies and fiefdoms of old, and Germany and Italy would rise to challenge the might of Britain and France. Tsarist Russia would soon meet its own destiny, in revolutionary change.

All the while the grown-up children of the Enlightenment wrestled with its liberal legacy, a core question being: are all people really equal, regardless of race and creed? This brought a great moral debate into sharp focus in Britain and America, beginning with the pleas of William Wilberforce (1759–1833), and other like-minded abolutionists in Britain, for an end to the Atlantic slave trade. The argument became increasingly heated over the decades, climaxing in the American Civil War (1861–65) across the Atlantic, which saw American killing fellow American, and the emergence of a new United States.

William Wilberforce

'A Trade Founded in Iniquity'

Speech advocating the abolition of slavery made to the House of Commons, London, 12 May 1789.

British statesman William Wilberforce, who brought about the abolition of slavery in the British West Indies, 1820s.

The great British reformer and anti-slavery campaigner William Wilberforce was born into the well-to-do family of a Yorkshire merchant in 1759. He studied at St John's College, Cambridge, where he began a longtime friendship with future prime minister, William Pitt the Younger (1759–1806).

Wilberforce was elected to Parliament at the age of 21, and four years later, he became an evangelical Christian. This changed his approach to life entirely: Wilberforce led a series of campaigns for social reform, beginning with the improvement of the appalling conditions of Britain's workers in the factories of the Industrial Revolution.

He also championed the abolitionist cause against slavery, helping to found the Anti-Slavery Society. In the following speech to the House of Commons, Wilberforce outlines the terrible circumstances endured by African slaves being transported on British ships on the Middle Passage from Africa to the New World of the Americas.

'...I must speak of the transit of the slaves in the West Indies. This I confess, in my own opinion, is the most wretched part of the whole subject. So much misery condensed in so little room, is more than the human imagination had ever before conceived...

Let any one imagine to himself 600 or 700 of these wretches chained two and two, surrounded with every object that is nauseous and disgusting, diseased, and struggling under every kind of wretchedness! How can we bear to think of such a scene as this?

One would think it had been determined to heap upon them all the varieties of bodily pain, for the purpose of blunting the feelings of the mind; and yet, in this very point, to show the power of human prejudice, the situation of the slaves has been described by Mr Norris, one of the Liverpool delegates, in a manner which, I am sure will convince the House how interest can draw a film across the eyes, so thick, that total blindness could do no more; and how it is our duty therefore to trust not to the reasonings of interested men, or to their way of colouring a transaction.

"Their apartments," says Mr Norris, "are fitted up as much for their advantage as circumstances will admit. The right ankle of one, indeed is connected with the left ankle of another by a small iron fetter, and if they are turbulent, by another on their wrists. They have several meals a day; some of their own country provisions, with the best sauces of African cookery; and by way of variety, another meal of pulses etcetera, according to European taste.

"After breakfast they have water to wash themselves, while their apartments are perfumed with frankincense and lime-juice. Before dinner, they are amused after the manner of their country. The song and dance are promoted," and, as if the whole was really a scene of pleasure and dissipation, it is added, that games of chance are furnished.

"The men play and sing, while the women and girls make fanciful ornaments with beads, which they are plentifully supplied with."

Such is the sort of strain in which the Liverpool delegates, and particularly Mr Norris, gave evidence before the Privy Council. What will the House think when, by the concurring testimony of other witnesses, the true history is laid open. The slaves who are sometimes described as rejoicing at their captivity, are so wrung with misery at leaving their country, that it is the constant practice to set sail at night, lest they should be sensible of their departure.

The pulses which Mr Norris talks of are horse beans; and the scantiness, both of water and provision, was suggested by the very legislature of Jamaica in the report of their committee, to be a subject that called for the interference of Parliament. Mr Norris talks of frankincense and lime juice; when surgeons tell you the slaves are stowed so close that there is not room to tread among them: and when you have it in evidence from Sir George Yonge, that even in a ship which wanted 200 of her complement, the stench was intolerable.

The song and the dance, says Mr Norris, are promoted. It had been more fair, perhaps, if he had explained that word "promoted". The truth is, that for the sake of exercise, these miserable wretches, loaded with chains, oppressed with disease and wretchedness, are forced to dance by the terror of the lash, and sometimes by the actual use of it. "I," says one of the other evidences, "was employed to dance the men, while another person danced the women."

Such, then is the meaning of the word "promoted"; and it may be observed too, with respect to food, that an instrument is sometimes carried out, in order to force them to eat which is the same sort of proof how much they enjoy themselves in that instance also. As to their singing, what shall we say when we are told that their songs are songs of lamentation upon their departure which, while they sing, are always in tears, insomuch that one captain, more humane as I should conceive him, therefore, than the rest, threatened one of the women with a flogging, because the mournfulness of her song was too painful for his feelings.

In order, however, not to trust too much to any sort of description, I will call the attention of the House to one species of evidence which is absolutely infallible. Death, at least, is a sure ground of evidence, and the proportion of deaths will not only confirm, but if possible will even aggravate our suspicion of their misery in the transit.

It will be found upon an average of all the ships of which evidence has been given at the privy council, that exclusive of those who perish before they sail, not less than 12½ per cent perish in the passage. Besides these, the Jamaica report tells you, that not less than 4½ per cent die on shore before the day of sale, which is only a week or two from the time of landing.

One third more die in the seasoning, and this in a country exactly like their own, where they are healthy and happy as some of the evidences would pretend. The diseases, however, which they contract on shipboard, the astringent washes which are to hide their wounds, and the mischievous tricks used to make them up for sale, are, as the Jamaica report says,—a most precious and valuable report, which I shall often have to advert to—one principle cause of this mortality.

Upon the whole, however, here is a mortality of about 50 per

'Here is a mortality of about 50 per cent, and this among negroes who are not bought unless, as the phrase is with cattle, they are sound in wind and limb. How then can the House refuse its belief to the multiplied testimonies before the privy council, of the savage treatment of the negroes.'

cent, and this among negroes who are not bought unless, as the phrase is with cattle, they are sound in wind and limb. How then can the House refuse its belief to the multiplied testimonies before the privy council, of the savage treatment of the negroes in the Middle Passage?

Nay, indeed, what need is there of any evidence? The number of deaths speaks for itself, and makes all such enquiry superfluous. As soon as ever I had arrived thus far in my investigation of the slave trade, I confess to you sir, so enormous, so dreadful, so irremediable did its wickedness appear that my own mind was completely made up for the abolition. A trade founded in iniquity, and carried on as this was, must be abolished, let the policy be what it might, let the consequences be what they would, I from this time determined that I would never rest till I had effected its abolition.'

It would be nearly 20 more years until Parliament acceded to the demands of Wilberforce and his abolitionist supporters, by outlawing the slave trade in the British West Indies in 1807. Wilberforce then began a new campaign to have slavery banned entirely, freeing those who were already slaves. Every slave throughout the British Empire finally gained his or her freedom in 1833. Wilberforce lived to see Parliament pass the Slavery Abolition Act, but died shortly after.

During his busy life, the great philanthropist had also campaigned for better living conditions for all British children, and was a stalwart supporter of the Royal Society for the Prevention of Cruelty to Animals. He is buried in Westminster Abbey, London, near his old friend William Pitt.

Thomas Jefferson

'The Essential Principles of Our Government'

**First Inaugural Address,
Washington, DC, 4 March 1801.**

Thomas Jefferson, the 3rd President of the United States of America, 1801.

The name Thomas Jefferson (1743–1826) is known to us in history as one of the Founders of the American republic. The man who swore himself to 'eternal hostility against every form of tyranny over the mind of man' was a child of the Enlightenment and a dedicated liberal statesman. He was one of the most powerful advocates for the pursuit of liberty, a subject which suffuses the American ethos still today.

Jefferson was born into the well-off family of a Virginia planter and surveyor. He studied law and entered politics in 1769, becoming an ardent supporter of the cause for independence of the American colonies from Britain. He primarily drafted the Declaration of Independence in 1776 during the American War of Independence (1775–83).

Jefferson served George Washington (1732–99), the first US president, in the government of the new republic as envoy to France. There, he witnessed firsthand the start of the French Revolution in 1789. He later became the first secretary of state under Washington. He founded the Republican Party to counter the centralist 'Federalism' of Alexander Hamilton (c.1755/57–1804), and twice contested the presidency against John Adams (1735–1826), under whom he served as vice-president (1797–1801). Adams defeated him in 1796, but Jefferson narrowly defeated him, in turn, in 1800.

In his first Inaugural Address as third president of the United States, in the new capital Washington, DC, which he himself had helped design, Jefferson restates clearly the values he holds most dear, those which he will pursue during his presidency.

'Friends and Fellow-Citizens,

Called upon to undertake the duties of the first executive office of our country, I avail myself of the presence of that portion of my fellow-citizens which is here assembled to express my grateful thanks for the favour with which they have been pleased to look toward me, to declare a sincere consciousness that the task is above my talents, and that I approach it with those anxious and awful presentiments which the greatness of the charge and the weakness of my powers so justly inspire.

A rising nation, spread over a wide and fruitful land, traversing all the seas with the rich productions of their industry, engaged in commerce with nations who feel power and forget right, advancing rapidly to destinies beyond the reach of mortal eye—when I contemplate these transcendent objects, and see the honour, the happiness, and the hopes of this beloved country committed to the issue, and the auspices of this day, I shrink from the contemplation, and humble myself before the magnitude of the undertaking.

Utterly, indeed, should I despair did not the presence of many whom I here see remind me that in the other high authorities provided by our Constitution I shall find resources of wisdom, of virtue, and of zeal on which to rely under all difficulties. To you, then, gentlemen, who are

'And let us reflect that, having banished from our land that religious intolerance under which mankind so long bled and suffered, we have yet gained little if we countenance a political intolerance as despotic, as wicked, and capable of as bitter and bloody persecutions.'

charged with the sovereign functions of legislation, and to those associated with you, I look with encouragement for that guidance and support which may enable us to steer with safety the vessel in which we are all embarked amidst the conflicting elements of a troubled world.

During the contest of opinion through which we have passed the animation of discussions and of exertions has sometimes worn an aspect which might impose on strangers unused to think freely and to speak and to write what they think; but this being now decided by the voice of the nation, announced according to the rules of the Constitution, all will, of course, arrange themselves under the will of the law, and unite in common efforts for the common good.

All, too, will bear in mind this sacred principle, that though the will of the majority is in all cases to prevail, that will to be rightful must be reasonable; that the minority possess their equal rights, which equal law must protect, and to violate would be oppression. Let us, then, fellow-citizens, unite with one heart and one mind. Let us restore to social intercourse that harmony and affection without which liberty and even life itself are but dreary things. And let us reflect that, having banished from our land that religious intolerance under which mankind so long bled and suffered, we have yet gained little if we countenance a political intolerance as despotic, as wicked, and capable of as bitter and bloody persecutions.

During the throes and convulsions of the ancient world, during the agonising spasms of infuriated man, seeking through blood and slaughter his long-lost liberty, it was not wonderful that the agitation of the billows should reach even this distant and peaceful shore; that this should be more felt and feared by some and less by others, and should divide opinions as to measures of safety. But every difference of opinion is not a difference of principle. We have called by different names brethren of the same principle. We are all Republicans, we are all Federalists. If there be any among us who would wish to dissolve this Union or to change its republican form, let them stand undisturbed as monuments of the safety with which error of opinion may be tolerated where reason is left free to combat it.

I know, indeed, that some honest men fear that a republican government can not be strong, that this Government is not strong enough; but would the honest patriot, in the full tide of successful experiment, abandon a government which has so far kept us free and firm on the theoretic and visionary fear that this Government, the world's best hope, may by possibility want energy to preserve itself? I trust not. I believe this, on the contrary, the strongest government on earth. I believe it the only one where every man, at the call of the law, would fly to the standard of the law, and would meet invasions of the public order as his own personal concern. Sometimes it is said that man can not be trusted with the government of himself. Can he, then, be trusted with the government of others? Or have we found angels in the forms of kings to govern him? Let history answer this question.

Let us, then, with courage and confidence pursue our own Federal and Republican principles, our attachment to union and representative government. Kindly separated by nature and a wide ocean from the exterminating havoc of one quarter of the globe; too high-minded to endure the degradations of the others; possessing a chosen country, with room enough for our descendants to the thousandth and thousandth generation; entertaining a due sense of our equal right to the use of our own faculties, to the acquisitions of our own industry, to honour and confidence from our fellow-citizens, resulting not from birth, but from our actions and their sense of them; enlightened by a benign religion, professed, indeed, and practiced in various forms, yet all of them inculcating honesty, truth, temperance, gratitude, and the love of man; acknowledging and adoring an overruling Providence, which by all its dispensations proves that it delights in the happiness of man here and his greater happiness hereafter—with all these blessings, what more is necessary to make us a happy and a prosperous people?

Still one thing more, fellow-citizens—a wise and frugal Government, which shall restrain men from injuring one another, shall leave them otherwise free to regulate their own pursuits of industry and improvement, and shall not take from the mouth of labor the bread it has earned. This is the sum of good government, and this is necessary to close the circle of our felicities.

About to enter, fellow-citizens, on the exercise of duties which comprehend everything dear and valuable to you, it is proper you should understand what I deem the essential principles of our Government, and consequently those which ought to shape its Administration. I will compress them within the narrowest compass they will bear, stating the general principle, but not all its limitations.

Equal and exact justice to all men, of whatever state or persuasion, religious or political; peace, commerce, and honest friendship with all nations, entangling alliances with none; the support of the state governments in all their rights, as the most competent administrations for our domestic concerns and the surest bulwarks against anti-republican tendencies; the preservation of the General Government in its whole constitutional vigour, as the sheet anchor of our peace at home and safety abroad; a jealous care of the right of election by the people—a mild and safe corrective of abuses which are lopped by the sword of revolution where peaceable remedies are unprovided; absolute acquiescence in the decisions of the majority, the vital principle of republics, from which is no appeal but to force, the vital principle and immediate parent of despotism; a well disciplined militia, our best reliance in peace and for the first moments of war, till regulars may relieve them; the supremacy of the civil over the military authority; economy in the public expense, that labor may be lightly burthened; the honest payment of our debts and sacred preservation of the public faith; encouragement of agriculture, and of commerce as its handmaid; the diffusion of information and arraignment of all abuses at the bar of the public reason; freedom of religion; freedom of the press, and freedom of person under the protection of the habeas corpus, and trial by juries impartially selected. These

'Sometimes it is said that man can not be trusted with the government of himself. Can he, then, be trusted with the government of others? Or have we found angels in the forms of kings to govern him? Let history answer this question.'

principles form the bright constellation which has gone before us and guided our steps through an age of revolution and reformation. The wisdom of our sages and blood of our heroes have been devoted to their attainment. They should be the creed of our political faith, the text of civic instruction, the touchstone by which to try the services of those we trust; and should we wander from them in moments of error or of alarm, let us hasten to retrace our steps and to regain the road which alone leads to peace, liberty, and safety.’

Jefferson served as president until 1809. During that time, he abolished the slave trade and oversaw the ‘Louisiana Purchase’ from France in 1803, which considerably enlarged the territories of the United States in the South and doubled the size of the United States at that time. After leaving office Jefferson retired to Monticello, the mountain-top home he designed himself in south-central Virginia, now a landmark US building. There, he devoted his remaining energies to building the campus at Charlottesville of the University of Virginia. He died on 4 July 1826, on the 50th anniversary of the signing of the Declaration of Independence.

Napoleon Bonaparte

'Adieu, My Friends'

The 'Farewell to the Old Guard', following the failed invasion of Russia, Fontainebleau, France, 20 April 1814.

Napoleon Bonaparte at Malmaison, France, 1804.

Napoleon Bonaparte (1769–1821) was born on the island of Corsica. It would be first of three islands he would live on, the others being Elba and St Helena, his prisons of exile.

He attended military school in Paris and graduated an artillery officer, rising to the rank of general. On 9–10 November 1799 he engineered a coup d'etat, installing himself as first consul, virtual dictator of France.

In 1804 he brought down the curtain on the 1,000-year-old Holy Roman Empire, defeating Emperor Francis II.

In the successful campaigns in the years that followed, Napoleon assembled an empire of his own, his military skills at the head of his half-million strong Grand Army too great for the combined might of England, Prussia and Austria. But his invasion of Russia, in 1812, proved a disastrous turning point. The Russians retreated but adopted a scorched-earth policy. After taking Moscow virtually unopposed and finding it unoccupied, a great fire broke out in the city, burning it virtually to the ground. With his supplies quickly dwindling, Napoleon had little option but to retreat.

The return march west through the Russia winter was the stuff of nightmares, with more than half the French army perishing—some 300,000 men lost—from cold, starvation and the guerrilla tactics of the Russians. The returning exhausted and decimated French army was later defeated by the unified forces of England, Austria, Prussia and Russia at the Battle of Nations (also known as the Battle of Leipzig) in 1813. After Paris was captured by the Allies in March 1814, Napoleon was forced to abdicate.

This short speech is Napoleon's address to the men who had remained loyal to him during his more than a decade of wars across Europe.

'With men such as you our cause could not be lost; but the war would have been interminable; it would have been civil war, and that would have entailed deeper misfortunes on France.'

'Soldiers of my Old Guard:

I bid you farewell. For 20 years I have constantly accompanied you on the road to honour and glory. In these latter times, as in the days of our prosperity, you have invariably been models of courage and fidelity. With men such as you our cause could not be lost; but the war would have been interminable; it would have been civil war, and that would have entailed deeper misfortunes on France.

I have sacrificed all of my interests to those of the country. I go, but you, my friends, will continue to serve France. Her happiness was my only thought. It will still be the object of my wishes. Do not regret my fate; if I have consented to survive, it is to serve your glory. I intend to write the history of the great achievements we have performed together. Adieu, my friends.

Would I could press you all to my heart.'

Napoleon was sent into exile on the tiny island of Elba, off the coast of Italy, but in 1815 he escaped and returned to Paris to public adulation. He gathered together his old comrades into an army again. For 100 days it seemed as if his grandiose imperial dream might be reborn, but at the Battle of Waterloo in June 1815, in Belgium, his over 70,000-strong forces met with both the battle-hardened Allied forces under the command of the Duke of Wellington (1769–1852), hero of the Napoleonic Wars, and the 45,000-strong Prussian army under the command of Gebhard Leberecht von Blücher (1742–1819). Despite the heroism of the Old Guard, Napoleon's forces were defeated.

Napoleon was exiled again, this time to the end of the earth, St Helena in the far South Atlantic. There, he whiled away his days writing and scheming, and gaining girth, and it was there that the soldier who once dreamed an empire saw out his final days, a pudgy captive on one of the most isolated specks on earth, a kingdom of penguins.

Abraham Lincoln

'Government of the People, by the People, for the People'

The Gettysburg Address,
Gettysburg, Pennsylvania, 19 November 1863.

Abraham Lincoln, 9 April 1865, five days before he was shot dead.

Abraham Lincoln (1809–65) rose from humble beginnings in a Kentucky log cabin to become a self-educated lawyer, then a reforming politician and perhaps America's best-loved president. A stirring orator, he first spoke out against slavery in the 1850s, and his resolve against it became ever firmer and more passionate. He found himself on a collision course with the slave-owning states of the American South, which ignited into Civil War soon after his inauguration in 1861.

Despite early Confederate successes, the Union's superior wealth, technology and infrastructure made its victory in the war virtually inevitable. Nonetheless some historians believe the entire outcome hung in the balance after General Robert E. Lee (1807–70) moved his Confederate army North to Gettysburg, Pennsylvania, in July 1863. Union troops engaged with them in battle there, the conflict raging on for three days, before Lee's men were defeated and forced into retreat. Both sides suffered terrible casualties, with estimates ranging up to 50,000 men in total.

Four-and-a-half months later, in November of 1863, Lincoln spoke at the dedication of the National Cemetery at Gettysburg, commemorating the fallen. His brief speech has become among the best-known of any American leader. In that respect, Lincoln was incorrect when he said 'the world will little note, nor long remember what we say here': the opposite is, in fact, true.

'Four score and seven years ago our fathers brought forth on this continent, a new nation, conceived in Liberty, and dedicated to the proposition that all men are created equal.

Now we are engaged in a great civil war, testing whether that nation, or any nation so conceived and so dedicated, can long endure.

We are met on a great battle-field of that war. We have come to dedicate a portion of that field, as a final resting place for those who here gave their lives that that nation might live. It is altogether fitting and proper that we should do this. But, in a larger sense, we can not dedicate—we can not consecrate—we can not hallow—this ground. The brave men, living and dead, who struggled here, have consecrated it, far above our poor power to add or detract.

The world will little note, nor long remember what we say here, but it can never forget what they did here. It is for us the living, rather, to be dedicated here to the unfinished work which they who fought here have thus far so nobly advanced. It is rather for us to be here dedicated to the great task remaining before us—that from these honoured dead we take increased devotion to that cause for which they gave the last full measure of devotion—that we here highly resolve that these dead shall not have died in

'The world will little note, nor long remember what we say here, but it can never forget what they did here. It is for us the living, rather, to be dedicated here to the unfinished work which they who fought here have thus far so nobly advanced.'

vain—that this nation, under God, shall have a new birth of freedom—and that government of the people, by the people, for the people, shall not perish from the earth.'

By the time of Lincoln's re-election the next year, the end loomed for the Confederates. The South had formally surrendered less than a week when, on the evening of 14 April 1865, the president and his wife set off for a night out in Washington. They were in private box at Ford's Theatre watching the hit show *Our American Cousin*, when John Wilkes Booth (1838–65), an embittered actor, managed to slip past guards, place a Derringer pistol to the back of Lincoln's head and fire a single fatal shot.

Though generally viewed as a conspiratorial act of revenge by beaten and bitter elements of the South, there are many other theories about the assassination, ranging from the plausible to the bizarre. However, the most likely explanation remains that while he sat watching a play on stage, Lincoln was murdered in cold blood by a disaffected rebel without a cause.

The World at War

It is increasingly common for modern historians to consider World War I ('The Great War'; 1914–18) and World War II (1939–45), as a single conflict. These wars are now often seen as leading inexorably from one to the other, largely from the conditions imposed upon a defeated Germany by the Allies in the 1919 Treaty of Versailles.

Advocates of this viewpoint argue that with the collapse of the German economy during the Weimar Republic (1919–33), and the hardships suffered by the German people, renewed conflict, as seen under the National Socialist Party (the Nazis; 1933–45), was virtually inevitable.

The origins of World War I, and thus the root cause of the global conflict as a whole, remain as debated today as they were when the 'war to end all wars' broke out in 1914. A perhaps less contested summary would include economic rivalry between the imperial European powers of Britain, Germany, France, Russia and Austria–Hungary. Industrial and trading competition, imperial pomp and fervent patriotism, secrecy, paranoia and the guile of diplomacy, all helped create the backdrop to war. The various international powers raised armies in their tens of millions, and there was a concerted military build-up by Germany, especially of its naval forces, against the ruler of the waves, Britain.

The spark for the conflagration which would devour a generation of young lives came from friction between Serbia and Austria–Hungary over the empire's hold on Bosnia, which climaxed in the assassination of the heir to the Austro–Hungarian empire, Archduke Franz Ferdinand (1863–1914), in Sarajevo in modern-day Bosnia and Herzegovina.

Although warned of the dangers, on 28 June 1914 the Archduke and his pregnant wife, Sophie, Countess von Chotek (1868–1914), were on a state visit to the Bosnian capital when their car was fired upon by Serbian nationalist Gavrilo Princip (1894–1918). After the shots, the countess saw blood at the corner of her husband's mouth and cried out, 'For God's sake, what has happened to you?' Moments later she slid to the floor of the car, having herself been shot. Franz Ferdinand pleaded 'Sophie, Sophie, don't die.' As others in the car tried to assist the bleeding Archduke, as he drifted into unconsciousness, he murmured reassuringly, 'It is nothing, it's nothing…'.

Both Archduke Ferdinand and his wife died quickly. Princip was captured and spent the rest of his years in chains. But the shots he had fired were famously heard around the world, setting into motion the meetings, schemes, proposals, counter-proposals and ultimatums between Austria–Hungary and its ally Germany, and Serbia and its allies, Russia, Britain and France, factors that led to Austria's declaration of war on Serbia, signifying the outbreak of World War I, just weeks after the assassinations in Sarajevo.

Herbert H. Asquith, 1st Earl of Oxford and Asquith

'A Strong and Overmastering Power'

Speech to the House of Commons, London, 3 August 1914.

Herbert Henry Asquith, the Earl of Oxford and Asquith, 1916.

The failure of moves to maintain the peace, and the coming of war, was articulated to Parliament by Britain's Liberal Prime Minister Herbert Henry Asquith (1852–1928).

The Yorkshire-born Asquith had a successful law career before becoming Liberal Member of Parliament for East Fife in 1886. He rose to become chancellor of the exchequer in 1905, before standing for and being elected prime minister in 1908. Asquith's popularity began to fall after Britain suffered early defeats in World War I, and he was deposed at the end of 1916.

He made the following war speech to Parliament on 3 August 1914, following an attack on Belgium by German forces.

'Simultaneously, we received from the Belgian Legation in London the following telegram from the Belgian Minister for Foreign Affairs: "The General Staff announce that territory has been violated at Verviers, near Aix-la-Chapelle. Subsequent information tends to show that a German force has penetrated still further into Belgian territory."

We also received this morning from the German Ambassador here a telegram sent to him from the German Foreign Secretary: "Please dispel any distrust that must exist on the part of the British Government with regard to our intentions by repeating, most positively, the formal assurance that, even in case of armed conflict with Belgium, Germany will not, under any pretence whatever, annexe Belgian territory. Please impress upon Sir Edward Grey that the German Army could not be exposed to a French attack across Belgium, which was planned according to absolutely unimpeachable information."

I have to add this on behalf of the Government: we cannot regard this as in any sense a satisfactory communication. We have, in reply to it, repeated the request we made last week to the German Government that they should give us the same assurance with regard to Belgian neutrality as was given to us and to Belgium by France last week.

We have asked that a reply to that request and a satisfactory answer to the telegram of this morning, which I have read to the House should be given before midnight...

If I am asked what we are fighting for, I can reply in two sentences. In the first place, to fulfil a solemn international obligation... an obligation of honour which no self-respecting man could possibly have repudiated. I say, secondly we are fighting to vindicate the principal that small nationalities are not to be crushed in defiance of international good faith at the arbitrary will of a strong and overmastering Power.'

'We are fighting to vindicate the principal that small nationalities are not to be crushed in defiance of international good faith at the arbitrary will of a strong and overmastering Power.'

After Asquith's speech, British King George V (1865–1936; reigned 1910–36) was cheered on by patriotic crowds outside Buckingham Palace, London. He sent a message to the head of the Navy, Admiral Sir John Jellicoe (1859–1935).

'At this grave moment in our national history I send to you and, through you, to the officers and men of the fleets, of which you have assumed command, the assurance of my confidence that under your direction they will revive and renew the old glories of the Royal Navy, and prove once again the sure shield of Britain and of her Empire in the hour of trial.'

The war inevitably aroused great and often conflicting passions—of patriotism, fear, passionate opposition to conscription, pacifistic opposition to all war, and American isolationism.

Woodrow Wilson

'The World Must Be Made Safe for Democracy'

**Speech to US Congress, 2 April 1917,
as the United States enters the World War I.**

Woodrow Wilson, 28th President of the United States.

In 1917 President (Thomas) Woodrow Wilson (1856–1924) felt compelled to involve America in World War I, despite powerful support within the United States for the country to retain an isolationist stance—a stance that Wilson had himself at one point shared. He addressed the US Congress on 2 April. Four days later, the United States declared war on Germany and entered the war on the Allied side.

Woodrow Wilson had been educated at Princeton University, and had practised as a lawyer before entering politics. He joined the Democratic Party and became governor of New Jersey in 1911, before being elected US president for the first time in 1912. A liberal progressive and social reformer, Wilson was re-elected to the post in 1916. By then, however, he had become increasingly uncomfortable with the US position of neutrality, especially after a German U-boat torpedoed the passenger liner the Lusitania off the Irish coast in 1915, resulting in the loss of nearly 1,200 lives.

By early 1917, Wilson had come to the conclusion that the US had to enter the war 'to make the world safe for democracy'. On 2 April, he made a speech (extracted below) to the US Congress in Washington, DC, arguing the case for the United States to declare war on Germany. His remarks regarding submarines underline the new technological war in which the world found itself—of guns that could cut down a field of men in moments, aircraft that could drop bombs on trenches, poison gas and the lethal new warships lurking undetected beneath the waves.

'...The present German submarine warfare against commerce is a warfare against mankind. It is a war against all nations. American ships have been sunk, American lives taken, in ways which it has stirred us very deeply to learn of, but the ships and people of other neutral and friendly nations have been sunk and overwhelmed in the waters in the same way. There has been no discrimination.

The challenge is to all mankind. Each nation must decide for itself how it will meet it. The choice we make for ourselves must be made with a moderation of counsel and a temperateness for judgement befitting our character and our motives as a nation. We must put excited feeling away. Our motive will not be revenge or the victorious assertion of the physical might of the nation, but only the vindication of right, of human right, of which we are only a single champion.

'We must put excited feeling away. Our motive will not be revenge or the victorious assertion of the physical might of the nation, but only the vindication of right, of human right, of which we are only a single champion.'

When I addressed the Congress on the 26th of February last, I thought that it would suffice to assert our neutral rights with arms, our right to use the seas against unlawful interference, our right to keep our people safe against unlawful violence.

But armed neutrality, it now appears, is impracticable. Because submarines are in effect outlaws when used as the German submarines have been used against merchant shipping, it is impossible to defend ships against their attacks as the law of nations has assumed that merchantmen would defend themselves against privateers or cruisers, visible craft giving chase upon the open sea. It is common prudence in such circumstances, grim necessity indeed, to endeavour to destroy them before they have shown their own intention.

They must be dealt with upon sight, if dealt with at all. The German Government denies the right of neutrals to use arms at all within the areas of the sea which it has proscribed, even in the defence of rights which no modern publicist has ever before questioned their right to defend.

The intimation is conveyed that the armed guards which we have placed on our merchant ships will be treated as beyond the pale of law and subject to be dealt with as pirates would be. Armed neutrality is ineffectual enough at best; in such circumstances and in the face of such pretensions it is worse than ineffectual: it is likely only to produce what it was meant to prevent; it is practically certain to draw us into the war without either the rights or the effectiveness of belligerents.

'It was a war determined upon as wars used to be determined upon in the old, unhappy days when peoples were nowhere consulted by their rulers and wars were provoked and waged in the interest of dynasties or of little groups of ambitious men who were accustomed to use their fellow men as pawns.'

There is one choice we cannot make, we are incapable of making: we will not choose the path of submission and suffer the most sacred rights of our nation and our people to be ignored or violated. The wrongs against which we now array ourselves are no common wrongs; they cut to the very roots of human life. With a profound sense of the solemn and even tragical character of the step I am taking and of the grave responsibilities which it involves, but in unhesitating obedience to what I deem my constitutional duty, I advise that the Congress declare the recent course of the Imperial German Government to be in fact nothing less than war against the government and people of the United States; that it formally accept the status of belligerent which has thus been thrust upon it; and that it take immediate steps not only to put the country in a more thorough state of defence but also to exert all its power and employ all its resources to bring the Government of the German Empire to terms and end the war...

We have no quarrel with the German people. We have no feeling towards them but one of sympathy and friendship. It was not upon their impulse that their government acted in entering this war. It was not with their previous knowledge or approval. It was a war determined upon as wars used to be determined upon in the old, unhappy days when peoples were nowhere consulted by their rulers and wars were provoked and waged in the interest of dynasties or of little groups of ambitious men who were accustomed to use their fellow men as pawns and tools.

We are accepting this challenge of hostile purpose because we know that in such a Government, following such methods, we can never have a friend; and that in the presence of its organized power, always lying in wait to accomplish we know not what purpose, there can be no assured security for the democratic Governments of the world.

We are now about to accept gauge of battle with this natural foe to liberty and shall, if necessary, spend the whole force of the nation to check and nullify its pretensions and its power. We are glad, now that we see the facts with no veil of false pretence about them, to fight thus for the ultimate peace of the world and for the liberation of its peoples, the German peoples included: for the rights of nations great and small and the privilege of men everywhere to choose their way of life and of obedience.

The world must be made safe for democracy. Its peace must be planted upon the tested foundations of political liberty. We have no selfish ends to serve. We desire no conquest, no dominion. We seek no indemnities for ourselves, no material compensation for the sacrifices we shall freely make. We are but one of the champions of the rights of mankind. We shall be satisfied when those rights have been made as secure as the faith and the freedom of nations can make them. ’

Emma Goldman

'Guns and Bayonets Have Never Solved Any Problems'

Speech against the war and conscription at Forward Hall, New York City, 14 June 1917.

Feminist and labour rights campaigner Emma Goldman, 1919.

As the Great War continued, and millions went to their deaths as cannon fodder, the movement against the conflict and opposing conscription grew. The entry of the United States into the war in 1917 brought a new array of activists to the fore, none more outspoken than feminist and labour rights campaigner Emma Goldman (1869–1940).

Goldman was born in Lithuania, but after her Jewish family moved to Russia, they were forced to flee to Germany to avoid persecution. In 1885, Goldman emigrated to the United States, where she became a political and social activist, arguing for such causes as the right to effective contraception, and against conscription and America's participation in the war. Her outspokenness, as typified by this speech to a meeting of workers in New York City, led to the US authorities jailing her for two years. They later deported her to Russia, although she did return to the United States in 1924. She subsequently settled in France.

'...Friends, tomorrow morning I am sure that you will read the report that a meeting took place on the East Side attended by foreigners, by workmen, and ill-kempt, poorly washed people of the East Side—foreigners who are being jeered at the present time in this country, foreigners who are being ridiculed because they have an idea. Well, friends, if the Americans are to wait until Americans wake up the country, they will have to resurrect the Indians who were killed in America and upon whose bodies this so-called democracy was established, because every other American, if you scratch him, you will find him to be an Englishman, Dutchman, Frenchman, Spaniard, a Jew and a German and a hundred and one other nationalities who sent their young men and their women to this country in the foolish belief that liberty was awaiting them at the American Harbour, Liberty holding a torch.

That torch has been burning dimly in the United States for a very long time. It is because the Goddess of Liberty is ashamed of the American people and what they have done in the name of liberty to liberty in the United States. And yet, friends, I am not sorry for the things that are happening in America today. I have come to the conclusion that every nation is like an individual, it must have its own experience and it does not accept the experience of other nations any more than you accept the experience of another individual, for if it were possible for a nation to learn by the bitter and tragic experiences of other nations, America today could not be in war and America today could not have inaugurated a reign of terror which is sweeping across the country from one end to another. America had Europe before its face as an example, with all the murders and bloodshed and corpses and millions of lives lost. America had the trenches and the battlefields of the last, nearly, three years of Europe before her. America realized that this war is one

'For 25 or 30 years we have told you that the United States of America is appropriating more power every day until the time will come when individual men or women will be nothing but cogs in a machine of this centralised, cruel, bloodthirsty government known as the United States.'

of the bloodiest and most criminal wars that has ever been fought by civilized people. America had the lesson that the working people and the sons of working women are being sacrificed in the name of Kultur and they want democracy upon the battlefields of Europe, and if America had been a grown man instead of a child it would have learned the lesson that no matter how great the cause it is never great enough to sacrifice millions of people in the trenches and on the battlefield in the name of democracy or liberty.

Evidently, America has to learn a salutary lesson and it is going to pay a terrible price. It is going to shed oceans of blood, it is going to heap mountains of human sacrifices of men of this country who are able to create and produce, to whom the future belongs. They are to be slaughtered in blood and in sacrifice in the name of a thing which has never yet existed in the United States of America, in the name of democracy and liberty.

My friends, there are people who say and tell you that when they prophecy something the prophecy comes true. I am sorry to say that I am one such and I have to say the same. For 30 years we have pointed out to you that this democratic State which is a government supposedly of the people, by the people and for the people has now become one of the most imperialistic that the world has ever laid its eyes upon. For 25 or 30 years we have told you that the United States of America is appropriating more power every day until the time will come when individual men or women will be nothing but cogs in a machine of this centralised, cruel, bloodthirsty government known as the United States.

'Guns and bayonets have never solved any problems. Bloodshed has never solved a problem. Never on earth, men and women, have such methods of violence, concentrated and organized violence, ever solved a single problem.'

We told you that, and you said, you are alarmists. You said, you are too extreme, that will never happen in the United States. And here you are, friends. It has happened in the United States. A Tsar was imposed upon you without the consent of the people. The people were never asked whether they wanted war. Indeed, the people of America placed Mr Wilson in the White House and in the chair of the presidency because he told the people that he would keep them out of war, and as one of his political advertisements billposters were posted all over the city with the picture of a working woman and her children saying, 'He has kept us out of war'. He promised you heaven, he promised you everything if you would only place him in power. What made you place him in power? You expected peace and not war. The moment you placed him in power, however, he forgot his promises and he is giving you hell.

...Guns and bayonets have never solved any problems. Bloodshed has never solved a problem. Never on earth, men and women, have such methods of violence, concentrated and organized violence, ever solved a single problem. Nothing but the human mind, nothing but human emotions, nothing but an intense passion for a great ideal, nothing but perseverance and devotion and strength of character—nothing else ever solved any problem.

And so, men and women, workmen and workwomen, you of the East Side, you who are sweated and bled to create the wealth of this country, you who are being sneered at because you are foreigners—very well, then, if you are good enough to create the wealth of America, if America had to go to Europe for her art, if America had to go to Europe for her literature, if America had to go to Europe for her music and her ideals, by God you will have to go to the foreigners for liberty.

I wish to say here, and I don't say it with any authority and I don't say it as a prophet, I merely tell you—I merely tell you the more people you lock up, the more will be the idealists who will take their place; the more of the human voice you suppress, the greater and louder and the profounder will be the human voice. At present it is a mere rumbling, but that rumbling is increasing in volume, it is growing in depth, it is spreading all over the country until it will be raised into a thunder and people of America will rise and say, we want to be a democracy, to be sure, but we want the kind of democracy which means liberty and opportunity to every man and woman in America.'

David Lloyd George

'The Most Critical Hour in This Terrible Conflict'

Address to the House of Commons, London, 5 January 1918.

David Lloyd George (left) and Winston Churchill, 1916.

After nearly four years of war, in early 1918 British Prime Minister David Lloyd George (1863–1945) addressed Parliament to affirm what the British had been fighting for during the long and bloody struggle, a conflict that had already claimed the lives of tens of millions of people.

Born in Manchester, England, Lloyd George was brought up in Wales. He practised as a solicitor before standing for Parliament for the Liberal Party and was elected in 1890. He became chancellor of the exchequer under Asquith (see pages 34–36), whom he overthrew at the end of 1916 to become prime minister.

As Lloyd George addressed the House of Commons in the midwinter of January 1918, the outcome of World War I still hung in the balance.

'When men by the million are being called upon to suffer and die, and vast populations are being subjected to the sufferings and privations of war on a scale unprecedented in the history of the world, they are entitled to know for what cause or causes they are making the sacrifice. It is only the clearest, greatest and justest of causes that can justify the continuance even for one day of this unspeakable agony of the nations, and we ought to be able to state clearly and definitely, not only the principles for which we are fighting, but also their definite and concrete application to the war map of the world.

We have arrived at the most critical hour in this terrible conflict, and before any government takes the fateful decision as to the conditions under which it ought either to terminate or continue the struggle, it ought to be satisfied that the conscience of the nation is behind these conditions, for nothing else can sustain the effort which is necessary to achieve a righteous end to this war...

We may begin by clearing away some misunderstandings and stating what we are not fighting for. We are not fighting a war of aggression against the German people. Their leaders have persuaded them that they are fighting a war of self-defence against a league of rival nations bent on the destruction of Germany. That is not so. The destruction or disruption of Germany or the German people has never been a war aim with us from the first day of this war to this day.

Most reluctantly, and indeed quite unprepared for the dreadful ordeal, we were forced to join in this war in self-defence. In defence of the violated public law of Europe, and in vindication of the most solemn treaty obligation on which the public system of Europe rested, and on which Germany had ruthlessly trampled in her invasion of Belgium, we had to join in the struggle or stand aside and see Europe go under and brute force triumph over public right and international justice. It was only the realization of that dreadful alternative that forced the British people into the war.

And from that original attitude they have never swerved. They have never aimed at the break-up of the German peoples or the disintegration of their state or country. Germany has occupied a great position in the world. It is not our wish or intention to question or destroy that position for the future, but rather to turn her aside from hopes and schemes of military domination, and to see her devote all her strength to the great beneficent tasks of the world. Nor are we fighting to destroy Austria-Hungary or to deprive Turkey of its capital, or of the rich and renowned lands of Asia Minor and Thrace, which are predominantly Turkish in race.

Nor did we enter this war merely to alter or destroy the imperial constitution of Germany, much as we consider that military, autocratic constitution a dangerous anachronism in the 20th century. Our point of view is that the adoption of a really democratic constitution by Germany would be the most convincing evidence that in her the old spirit of military domination had indeed died in this war, and would make it much easier for us to conclude a broad democratic peace with her. But, after all, that is a question for the German people to decide...

So long as the possibility of dispute between nations continues—that is to say, so long as men and women are dominated by passion and ambition, and war is the only means of settling a dispute—all nations must live under the burden, not only of having from time to time to engage in it, but of being compelled to prepare for its possible outbreak. The crushing weight of modern armaments, the increasing evil of compulsory military service, the vast waste of wealth and effort involved in warlike preparation, these are blots on our civilization of which every thinking individual must be ashamed.

For these and other similar reasons, we are confident that a great attempt must be made to establish by some international organization an alternative to war as a means of settling international disputes. After all, war is a relic of barbarism and, just as law has succeeded violence as the means of settling disputes between individuals, so we believe that it is destined ultimately to take the place of war in the settlement of controversies between nations.

'The crushing weight of modern armaments, the increasing evil of compulsory military service, the vast waste of wealth and effort involved in warlike preparation, these are blots on our civilization.'

If, then, we are asked what we are fighting for, we reply as, we have often replied: we are fighting for a just and lasting peace, and we believe that before permanent peace can be hoped for three conditions must be fulfilled: firstly, the sanctity of treaties must be established; secondly, a territorial settlement must be secured, based on the right of self-determination or the consent of the governed; and, lastly, we must seek by the creation of some international organization to limit the burden of armaments and diminish the probability of war.

On these conditions the British Empire would welcome peace; to secure these conditions its peoples are prepared to make even greater sacrifices than those they have yet endured.'

By the time World War I ended, on 11 November 1918, having involved soldiers from as far afield as the United States, Canada, Australia and New Zealand, as well as Turkish, Hungarian and Italian military, some 20 million people had lost their lives in the 'war to end all wars'.

Neville Chamberlain

'He Can Only Be Stopped By Force'

Broadcast to the British people making a declaration of war on Germany, 3 September 1939.

Neville Chamberlain on his return from Munich after meeting with Hitler, 30 September 1938.

During World War I and in the period after it ended, Germany's economy, and authority and prestige in the world arena were severely effected. Through the 1920s and into the 1930s, the nation was plagued with economic problems, unemployment and a collapse of its currency. It also saw the collapse of the Weimar Republic in 1933, and the steady rise to prominence of the National Socialist Party (the Nazis), headed by Adolf Hitler (1889–1945). Germany witnessed great conflict between the Nazis and the Communists, among other factions.

Hitler, or Der Führer (the 'Leader') as he became known, became chancellor in 1933, taking around one-third of the vote. Although he had already written *Mein Kampf* (1925), which outlined many of his opinions on the German people and the Jewish race, his rhetoric became openly more hostile and the Nazis' violent action against Germany's Jewish population more overt. He also began a programme of rearmament, in breach of the Treaty of Versailles, signed at the end of World War I. This, and Hitler's support of territorial expansion to increase the German people's 'living space', plus promises to increase employment, improve the economy and defend German honour, helped make Hitler increasingly popular. While secretly plotting war, Hitler formed the Rome–Berlin axis in 1936, allying himself with Italian fascist leader 'Il Duce', Benito Mussolini (1883–1945).

In 1937 Neville Chamberlain (1869-1940) became prime minister of Britain. He followed fellow Conservative Stanley Baldwin (1867–1947), who had failed to respond to aggressive German rearmament and war preparations, and Chamberlain essentially continued the policy of so-called 'appeasement'.

Hitler took over the Sudetenland (historically made up of sections of northern and western Bohemia and northern Moravia) and annexed Austria, without a shot being fired. Britain and France continued to try to appease him by acquiescing to his demands over Czechoslovakia in the Munich Agreement of September 1938, a document which Chamberlain flourished from the steps of his aircraft with the triumphant pronouncement of: 'Peace in our time!'.

Statesman Winston Churchill (1874–1965) remarked: 'An appeaser is one who feeds a crocodile, hoping it will eat him last.' Churchill's judgement was sound. The Nazis never had any intention of honouring their word and, in 1939 Hitler invaded Poland, and Europe and the rest of the world entered yet another war. A broken man, Chamberlain broadcast the news to Britons in their homes.

'I am speaking to you from the cabinet room of 10 Downing Street. This morning the British Ambassador in Berlin handed the German Government a final note stating that, unless we

'This is a sad day for all of us, and to none sadder than to me. Everything that I have worked for, everything that I have hoped for, everything that I have believed in during my public life, has crashed into ruins.'

heard from them by 11 o'clock that they were prepared at once to withdraw their troops from Poland, a state of war would exist between us. I have to tell you now that no such undertaking has been received, and that consequently this country is at war with Germany.

You can imagine what a bitter blow it is to me that all my long struggle to win peace has failed. Yet I cannot believe that there is anything more, or anything different, that I could have done, and that would have been more successful. Up to the very last it would have been quite possible to have arranged a peaceful and honourable settlement between Germany and Poland. But Hitler would not have it; he had evidently made up his mind to attack Poland whatever happened. And although he now says he put forward reasonable proposals which were rejected by the Poles, that is not a true statement. The proposals were never shown to the Poles, nor to us. And though they were announced in the German broadcast on Thursday night, Hitler did not wait to hear comments on them but ordered his troops to cross the Polish frontier the next morning.

His action shows convincingly that there is no chance of expecting that this man will ever give up his practice of using force to gain his will. He can only be stopped by force, and we and France are today in fulfilment of our obligations going to the aid of Poland who is so bravely resisting this wicked and unprovoked attack upon her people.

We have a clear conscience, we have done all that any country could do to establish peace, but a situation in which no word given by Germany's ruler could be trusted, and no people or country could feel itself safe, had become intolerable. And now that we have resolved to finish it, I know that you will all play your parts with calmness and courage.'

In a speech to the House of Commons on the same day, Chamberlain revealed just what a bitter blow to him personally the failure to stave off a return to the battlefield had been.

'This is a sad day for all of us, and to none sadder than to me. Everything that I have worked for, everything that I have hoped for, everything that I have believed in during my public life, has crashed into ruins. There is only one thing left for me to do: that is, to devote what strength and powers I have to forwarding the victory of the cause for which we have to sacrifice so much. I cannot tell what part I may be allowed to play myself; I trust I may live to see the day when Hitlerism has been destroyed and a liberated Europe has been re-established.'

Neville Chamberlain was not allowed to play a part for long: Churchill succeeded him as prime minister in May 1940, when Britain's fortunes were at their lowest ebb. Chamberlain died from cancer in November that same year.

Winston Churchill

'The Few'

The Battle of Britain speech to the House of Commons, London, 20 August 1940.

Winston Churchill broadcasting from Downing Street, London, 1942.

When Winston Churchill became British prime minister in May 1940, he found himself in charge of a nation poorly prepared for war, one facing the drilled and marshalled forces of a fanatical foe.

Churchill was a soldier–statesman and was educated at both Harrow and Sandhurst Military College. He served with the British forces in India and the Sudan, and in 1900 stood for the Conservatives for the House of Commons. Lord of the Admiralty at the outbreak of World War I in 1914, he oversaw the British–Anzac landing at Gallipoli, Turkey, and resigned after its disastrous failure. He was soon recalled however, as minister of munitions.

A headstrong, sometimes erratic and capricious man, Churchill called for a hard line during the General Strike in Britain of 1926. He opposed any moves for Indian independence from Britain, famously dubbing Mahatma Gandhi, one of the leading figures of the Quit India movement, a 'half-naked fakir'.

He recognized early on the threat posed by Hitler, however, and was strongly opposed to the appeasement policy followed by both Baldwin and Chamberlain. As Nazi panzers tore into France in May 1940, Churchill accepted the post of prime minister stating: 'I have nothing to offer but blood, toil, tears and sweat.'

During the dark days that followed, Churchill, a great orator, made memorable speeches to try to keep up the spirits of his people. 'Let us therefore brace ourselves to our duties and so bear ourselves that if the British Empire and its Commonwealth last for 1,000 years men will still say "This was their finest hour", and proclaiming "We shall never surrender". He worked night and day while German bombers overhead pounded London, snatching what sleep he could on a camp bed down in a Whitehall bunker.

In the following speech, as the fighter pilots of the Royal Air Force battled against the German bombers striving to pave the way for a planned Nazi invasion of the British Isles, Churchill famously commented of the Battle of Britain pilots: 'Never in the field of human conflict was so much owed by so many to so few.'

'Almost a year has passed since the war began, and it is natural for us, I think, to pause on our journey at this milestone and survey the dark, wide field. It is also useful to compare the first year of this second war against German aggression with its forerunner a quarter of a century ago. Although this war is in fact only a continuation of the last, very great differences in its character are apparent.

In the last war millions of men fought by hurling enormous masses of steel at one another. "Men and shells" was the cry, and prodigious slaughter was the consequence. In this war nothing of this kind has yet appeared. It is a conflict of strategy, of organization, of technical apparatus, of science, mechanics, and morale. The British casualties in the first 12 months of the Great War amounted to 365,000. In this war, I am thankful to say, British killed, wounded, prisoners, and missing, including civilians, do not exceed 92,000, and of these a large proportion are alive as prisoners of war. Looking more widely around, one may say that throughout all Europe for one man killed or wounded in the first year perhaps five were killed or wounded in 1914–15.

The slaughter is only a small fraction, but the consequences to the belligerents have been even more deadly. We have seen great countries with powerful armies dashed out of coherent existence in a few weeks. We have seen the French Republic and the renowned French Army beaten into complete and total submission with less than the casualties which they suffered in any one of half a dozen of the battles of 1914–18.

'The whole of the warring nations are engaged, not only soldiers, but the entire population, men, women, and children. The fronts are everywhere. The trenches are dug in the towns and streets. Every village is fortified. Every road is barred. The front line runs through the factories.'

The entire body—it might almost seem at times the soul—of France has succumbed to physical effects incomparably less terrible than those which were sustained with fortitude and undaunted willpower 25 years ago.

Although up to the present the loss of life has been mercifully diminished, the decisions reached in the course of the struggle are even more profound upon the fate of nations than anything that has ever happened since barbaric times. Moves are made upon the scientific and strategic boards, advantages are gained by mechanical means, as a result of which scores of millions of men become incapable of further resistance, or judge themselves incapable of further resistance, and a fearful game of chess proceeds from check to mate by which the unhappy players seem to be inexorably bound.

There is another more obvious difference from 1914. The whole of the warring nations are engaged, not only soldiers, but the entire population, men, women, and children. The fronts are everywhere. The trenches are dug in the towns and streets. Every village is fortified. Every road is barred. The front line runs through the factories. The workmen are soldiers with different weapons but the same courage. These are great and distinctive changes from what many of us saw in the struggle of a quarter of a century ago.

There seems to be every reason to believe that this new kind of war is well suited to the genius and the resources of the British nation and the British Empire and that, once we get properly equipped and properly started, a war of this kind will be more favourable to us than the sombre mass slaughters of the Somme and Passchendaele. If it is a case of the whole nation fighting and suffering together, that ought to suit us, because we are the most united of all the nations, because we entered the war upon the national will and with our eyes open, and because we have been nurtured in freedom and individual responsibility and are the products, not of totalitarian uniformity but of tolerance and variety.

If all these qualities are turned, as they are being turned, to the arts of war, we may be able to show the enemy quite a lot of things that they have not thought of yet. Since the Germans drove

'It would have seemed incredible that at the end of a period of horror and disaster, or at this point in a period of horror and disaster, we should stand erect, sure of ourselves, masters of our fate and with the conviction of final victory burning unquenchable in our hearts.'

the Jews out and lowered their technical standards, our science is definitely ahead of theirs. Our geographical position, the command of the sea, and the friendship of the United States enable us to draw resources from the whole world and to manufacture weapons of war of every kind, but especially of the superfine kinds, on a scale hitherto practised only by Nazi Germany.

Hitler is now sprawled over Europe. Our offensive springs are being slowly compressed, and we must resolutely and methodically prepare ourselves for the campaigns of 1941 and 1942. Two or three years are not a long time, even in our short, precarious lives. They are nothing in the history of the nation, and when we are doing the finest thing in the world, and have the honour to be the sole champion of the liberties of all Europe, we must not grudge these years or weary as we toil and struggle through them...

Rather more than a quarter of a year has passed since the new Government came into power in this country. What a cataract of disaster has poured out upon us since then. The trustful Dutch overwhelmed; their beloved and respected Sovereign driven into exile; the peaceful city of Rotterdam the scene of a massacre as hideous and brutal as anything in the Thirty Years' War. Belgium invaded and beaten down; our own fine Expeditionary Force, which King Leopold called to his rescue, cut off and almost captured, escaping as it seemed only by a miracle and with the loss of all its equipment; our Ally, France, out; Italy in against us; all France in the power of the enemy, all its arsenals and vast masses of military material converted or convertible to the enemy's use; a puppet Government set up at Vichy which may at any moment be forced to become our foe; the whole Western seaboard of Europe from the North Cape to the Spanish frontier in German hands; all the ports, all the airfields on this immense front, employed against us as potential springboards of invasion. Moreover, the German air power, numerically so far outstripping ours, has been brought so close to our island that what we used to dread greatly has come to pass and the hostile bombers not only reach our shores in a few minutes and from many directions, but can be escorted by their fighting aircraft.

Why, Sir, if we had been confronted at the beginning of May with such a prospect, it would have seemed incredible that at the end of a period of horror and disaster, or at this point in a period of horror and disaster, we should stand erect, sure of ourselves, masters of our fate and with the conviction of final victory burning unquenchable in our hearts. Few would have believed we could survive; none would have believed that we should today not only feel stronger but should actually be stronger than we have ever been before.

Let us see what has happened on the other side of the scales. The British nation and the British Empire finding themselves alone, stood undismayed against disaster. No-one flinched or wavered; nay, some who formerly thought of peace, now think only of war. Our people are united and resolved, as they have never been before. Death and ruin have become small things compared with the shame of defeat or failure in duty.

We cannot tell what lies ahead. It may be that even greater ordeals lie before us. We shall face whatever is coming to us. We are sure of ourselves and of our cause and that is the supreme fact which has emerged in these months of trial.

Meanwhile, we have not only fortified our hearts but our island. We have rearmed and rebuilt our armies in a degree which would have been deemed impossible a few months ago. We have ferried across the Atlantic, in the month of July, thanks to our friends over there, an immense mass of munitions of all kinds, cannon, rifles, machine-guns, cartridges, and shell, all safely landed without the loss of a gun or a round. The output of our own factories, working as they have never worked before, has poured forth to the troops. The whole British Army is at home. More than 2 million determined men have rifles and bayonets in their hands tonight and three-quarters of them are in regular military formations. We have never had armies like this in our island in time of war. The whole island bristles against invaders, from the sea or from the air.

As I explained to the House in the middle of June, the stronger our Army at home, the larger must the invading expedition be, and the larger the invading expedition, the less difficult will be the task of the Navy in detecting its assembly and in intercepting and destroying it on passage; and the greater also would be the difficulty of feeding and supplying the invaders if ever they landed, in the teeth of continuous naval and air attack on their communications. All this is classical and venerable doctrine. As in Nelson's day, the maxim holds, "Our first line of defence is the enemy's ports". Now air reconnaissance and photography have brought to an old principle a new and potent aid.

Our Navy is far stronger than it was at the beginning of the war. The great flow of new construction set on foot at the outbreak is now beginning to come in. We hope our friends across the ocean will send us a timely reinforcement to bridge the gap between the peace flotillas of 1939 and the war flotillas of 1941. There is no difficulty in sending such aid. The seas and oceans are open. The U-boats are contained. The magnetic mine is, up to the present time, effectively mastered. The merchant tonnage under the British flag, after a year of unlimited U-boat war, after eight months of intensive mining attack, is larger than when we began. We have, in addition, under our control at least 4 million tons of shipping from the captive countries which has taken refuge here or in the harbours of the Empire. Our stocks of food of all kinds are far more abundant than in the days of peace and a large and growing programme of food production is on foot.

Why do I say all this? Not assuredly to boast; not assuredly to give the slightest countenance to complacency. The dangers we face are still enormous, but so are our advantages and resources. I recount them because the people have a right to know that there are solid grounds for the confidence which we feel, and that we have good reason to believe ourselves capable, as I said in a very dark hour two months ago, of continuing the war "if necessary alone, if necessary for years". I say it also because the fact that the British Empire stands invincible, and that Nazidom is still

'More than 2 million determined men have rifles and bayonets in their hands tonight and three-quarters of them are in regular military formations. We have never had armies like this in our island in time of war. The whole island bristles against invaders.'

‘The gratitude of every home in our island, in our Empire, and indeed throughout the world, except in the abodes of the guilty, goes out to the British airmen who, undaunted by odds, unwearied in their constant challenge and mortal danger, are turning the tide of the world war by their prowess and by their devotion. Never in the field of human conflict was so much owed by so many to so few.’

being resisted, will kindle again the spark of hope in the breasts of hundreds of millions of downtrodden or despairing men and women throughout Europe, and far beyond its bounds, and that from these sparks there will presently come cleansing and devouring flame.

The great air battle which has been in progress over this island for the last few weeks has recently attained a high intensity. It is too soon to attempt to assign limits either to its scale or to its duration. We must certainly expect that greater efforts will be made by the enemy than any he has so far put forth. Hostile air fields are still being developed in France and the Low Countries, and the movement of squadrons and material for attacking us is still proceeding.

It is quite plain that Herr Hitler could not admit defeat in his air attack on Great Britain without sustaining most serious injury. If, after all his boastings and blood-curdling threats and lurid accounts trumpeted round the world of the damage he has inflicted, of the vast numbers of our Air Force he has shot down, so he says, with so little loss to himself; if after tales of the panic-stricken British crushed in their holes cursing the plutocratic Parliament which has led them to such a plight; if after all this his whole air onslaught were forced after a while tamely to peter out, the Führer's reputation for veracity of statement might be seriously impugned...

The gratitude of every home in our island, in our Empire, and indeed throughout the world, except in the abodes of the guilty, goes out to the British airmen who, undaunted by odds, unwearied in their constant challenge and mortal danger, are turning the tide of the world war by their prowess and by their devotion. Never in the field of human conflict was so much owed by so many to so few.’

Despite the victory over Germany in 1945, Churchill was defeated in a landslide election in the same year by the Labour Party of Clement Attlee (1883–1965), about whom he quipped he that was ‘a modest man who has much to be modest about’. Churchill was re-elected in 1951, and served as prime minister until 1955. Before his death, in 1965, he remarked: ‘I am prepared to meet my maker. Whether my maker is prepared for the great ordeal of meeting me is another matter.’

Benito Mussolini

'We Call Bread Bread, and Wine Wine'

Addressing the Blackshirts, Rome, 23 February 1941.

Dictator Benito Mussolini saluting during a public address, 1938.

The Italian dictator, also known as 'Il Duce' ('The Leader') once commented that 'war is to men what maternity is to women'—certainly, conflict seemed to come naturally to him. Mussolini (1883–1945) was the son of a part-time journalist and blacksmith and a teacher. A socialist as a young man, Mussolini's fervent nationalism led him eventually to a parting of ideological ways with that earlier favoured political doctrine.

He enlisted in the Italian Army during World War I and was wounded in 1917. Two years later, he founded the Fascio di Combattimento ('fighting bands') organisation for World War I veterans, and Fascism was born. Soldiers returning to an Italy stricken with political, economic and industrial turmoil found his posturing machismo and hectoring rhetoric irresistible, and outfitted in their signature black shirts they became Mussolini's private army.

In 1922, with the government in crisis, Mussolini led the Blackshirts in their 'March On Rome', a coup d'etat. During the 1920s he suspended constitutional rule, curtailed civil rights, and crushed opposition. Dreaming of emulating ancient imperial Rome, in 1935 he felt ready to embark on empire-building, and launched brutal invasions of Ethiopia and Albania. Along with Hitler, he supported General Francisco Franco (1892–1975) during the Spanish Civil War (1936–39), and in 1940 entered World War II on the Nazi side in the so-called Axis.

In this speech to his followers, the year after Italy entered the war, he seeks to justify his actions, extolls fascist Italy with pomp and vainglory, and declares himself unafraid of speaking openly about Italy's first disasters during the war.

'We have actually been at war since 1922—that is, from the day when we lifted the flag of our revolution, which was then defended by a handful of men against the Masonic, democratic, capitalistic world. From that day world liberalism, democracy and plutocracy declared and waged war.'

'Blackshirts of Rome! I come among you to look you firmly in the eyes, feel your temperature and break the silence which is dear to me, especially in wartime. Have you ever asked yourselves in an hour of meditation, which every one finds during the day, how long we have been at war? Not only eight months, as a superficial observer of events might believe, not from September the first 1939, when through guarantees to Poland, Britain unleashed the conflagration with a criminal and premeditated will. We have been at war six years, precisely from 1 February 1935, when the first communiqué announcing the mobilization of Peloritana was issued.

The Ethiopian war was hardly finished when from the other shore of the Mediterranean there reached us appeals from General Franco, who had begun his national revolution. Could we Fascisti leave without answering that cry and remain indifferent in the face of the perpetuation of the bloody crimes of the so-called popular fronts? Could we refuse to give our aid to the movement of salvation that had found in Antonio Primo de Rivera its creator, ascetic and martyr? No. Thus our first squadron of aeroplanes left on 27 July 1936, and during the same day we had our first dead.

We have actually been at war since 1922—that is, from the day when we lifted the flag of our revolution, which was then defended by a handful of men against the Masonic, democratic, capitalistic world. From that day world liberalism, democracy and plutocracy declared and waged war against us with press campaigns, spreading libellous reports, financial sabotage, attempts and plots even when we were intent upon the work of international reconstruction which is and will remain for centuries, as the undestroyable documentation of our creative will...

But developments in history, which sometimes are speeded up, cannot be halted any more than the fleeting moment of Faust could be halted. History takes one by the throat and forces a decision. This is not the first time this has occurred in the history of Italy! If we had been 100 per cent ready we would have entered the war in September 1939, and not in June 1940. During that brief period of time we faced and overcame exceptional difficulties.

The lightning-like and crushing victory of Germany in the West eliminated the eventuality of a long continental war. Since then the land war on the Continent has ended and it cannot flare back. The German victory was facilitated by Italian non-belligerency which immobilized heavy naval, air and land forces of the Anglo–French bloc. Some people who today apparently think Italy's intervention was premature were probably the same who then deemed it too late.

In reality the moment was timely because if it is true that one enemy was in the course of liquidation there remained the other, the bigger one, the most powerful enemy number one against whom we are engaged and against whom we will continue the struggle to the last drop of blood.

Having definitely liquidated Britain's armies on the European Continent, the war could not but assume a naval, air and, for us, also a colonial character. It is the geographic and historic order of things that the most difficult and most faraway theatres of war are reserved for Italy. War beyond the sea and in the desert. Our fronts stretch for thousands of kilometres and are thousands of kilometres away. Some ignorant foreign commentators should take due account of this. However, during the first four months of the war we were able to inflict grave naval, air and land blows to the forces of the British Empire.

Since 1935 the attention of our general staff has been focused on Libya. All the work of the Governors who succeeded each other in Libya was aimed at strengthening economically and militarily that large region, transforming the former desert or desert zones into fecund land. Miracles! This word is able to sum up what has been done down there. With European tension becoming graver, and following the events of 1935 and 1936, Libya, reconquered by Fascism, was considered one of the most delicate

'But developments in history, which sometimes are speeded up, cannot be halted any more than the fleeting moment of Faust could be halted. History takes one by the throat and forces a decision. This is not the first time this has occurred in the history of Italy!'

'We haven't elevated lying into a government art nor into a narcotic for the people the way the London government has done. We call bread bread, and wine wine, and when the enemy wins a battle it is useless and ridiculous to seek, as the English do in their incomparable hypocrisy, to deny or diminish it.'

points in our general strategic set-up, since it could be attacked from two fronts.

The effort carried out militarily to strengthen Libya is shown by these figures. During the period only from 1 October 1937 to 31 January 1940, we sent to Libya 14,000 officers and 396,358 soldiers, and organized two armies—the fifth and 10th. This latter had 10 divisions. In the same period were sent 1,924 cannon of all calibres and many of them of recent construction and model; 15,386 machine-guns; 11,000,000 rounds of shells; 1,344,287,275 bullets for light arms; 127,877 tons of engineers' materials; 779 tanks with a certain per centage of heavy tanks; 9,584 auto vehicles of various kinds; 4,809 motorcycles.

These figures show that to the preparation of the Libyan defence we devoted an effort which can be described as imposing. The same thing can be said as far as East Africa is concerned, where we were prepared to resist despite the distance and total isolation, which is a tribute to the will and courage of our soldiers. The soldiers who are fighting in the empire—without any hope of help—are farthest but therefore nearest our hearts. Commanded by the born soldier the Viceroy is and by a group of generals of great valour, the national and native soldiers will cause great trouble to the enemy.

It was during October and November that Great Britain gathered and lined up against us the mass of her imperial forces, recruited from three continents and armed by a fourth. She concentrated in Egypt 15 divisions and a considerable mass of armoured means and hurled them against our lines in Marmarica where on the first line were Libyan divisions, brave and faithful but unsuited to bear the attack of enemy machines. In December a battle was thus started, which was only five or 10 days in advance of ours, and which brought the enemy to Bengazi.

We are not like the English. We boast that we are not like them. We haven't elevated lying into a government art nor into a narcotic for the people the way the London government has done. We call bread bread, and wine wine, and when the enemy wins a battle it is useless and ridiculous to seek, as the English do in their incomparable hypocrisy, to deny or diminish it. One entire army—the 10th—was broken up almost completely with its men and cannon. The Fifth Air Squadron was literally sacrificed, almost entirely. Where possible we resisted strongly and furiously.

Since we recognize these facts it is useless for the enemy to exaggerate the figures of its booty. It is because we are certain regarding the grade of national maturity reached by the Italian people and regarding the future development of events that we continue to follow the cult of truth and repudiate all falsification.

The events during these months exasperate our will and must accentuate against the enemy that cold, conscious, implacable hate, hate in every home, which is indispensable for victory. Great Britain's last support on the Continent was and is Greece, the only nation that did not want to renounce the British guarantee. It was necessary to face Greece, and on this point the accord of all responsible military leaders was absolute. I add that the operative plan, prepared by the superior command of the armed forces of Albania, was unanimously approved without reservations. Between the decision and the start of action there was a delay of only two days.

Let it be said once and for all that the Italian soldiers in Albania combated superbly. Let it be said in particular that the Alpini wrote pages of blood and glory that would honour any army. When the sufferings of the march by the Julia division almost up to Metzovo are known all will appear legendary.

Neutrals of every continent who are spectators at the bloody clashes between the armed masses must have sufficient shame to keep quiet and not express libellous provocative opinions.

The Italian prisoners who fell into the hands of the Greeks are a few thousand, most of them wounded. The Greek successes do not go out of the tactical field and only megalomania has magnified them. The Greek losses are very high and shortly it will be spring, and as befits such a season our season—beautiful things will grow. I say beautiful things will be seen in every one of the four cardinal points.

Not less heavy are the losses we inflicted on the English. To state as they do that their losses in the battle of 60 days in Cyrenaica are not above 2,000 dead and wounded means adding a grotesque note to the drama. It means attempting to exceed themselves as far as shameless lies are concerned, which should seem difficult for the English. They must add at least one zero to the figures of their communiqués.

From November to when English torpedo planes, which took off not from Greek bases but from an aircraft carrier, succeeded with their coup at Taranto, which we admitted, we met adversity in the war. We must recognize this. We had grey days.

This happens in all wars, in all times. Think of the Punic Wars, when the Battle of Cannae threatened to crush Rome. But at Zama, Rome destroyed Carthage and wiped it out from geography and history forever. Our capacity to recuperate in moral and material fields is really formidable and constitutes one of the peculiar characteristics of our race.

'Think of the Punic Wars, when the Battle of Cannae threatened to crush Rome. But at Zama, Rome destroyed Carthage and wiped it out from geography and history forever. Our capacity to recuperate in moral and material fields is really formidable.'

Especially in this war, which has the world as its theatre and pits continents directly or indirectly one against another. On land and sea and in the air it is the final battle that counts. That we shall have to fight hard is certain, that we shall have to fight long is also probable, but the final result will be an Axis victory.

Great Britain cannot win the war. I can prove this logically and in this case belief is corroborated by fact. This proof begins with the dogmatic premise that although anything may happen Italy will march with Germany, side by side, to the end.

Those who may be tempted to imagine something different forget that the alliance between Italy and Germany is not only between two States or two armies or two diplomacies but between two peoples and two revolutions and is destined to give its imprint upon the century.

'Americans who will read what I say should be calm and not believe in the existence of a big bad wolf who wants to devour them. In all cases it is more likely that the United States, before it is attacked by Axis soldiers, will be attacked by the not well known but very warlike inhabitants of the planet Mars.'

The collaboration offered by the Führer and that which the German air and armoured units are giving in the Mediterranean are proof that all fronts are common and that our efforts are common. The Germans know that Italy today has on her shoulders the weight of 1 million British and Greek soldiers, of from 1,500 to 2,000 planes, of as many tanks, of thousands of cannon, of at least 500,000 tons of military shipping.

Co-operation between the two armed forces occurs on the plan of comradely, loyal, spontaneous solidarity. Let it be said for foreigners who are always ready to libel that the comportment of German soldiers in Sicily and Libya is under all respects perfect and worthy of a strong army and a strong people brought up under severe discipline...

Churchill has not the least idea of the spiritual forces of the Italian people or of what Fascism can do. We can understand Churchill's ordering the shelling of industrial plants at Genoa to disrupt work, but to shell the city in order to break down its morale is a childish illusion. It means that the British do not at all know the race temperament of the Ligurian people in general and the Genoese in particular. It means that they are ignorant of the civilian virtues and proud patriotism of the people who gave the fatherland Columbus, Garibaldi and Mazzini...

Let me say now that what is occurring in the United States is one of the most colossal mystifications in all history. Illusion and lying are the basis of American interventionism—illusion that the United States is still a democracy, when instead it is a political and financial oligarchy dominated by Jews, through a personal form of dictatorship. The lie is that the Axis powers, after they finish Great Britain, want to attack America.

Neither in Rome nor Berlin are such fantastic plans as this prepared. These projects could not be made by those who have an inclination for the madhouse. Though we certainly are totalitarian and will always be so, we have our feet on hard ground. Americans who will read what I say should be calm and not believe in the existence of a big bad wolf who wants to devour them.

In all cases it is more likely that the United States, before it is attacked by Axis soldiers, will be attacked by the not well known but very warlike inhabitants of the planet Mars, who will descend from the stratosphere in unimaginable flying fortresses.

Rome comrades! Through you I want to speak to the Italian people, to the authentic, real, great Italian people, who fight with the courage of lions on land, sea and air fronts; people who early in the morning are up to go to work in fields, factories and offices; people who do not permit themselves luxuries, not even innocent ones.

They absolutely must not be confused or contaminated by the minority or well-known poltroons, anti-social individuals and complainers, who grumble about rations and regret their suspended comforts, or by snakes, the remains of the Masonic lodges, whom we will crush without difficulties when and how we want.

The Italian people, the Fascist people deserve and will have victory. The hardships, suffering and sacrifices that are faced with exemplary courage and dignity by the Italian people will have their day of compensation when all the enemy forces are crushed on the battlefields by the heroism of our soldiers and a triple, immense cry will cross the mountains and oceans like lightning and light new hopes and give new certainties to spirit multitudes: Victory, Italy, peace with justice among peoples! ’

Whatever the beliefs of Mussolini, the Italians made poor allies for the Germans and were defeated virtually wherever they took to the field. When the Allies invaded Sicily in 1943, Mussolini was removed from office and placed under arrest. Rescued in a raid by German paratroopers, he became a puppet of the Nazis, heading a powerless splinter regime. Il Duce and his mistress Clara Petacci attempted to escape to Switzerland in the closing days of the war in 1945, but they were captured and executed. Their bodies were strung up by their heels on the streets of Milan where mobs mocked and jeered at the dead dictator.

Adolf Hitler

'The Most Bloodthirsty or Amateurish Strategist that History Has Ever Known'

**Speech to the Reichstag,
Berlin, 4 May 1941.**

Adolf Hitler gives a May Day address at the Lustgarten, Berlin in 1935.

The name Adolf Hitler was once revered by Germans at the height of his wartime success, but after his downfall it became synonymous for peoples across the world with treachery, cruelty and mass murder. The Austrian-born German dictator's creed of racial hatred, fanatical mythic-nationalism and territorial expansion stole the lives of tens of millions of people around the world.

A would-be artist, Hitler failed to gain entry to the Vienna School of Art, and sold his watercolours on the street. He enlisted in the German army during World War I, and was promoted to corporal and awarded the Iron Cross. After the war had ended, he joined the National Socialist German Workers' (Nazi) Party, discovering in himself a skill in oratory. He went on to become party leader.

Imprisoned after the failure of the 'Beer Hall Putsch' in Munich in 1923, Hitler wrote his manifesto *Mein Kampf* (My Struggle), espousing anti-semitism and German territorial expansionism, among other things. Upon his release, Hitler found the ground fertile for his extreme political and cultural views, as Germans were suffering from severe post-war economic hardship. His Nazi party battled with the Communist Party, which many people also found attractive, and made several attempts to win power through the ballot box. He became Germany's chancellor in 1933 and its president in 1934. He staged massive torchlight rallies to emphasize resurgent German power, built concentration camps to deal with political dissidents, social deviants, Jews, Slavs and other people that he deemed unfit. He also intensified the Nazi campaign of violence against the Jews.

His armies invaded Poland in September 1939, and Britain and France subsequently declared war on Germany. The Nazi mechanized formations of panzer tanks and dive-bombers wrought havoc on Poland. They repeated their blitzkrieg victory in France in May 1940, skirting the 'impregnable' Maginot Line, and smashing their way through outmanoeuvred French and British forces. With France fallen, Italy in alliance with Hitler, Spain in de facto alliance and the USSR in a non-aggression pact, only Britain remained standing against him.

In this speech to the German assembly, made in May 1941, Hitler makes plain his irritation with Churchill (see pages 51–56), whom he has failed to defeat. Hitler's forces had suffered their first major reverse of the war in the summer of 1940, when the Luftwaffe lost the Battle of Britain, and an invasion of Britain was not deemed possible. Hitler devotes significant passages of the text that follows to delivering personal attacks on Churchill, while at the same time speaking about the situation in Greece and also glorifying German military prowess.

‘Deputies. Men of the German Reichstag.

At a time when only deeds count and words are of little importance, it is not my intention to appear before you, the elected representatives of the German people, more often than absolutely necessary. The first time I spoke to you was at the outbreak of the war when, thanks to the Anglo–French conspiracy against peace, every attempt at an understanding with Poland, which otherwise would have been possible, had been frustrated.

The most unscrupulous men of the present time had, as they admit today, decided as early as 1936 to involve the Reich, which in its peaceful work of reconstruction was becoming too powerful for them, in a new and bloody war and, if possible, to destroy it. They had finally succeeded in finding a state that was prepared for their interests and aims, and that state was Poland.

‘The man behind this fanatical and diabolical plan to bring about war at whatever cost was Mr Churchill. His associates were the men who now form the British Government. These endeavours received most powerful support, both openly and secretly, from the so-called great democracies on both sides of the Atlantic.’

All my endeavours to come to an understanding with Britain were wrecked by the determination of a small clique which, whether from motives of hate or for the sake of material gain, rejected every German proposal for an understanding due to their resolve, which they never concealed, to resort to war, whatever happened.

The man behind this fanatical and diabolical plan to bring about war at whatever cost was Mr Churchill. His associates were the men who now form the British Government. These endeavours received most powerful support, both openly and secretly, from the so-called great democracies on both sides of the Atlantic. At a time when the people were more and more dissatisfied with their deficient statesmanship, the responsible men over there believed that a successful war would be the most likely means of solving problems that otherwise would be beyond their power to solve.

Behind these men there stood the great international Jewish financial interests that control the banks and the Stock Exchange as well as the armament industry. And now, just as before, they sensed the opportunity of doing their unsavoury business. And so, just as before, there was no scruple about sacrificing the blood of the peoples. That was the beginning of this war. A few weeks later the state that was the third country in Europe, Poland, but had been reckless enough to allow herself to be used for the financial interests of these warmongers, was annihilated and destroyed.

In these circumstances I considered that I owed it to our German people and countless men and women in the opposite camps, who as individuals were as decent as they were innocent of blame, to make yet another appeal to the common sense and the conscience of these statesmen. On 6 October 1939, I therefore once more publicly stated that Germany had neither demanded nor intended to demand anything either from Britain or from France, that it was madness to continue the war and, above all, that the scourge of modern weapons of warfare, once they were brought into action, would inevitably ravage vast territories.

But just as the appeal I made on 1 September 1939, proved to be in vain, this renewed appeal met with indignant rejection. The British and their Jewish capitalist backers could find no other explanation for this appeal, which I had made on humanitarian grounds, than the assumption of weakness on the part of Germany. They assured the people of Britain and France that Germany dreaded the clash to be expected in the spring of 1940 and was eager to make peace for fear of the annihilation that would then inevitably result.

Already at that time the Norwegian Government, misled by the stubborn insistence of Mr. Churchill's false prophecies, began to toy with the idea of a British landing on their soil, thereby contributing to the destruction of Germany by permitting their harbours and Swedish iron ore fields to be seized. So sure were Mr. Churchill and Paul Reynaud of the success of their new scheme that finally, whether from sheer recklessness or perhaps under the influence of drink, they deemed it no longer necessary to make a secret of their intentions.

It was thanks to these two gentlemen's tendency to gossip that the German Government at that time gained cognizance of the plans being made against the Reich. A few weeks later this danger to Germany was eliminated. One of the boldest deeds of arms in the whole history of warfare frustrated the attack of the British and French armies against the right flank of our line of defence.

Immediately after the failure of these plans, increased pressure was exerted by the British warmongers upon Belgium and Holland. Now that the attack upon our sources for the supply of iron ore had proved unsuccessful, they aimed to advance the front to the Rhine by involving the Belgian and Dutch states and thus to threaten and paralyse our production centres for iron and steel.

On 10 May of last year perhaps the most memorable struggle in all German history commenced. The enemy front was broken up in a few days and the stage was then set for the operation that culminated in the greatest battle of annihilation in the history of the world. Thus France collapsed, Belgium and Holland were already occupied, and the battered remnants of the British expeditionary force were driven from the European continent, leaving their arms behind.

'On 10 May of last year perhaps the most memorable struggle in all German history commenced. The enemy front was broken up in a few days and the stage was then set for the operation that culminated in the greatest battle of annihilation in the history of the world.'

On 19 July 1940, I then convened the German Reichstag for the third time in order to render that great account which you all still remember. The meeting provided me with the opportunity of expressing the thanks of the nation to its soldiers in a form suited to the uniqueness of the event. Once again I seized the opportunity of urging the world to make peace. And what I foresaw and prophesied at that time happened. My offer of peace was misconstrued as a symptom of fear and cowardice. The European and American warmongers succeeded once again in fogging the sound common sense of the masses, who can never hope to profit from this war, by conjuring up false pictures of new hope. Thus, finally, under pressure of public opinion, as formed by their press, they once more managed to induce the nation to continue this struggle.

Even my warnings against night bombings of the civilian population, as advocated by Mr Churchill, were interpreted as a sign of German impotence. He, the most bloodthirsty or amateurish strategist that history has ever known, actually saw fit to believe that the reserve displayed for months by the German Air Force could be looked upon only as proof of their incapacity to fly by night.

So this man for months ordered his paid scribblers to deceive the British people into believing that the Royal Air Force alone—and no others—was in a position to wage war in this way, and that thus ways and means had been found to force the Reich to its knees by the ruthless onslaught of the British Air Force on the German civilian population in conjunction with the starvation blockade.

Again and again I uttered these warnings against this specific type of aerial warfare, and I did so for over three and a half months. That these warnings failed to impress Mr Churchill does not surprise me in the least. For what does this man care for the lives of others? What does he care for culture or for architecture? When war broke out he stated clearly that he wanted to have his war, even though the cities of England might be reduced to ruins. So now he has got his war. My assurances that from a given moment every one of his bombs would be returned if necessary a hundredfold failed to induce this man to consider even for an instant the criminal nature of his action. He professes not to be in the least depressed and he even assures us that the British people, too, after such bombing raids, greeted him with a joyous serenity, causing him to return to London refreshed by his visits to the stricken areas.

It is possible that this sight strengthened Mr Churchill in his firm determination to continue the war in this way, and we are no less determined to continue to retaliate, if necessary, a hundred bombs for every one of his and to go on doing so until the British nation at last gets rid of this criminal and his methods.

The appeal to forsake me, made to the German nation by this fool and his satellites on May Day, of all days, are only to be explained either as symptomatic of a paralytic disease or of a drunkard's ravings.'

'That these warnings failed to impress Mr Churchill does not surprise me in the least. For what does this man care for the lives of others? What does he care for culture or for architecture? When war broke out he stated clearly that he wanted to have his war, even though the cities of England might be reduced to ruins.'

Unable to conquer Britain, a month after delivering this speech, Hitler made the fatal error of striking out to the East against the Soviets. His troops met the same fate as Napoleon's—initial success followed by bitter defeat, starvation and freezing death in the Russian winter.

Meanwhile Hitler set about turning the 'Final Solution' into a reality—the murder of 6 million Jews, gypsies, homosexuals and anyone else who had opposed him. Most died in concentration camps where they were gassed and their bodies incinerated. The most heinous crime of the century, and perhaps in human history, the Final Solution was conducted with cold-blooded bureaucratic and industrial efficiency.

The worsening reverses on the Eastern Front, and the entry of the US into the war, with an air campaign which devastated German cities and industry, led inexorably to defeat. Allied forces invaded France on D–Day, 6 June 1944, and overcoming initial resistance pushed north towards Germany, while the Soviets advanced from the East.

As Allied forces closed in, Hitler made a final broadcast on 30 January 1945, his last recorded public speech. To the end his message was one of ethnic conflict and triumphalism.

'However grave the crisis may be at the moment, through our unalterable will, our readiness for sacrifice and our own abilities we will overcome the crisis. We will endure. It is not Central Asia that will win, but Europe led by this nation, which for 1500 years has defended and will continue to defend Europe against the East, our Greater German Reich, the German nation.'

'However grave the crisis may be at the moment, through our unalterable will, our readiness for sacrifice and our own abilities we will overcome the crisis. We will endure. It is not Central Asia that will win, but Europe led by this nation.'

Three months later, on 30 April 1945, with Berlin under attack, Hitler married his long-time girlfriend Eva Braun, and the pair committed suicide. His legacy was Europe in ruins, a Jewish people ravaged and profoundly traumatised, and a German people forced to face up to accusations of complicity in its support of such horrific crimes against humanity.

Like many who commit unspeakable acts, Hitler has become an object of obsession and, even, admiration for some people in the decades since his death. Others believe that he was just an opportunist who exploited the suffering of his own people to achieve his own ends and ambitions, murdering countless innocents along the way. He took his own life rather than answer for his crimes to those people whose families and loved ones he had slain through his greed, cruelty and folly.

Joseph Goebbels

'Rise Up, and Let the Storm Break Loose'

Speech, Berlin, 18 February 1943.

Nazi politician Joseph Goebbels speaking at a military gathering in 1940.

While Hitler was considered a mesmerizing public speaker, one who could reduce the masses to either fawning adulation or raise them to seething fury, many held Joseph Goebbels, his propaganda minister, to be his near-equal.

Goebbels (1897–1945) was born into a poor family. A club foot absolved him from military service in World War I, allowing him instead to concentrate on his education. He gained a doctorate in literature which allowed him to use the title 'Dr'. Goebbels closely aligned himself with Adolf Hitler during the tumultuous 1920s and became editor of the Nazi paper *Völkische Freiheit.*

After Hitler became Chancellor in 1933, Goebbels was given the somewhat Orwellian title of Minister of Public Enlightenment and Propaganda. His comprehension of the persuasive power of public spectacles such as massed torchlit rallies, and of the new media of film and radio, as well as print graphics, made him a natural choice to help put forward the Nazi message to the German nation. His services were called upon after German forces were defeated at Stalingrad and the Eastern Front began to disintegrate for the Nazis.

In June 1941, Hitler ordered an invasion of the Soviet Union. Although German formations advanced deep into Soviet territory in the early summer days of the offensive, counter-attacks by Russian forces during the winter kept them out of Moscow. Nazi strategists then settled on a plan to take the city of Stalingrad (now Volgograd) south of Moscow.

The bitter siege, which lasted from July 1942 to February 1943, is said to be the largest battle ever fought, resulting in up to 2 million casualties and 500,000 German and their allied forces captured. It proved a turning point in the war. The Nazi machine had been vanquished by the enemy Hitler hated most, Communist Russia, and as the remaining troops were pushed back to the West, the Soviets pursued them, all the way back to Berlin. More than any other single event, the defeat at Stalingrad represented the beginning of the end for Hitler and the Reich.

As the Nazi regime allowed word to filter out to the German people about the disastrous campaign and its consequences, Hitler's chief propagandist addressed a rally in Berlin that was broadcast to the German people.

In a speech littered with virulently anti-semitic and anti-Soviet rhetoric, Goebbels incited all Germans to rise up and renew the fight.

'I do not know how many millions of people are listening to me over the radio tonight, at home and at the front. I want to speak to all of you from the depths of my heart to the depths of yours. I believe that the entire German people has a passionate interest in what I have to say tonight. I will therefore speak with holy seriousness and openness, as the hour demands.

The German people, raised, educated and disciplined by National Socialism, can bear the whole truth. It knows the gravity of the situation, and its leadership can therefore demand the necessary hard measures, yes even the hardest measures. We Germans are armed against weakness and uncertainty. The blows and misfortunes of the war only give us additional strength, firm resolve, and a spiritual and fighting will to overcome all difficulties and obstacles with revolutionary élan.

Now is not the time to ask how it all happened. That can wait until later, when the German people and the whole world will learn the full truth about the misfortune of the past weeks, and its deep and fateful significance. The heroic sacrifices of heroism of our soldiers in Stalingrad has had vast historical significance for the whole Eastern Front. It was not in vain. The future will make clear why.

When I jump over the past to look ahead, I do it intentionally. The time is short! There is no time for fruitless debates. We must act, immediately, thoroughly, and decisively, as has always been the National Socialist way.

The movement has from its beginning acted in that way to master the many crises it faced and overcame. The National Socialist state also acted decisively when faced by a threat. We are not like the ostrich that sticks its head in the sand so as not to see danger. We are brave enough to look danger in the face, to coolly and ruthlessly take its measure, then act decisively with our heads held high. Both as a movement and as a nation, we have always been at our best when we needed fanatic, determined wills to overcome and eliminate danger, or a strength of character sufficient to overcome every obstacle, or bitter determination to reach our goal, or an iron heart capable of withstanding every internal and external battle. So it will be today. My task is to give you an unvarnished picture of the situation, and to draw the hard conclusions that will guide the actions of the German government, but also of the German people.

We face a serious military challenge in the East. The crisis is at the moment a broad one, similar but not identical in many ways to that of the previous winter. Later we will discuss the causes. Now, we must accept things as they are and discover and apply the ways and means to turn things again in our favour. There is no point in disputing the seriousness of the situation. I do not want to give you a false impression of the situation that could lead to false conclusions, perhaps giving the German people a false sense of security that is altogether inappropriate in the present situation.

'We Germans are armed against weakness and uncertainty. The blows and misfortunes of the war only give us additional strength, firm resolve, and a spiritual and fighting will to overcome all difficulties and obstacles with revolutionary élan.'

The storm raging against our venerable continent from the steppes this winter overshadows all previous human and historical experience. The German army and its allies are the only possible defence. In his proclamation on 30 January, the Führer asked in a grave and compelling way what would have become of Germany and Europe if, on 30 January 1933, a bourgeois or democratic government had taken power instead of the National Socialists! What dangers would have followed, faster than we could then have suspected, and what powers of defence would we have had to meet them? Ten years of National Socialism have been enough to make plain to the German people the seriousness of the danger posed by Bolshevism from the East. Now one can understand why we spoke so often of the fight against Bolshevism at our Nuremberg party rallies. We raised our voices in warning to our German people and the world, hoping to awaken Western humanity from the paralysis of will and spirit into which it had fallen. We tried to open their eyes to the horrible danger from Eastern Bolshevism, which had subjected a nation of nearly 200 million people to the terror of the Jews and was preparing an aggressive war against Europe.

When the Führer ordered the army to attack the East on 22 June 1941, we all knew that this would be the decisive battle of this great struggle. We knew the dangers and difficulties. But we also knew that dangers and difficulties always grow over time, they never diminish. It was two minutes before midnight. Waiting any longer could easily have led to the destruction of the Reich and a total Bolshevization of the European continent.

'It is understandable that, as a result of broad concealment and misleading actions by the Bolshevist government, we did not properly evaluate the Soviet Union's war potential. Only now do we see its true scale. That is why the battle our soldiers face in the East exceeds in its hardness, dangers and difficulties all human imagining.'

It is understandable that, as a result of broad concealment and misleading actions by the Bolshevist government, we did not properly evaluate the Soviet Union's war potential. Only now do we see its true scale. That is why the battle our soldiers face in the East exceeds in its hardness, dangers and difficulties all human imagining. It demands our full national strength. This is a threat to the Reich and to the European continent that casts all previous dangers into the shadows. If we fail, we will have failed our historic mission. Everything we have built and done in the past pales in the face of this gigantic task that the German army directly and the German people less directly face...

In resisting the grave and direct threat with its weapons, the German people and its Axis allies are fulfilling in the truest sense of the word a European mission. Our courageous and just battle against this worldwide plague will not be hindered by the worldwide outcry of International Jewry. It can and must end only with victory.

The tragic battle of Stalingrad is a symbol of heroic, manly resistance to the revolt of the steppes. It has not only a military, but also an intellectual and spiritual significance for the German people. Here for the first time our eyes have been opened to the true nature of the war. We want no more false hopes and illusions. We want bravely to look the facts in the face, however hard and dreadful they may be. The history of our party and our state has proven that a danger recognized is a danger defeated. Our coming hard battles in the East will be under the sign of this heroic resistance. It will require previously undreamed of efforts by our soldiers and our weapons. A merciless war is raging in the East. The Führer was right when he said that in the end there will not be winners and losers, but the living and the dead.

The German nation knows that. Its healthy instincts have led it through the daily confusion of intellectual and spiritual difficulties. We know today that the Blitzkrieg in Poland

'In this hour of national reflection and contemplation, we believe firmly and unshakeably in victory. We see it before us, we need only reach for it. We must resolve to subordinate everything to it. That is the duty of the hour. Let the slogan be: Now, people rise up and let the storm break loose!'

and the campaign in the West have only limited significance to the battle in the East. The German nation is fighting for everything it has. We know that the German people are defending their holiest possessions: their families, women and children, the beautiful and untouched countryside, their cities and villages, their 2,000-year-old culture, everything indeed that makes life worth living...

We pledge to do all in our life and work that is necessary for victory. We will fill our hearts with the political passion, with the ever-burning fire that blazed during the great struggles of the party and the state. Never during this war will we fall prey to the false and hypocritical objectivism that has brought the German nation so much misfortune over its history.

When the war began, we turned our eyes to the nation alone. That which serves its struggle for life is good and must be encouraged. What harms its struggle for life is bad and must be eliminated and cut out. With burning hearts and cool heads we will overcome the major problems of this phase of the war. We are on the way to final victory. That victory rests on our faith in the Führer.

This evening I once again remind the whole nation of its duty. The Führer expects us to do that which will throw all we have done in the past into the shadows. We do not want to fail him. As we are proud of him, he should be proud of us.

The great crises and upsets of national life show who the true men and women are. We have no right any longer to speak of the weaker sex, for both sexes are displaying the same determination and spiritual strength. The nation is ready for anything. The Führer has commanded, and we will follow him. In this hour of national reflection and contemplation, we believe firmly and unshakeably in victory. We see it before us, we need only reach for it. We must resolve to subordinate everything to it. That is the duty of the hour. Let the slogan be: Now, people rise up and let the storm break loose! '

Goebbels was promoted to Minister for Total War, and before Hitler committed suicide, in 1945, he pronounced Goebbels his successor. But, by then, the few who remained of the Nazi Reich were huddled in their Berlin bunkers while Soviet tanks rolled into the streets above. The day after Hitler's suicide, on 1 May 1945, Goebbels killed his six children, his wife, and then himself.

Franklin D. Roosevelt

'The End of Nazism'

Presidential address on the Yalta conference to the US Congress, Washington, DC, 1 March 1945.

Franklin D. Roosevelt reports to the US Congress on the results of the Yalta summit conference, 1945.

It fell to the President Franklin Delano Roosevelt (1882–1945) to steer the United States through World War II. Roosevelt was born in New York and educated at Harvard and Columbia universities. He married a distant cousin, Eleanor Roosevelt (1884–1962), in 1905. Another distant cousin, Theodore 'Teddy' Roosevelt (1858–1919), was US president at the time.

Franklin D. Roosevelt worked in a New York law firm before standing for the US Senate in 1910. Ten years later, he ran for vice-president on the Democratic ticket, but the Republicans won that election. The following year he was stricken with polio. Despite a recovery demanding enormous effort and personal determination, he spent the rest of his life walking with the aid of crutches.

Elected Governor of New York in 1928, he showed signs of the liberal policies that would distinguish his presidency. That came in 1932, with a hard-fought party nomination followed by an easy victory over President Herbert Hoover.

The stock exchange crash of 1929 and the Great Depression that followed in the 1930s put many millions of Americans out of work. Banks closed, men and women tramped the highways and rode in railway boxcars looking for work. Economic and social collapse threatened the country. In his inaugural address Roosevelt famously reassured Americans that economic revival would come, and that 'the only thing that we have to fear is fear itself'.

When World War II broke out in 1939, despite Roosevelt's concerns about Hitler and Mussolini, Americans had little enthusiasm for involvement in another European conflict. The United States stayed out of the conflict initially, although it supplied large-scale aid to embattled Britain.

The Japanese attack on Pearl Harbor in December 1941 put an end to US isolationism, however, and the nation found itself at war in both the Pacific and Europe. As the tide of the conflict began to turn, Roosevelt engaged in a series of summits with Churchill and Stalin—the trio were nicknamed 'The Big Three'—to oversee the final defeat of the Axis powers and shape the postwar era. Early in February 1945, they held a week of meetings at the Crimean resort town of Yalta, on the Black Sea, and on his return to the United States, Roosevelt spoke to Congress on the outcome of this meeting from his wheelchair.

'I hope that you will pardon me for this unusual posture of sitting down during the presentation of what I want to say, but I know that you will realize that it makes it a lot easier for me not to have to carry about10 pounds of steel around on the bottom of my legs; and also because of the fact that I have just completed a 14,000-mile trip.

First of all, I want to say, it is good to be home. It has been a long journey. I hope you will also agree that it has been, so far, a fruitful one. Speaking in all frankness, the question of whether it is entirely fruitful or not lies to a great extent in your hands. For unless you here in the halls of the American Congress—with the support of the American people—concur in the general conclusions reached at Yalta, and give them your active support, the meeting will not have produced lasting results.

That is why I have come before you at the earliest hour I could after my return. I want to make a personal report to you—and, at the same time, to the people of the country. Many months of earnest work are ahead of us all, and I should like to feel that when the last stone is laid on the structure of international peace, it will be an achievement for which all of us in America have worked steadfastly and unselfishly together.

'Many months of earnest work are ahead of us all, and I should like to feel that when the last stone is laid on the structure of international peace, it will be an achievement for which all of us in America have worked steadfastly and unselfishly together.'

I am returning from this trip—that took me so far—refreshed and inspired. I was well the entire time. I was not ill for a second, until I arrived back in Washington, and there I heard all of the rumours which had occurred in my absence. I returned from the trip refreshed and inspired. The Roosevelts are not, as you may suspect, averse to travel. We seem to thrive on it!

Far away as I was, I was kept constantly informed of affairs in the United States. The modern miracles of rapid communication have made this world very small. We must always bear in mind that fact, when we speak or think of international relations. I received a steady stream of messages from Washington—I might say from not only the executive branch with all its departments, but also from the legislative branch—and except where radio silence was necessary for security purposes, I could continuously send messages any place in the world. And of course, in a grave emergency, we could have even risked the breaking of the security rule.

I come from the Crimea Conference with a firm belief that we have made a good start on the road to a world of peace. There were two main purposes in this Crimea Conference. The first was to bring defeat to Germany with the greatest possible speed, and the smallest possible loss of Allied men. That purpose is now being carried out in great force. The German Army, and the German people, are feeling the ever-increasing might of our fighting men and of the Allied armies. Every hour gives us added pride in the heroic advance of our troops in Germany—on German soil—toward a meeting with the gallant Red Army.

The second purpose was to continue to build the foundation for an international accord that would bring order and security after the chaos of the war, that would give some assurance of lasting peace among the Nations of the world.

Toward that goal also, a tremendous stride was made.

At Teheran, a little over a year ago, there were long-range military plans laid by the Chiefs of Staff of the three most powerful Nations. Among the civilian leaders at Teheran, however, at that time, there were only exchanges of views and expressions of opinion. No political arrangements were made—and none was attempted. At the Crimea Conference, however, the time had come for getting down to specific cases in the political field. There was on all sides at this

Conference an enthusiastic effort to reach an agreement. Since the time of Teheran, a year ago, there had developed among all of us a—what shall I call it? a greater facility in negotiating with each other, that augurs well for the peace of the world. We know each other better.

I have never for an instant wavered in my belief that an agreement to insure world peace and security can be reached…

Days were spent in discussing these momentous matters and we argued freely and frankly across the table. But at the end, on every point, unanimous agreement was reached. And more important even than the agreement of words, I may say we achieved a unity of thought and a way of getting along together.

Of course, we know that it was Hitler's hope and the German warlords'—that we would not agree, that some slight crack might appear in the solid wall of Allied unity, a crack that would give him and his fellow gangsters one last hope of escaping their just doom. That is the objective for which his propaganda machine has been working for many months.

But Hitler has failed.

'Unconditional surrender means something else. It means the end of Nazism. It means the end of the Nazi Party—and of all its barbaric laws and institutions. It means the termination of all militaristic influence in the public, private, and cultural life of Germany.'

Never before have the major Allies been more closely united—not only in their war aims but also in their peace aims. And they are determined to continue to be united with each other—and with all peace-loving Nations—so that the ideal of lasting peace will become a reality…

We made it clear again at Yalta, and I now repeat that unconditional surrender does not mean the destruction or enslavement of the German people. The Nazi leaders have deliberately withheld that part of the Yalta declaration from the German press and radio. They seek to convince the people of Germany that the Yalta declaration does mean slavery and destruction for them—they are working at it day and night for that is how the Nazis hope to save their own skins, and deceive their people into continued and useless resistance.

We did, however, make it clear at the Conference just what unconditional surrender does mean for Germany. It means the temporary control of Germany by Great Britain, Russia, France, and the United States. Each of these Nations will occupy and control a separate zone of Germany and the administration of the four zones will be co-ordinated in Berlin by a Control Council composed of representatives of the four Nations.

Unconditional surrender means something else. It means the end of Nazism. It means the end of the Nazi Party—and of all its barbaric laws and institutions.

It means the termination of all militaristic influence in the public, private, and cultural life of Germany.

It means for the Nazi war criminals a punishment that is speedy and just—and severe.

It means the complete disarmament of Germany; the destruction of its militarism and its military equipment; the end of its production of armament; the dispersal of all its armed forces; the permanent dismemberment of the German General Staff which has so often shattered the peace of the world. It means that Germany will have to make reparations in kind for the damage which has been done to the innocent victims of its aggression...

During my stay in Yalta, I saw the kind of reckless, senseless fury, the terrible destruction that comes out of German militarism. Yalta, on the Black Sea, had no military significance of any kind. It had no defences.

Before the last war, it had been a resort for people like the Tsars and princes and for the aristocracy of Russia—and the hangers-on. However, after the Red Revolution, and until the attack on the Soviet Union by Hitler, the palaces and the villas of Yalta had been used as a rest and recreation centre by the Russian people.

The Nazi officers took these former palaces and villas for their own use. The only reason that the so-called former palace of the Tsar was still habitable, when we got there, was that it had been given—or he thought it had been given—to a German general for his own property and his own use. And when Yalta was so destroyed, he kept soldiers there to protect what he thought would become his own, nice villa. It was a useful rest and recreation centre for hundreds of thousands of Russian workers, farmers, and their families, up to the time that it was taken again by the Germans. The Nazi officers took these places for their own use, and when the Red Army forced the Nazis out of the Crimea—almost just a year ago—all of these villas were looted by the Nazis, and then nearly all of them were destroyed by bombs placed on the inside. And even the humblest of the homes of Yalta were not spared.

There was little left of it except blank walls, ruins, destruction and desolation.

Sevastopol—that was a fortified port, about 40 or 50 miles away—there again was a scene of utter destruction—a large city with great navy yards and fortifications—I think less than a dozen buildings were left intact in the entire city.

'Sevastopol—that was a fortified port, about 40 or 50 miles away—there again was a scene of utter destruction—a large city with great navy yards and fortifications—I think less than a dozen buildings were left intact in the entire city.'

I had read about Warsaw and Lidice and Rotterdam and Coventry—but I saw Sevastopol and Yalta! And I know that there is not room enough on earth for both German militarism and Christian decency.

Of equal importance with the military arrangements at the Crimea Conference were the agreements reached with respect to a general international organization for lasting world peace... A conference of all the United Nations of the world will meet in San Francisco on 25 April 1945. There, we all hope, and confidently expect, to execute a definite charter of organization under which the peace of the world will be preserved and the forces of aggression permanently outlawed.

This time we are not making the mistake of waiting until the end of the war to set up the machinery of peace. This time, as we fight together to win the war finally, we work together to keep it from happening again.

I, as you know, have always been a believer in the document called the Constitution of the

United States. And I spent a good deal of time in educating two other Nations of the world in regard to the Constitution of the United States. The charter has to be—and should be—approved by the Senate of the United States, under the Constitution. I think the other nations all know it now. I am aware of that fact, and now all the other Nations are. And we hope that the Senate will approve of what is set forth as the Charter of the United Nations when they all come together in San Francisco next month.

The Senate of the United States, through its appropriate representatives, has been kept continuously advised of the program of this Government in the creation of the International Security Organization.

The Senate and the House of Representatives will both be represented at the San Francisco Conference. The Congressional delegates to the San Francisco Conference will consist of an equal number of Republican and Democratic members. The American Delegation is—in every sense of the word—bipartisan.

World peace is not a party question. I think that Republicans want peace just as much as Democrats. It is not a party question—any more than is military victory—the winning of the war.

When the Republic was threatened, first by the Nazi clutch for world conquest back in 1940 and then by the Japanese treachery in 1941, partisanship and politics were laid aside by nearly every American; and every resource was dedicated to our common safety. The same consecration to the cause of peace will be expected, I think, by every patriotic American, and by every human soul overseas.

The structure of world peace cannot be the work of one man, or one party, or one Nation. It cannot be just an American peace, or a British peace, or a Russian, a French, or a Chinese peace. It cannot be a peace of large Nations—or of small Nations. It must be a peace which rests on the co-operative effort of the whole world...

'The structure of world peace cannot be the work of one man, or one party, or one Nation. It cannot be just an American peace, or a British peace, or a Russian, a French, or a Chinese peace. It cannot be a peace of large Nations—or of small Nations. It must be a peace which rests on the co-operative effort of the whole world...'

No plan is perfect. Whatever is adopted at San Francisco will doubtless have to be amended time and again over the years, just as our own Constitution has been. No one can say exactly how long any plan will last. Peace can endure only so long as humanity really insists upon it, and is willing to work for it—and sacrifice for it.

Twenty-five years ago, American fighting men looked to the statesmen of the world to finish the work of peace for which they fought and suffered. We failed them then. We cannot fail them again, and expect the world again to survive.

The Crimea Conference was a successful effort by the three leading Nations to find a common ground for peace. It ought to spell the end of the system of unilateral action, the exclusive alliances, the spheres of influence, the balances of power, and all the other expedients that have been tried for centuries and have always failed. We propose to substitute for all these, a universal organization in which all peace-loving Nations will finally have a chance to join.

I am confident that the Congress and the American people will accept the results of this Conference as the beginnings of a permanent structure of peace upon which we can begin to build, under God, that better world in which our children and grandchildren, yours and mine, the children and grandchildren of the whole world must live, and can live.

And that, my friends, is the principal message I can give you. But I feel it very deeply, as I know that all of you are feeling it today, and are going to feel it in the future. ❜

'Twenty-five years ago, American fighting men looked to the statesmen of the world to finish the work of peace for which they fought and suffered. We failed them then. We cannot fail them again, and expect the world again to survive.'

The war ended even more quickly than President Roosevelt might have expected. Informed by the physicist Albert Einstein (1879–1955) about the possible military implications of atomic research on warfare, Roosevelt authorized the top-secret Manhattan Project (1942–45) to develop an atomic bomb in the belief that such a powerful weapon could significantly shorten the war.

Roosevelt died on 12 April 1945, a little more than two weeks before Hitler committed suicide in his Berlin bunker and the Third Reich collapsed. He neither lived to see the war's end nor the outcome of the Manhattan Project. Following the testing of the first atomic device in New Mexico, bombs were dropped on Hiroshima and Nagasaki in Japan in August 1945, on the orders of Roosevelt's former vice-president and successor, President Harry S. Truman (1884–1972). The Japanese surrendered days later.

Roosevelt was admired as a compassionate, creative and determined leader, and was deeply missed by the millions of Americans whose respect he had earned during his lifetime.

Harry S. Truman

'It Is An Atomic Bomb'

Radio address on 6 August 1945, announcing the dropping of the A-bomb on Hiroshima, Japan.

Harry S. Truman announcing the surrender of Japan in 1945.

Harry Truman was born into a Missouri farming family, and served in World War I. After the war, he studied law and rose to become a judge. In 1935 he was elected to the US Senate for the Democratic Party. He became Franklin D. Roosevelt's running mate for the 1944 presidential election, when Roosevelt was elected to an unprecedented fourth term. After FDR's death in April 1945, Truman succeeded to the presidency, overseeing the final phases of the war and the defeat of Germany and Japan and their allies. His actions included the order to drop the world's first atomic bombs on Hiroshima and Nagasaki in Japan.

'Sixteen hours ago an American airplane dropped one bomb on Hiroshima, an important Japanese Army base. That bomb had more power than 20,000 tons of TNT. It had more than 2,000 times the blast power of the British "Grand Slam" which is the largest bomb ever yet used in the history of warfare.

The Japanese began the war from the air at Pearl Harbor. They have been repaid many fold. And the end is not yet. With this bomb we have now added a new and revolutionary increase in destruction to supplement the growing power of our armed forces. In their present form these bombs are now in production and even more powerful forms are in development.

It is an atomic bomb. It is a harnessing of the basic power of the universe. The force from which the sun draws its power has been loosed against those who brought war to the Far East.

Before 1939, it was the accepted belief of scientists that it was theoretically possible to release atomic energy. But no one knew any practical method of doing it. By 1942, however, we knew that the Germans were working feverishly to find a way to add atomic energy to the other engines of war with which they hoped to enslave the world. But they failed. We may be grateful to Providence that the Germans got the V-1s and V-2s late and in limited quantities and even more grateful that they did not get the atomic bomb at all.

The battle of the laboratories held fateful risks for us as well as the battles of the air, land and sea, and we have now won the battle of the laboratories as we have won the other battles.

Beginning in 1940, before Pearl Harbour, scientific knowledge useful in war was pooled between the United States and Great Britain, and many priceless aids to our victories have come from that arrangement. Under that general policy the research on the atomic bomb was begun. With American and British scientists working together we entered the race of discovery against the Germans.

The United States had available the large number of scientists of distinction in the many needed areas of knowledge. It had the tremendous industrial and financial resources necessary for the project and they could be devoted to it without undue impairment of other vital war work.

In the United States the laboratory work and the production plants, on which a substantial start had already been made, would

'It is an atomic bomb. It is a harnessing of the basic power of the universe. The force from which the sun draws its power has been loosed against those who brought war to the Far East.'

be out of reach of enemy bombing, while at that time Britain was exposed to constant air attack and was still threatened with the possibility of invasion.

For these reasons Prime Minister Churchill and President Roosevelt agreed that it was wise to carry on the project here. We now have two great plants and many lesser works devoted to the production of atomic power.

Employment during peak construction numbered 125,000 and over 65,000 individuals are even now engaged in operating the plants. Many have worked there for two and a half years. Few know what they have been producing. They see great quantities of material going in and they see nothing coming out of these plants, for the physical size of the explosive charge is exceedingly small. We have spent 2 billion dollars on the greatest scientific gamble in history and won.

But the greatest marvel is not the size of the enterprise, its secrecy, nor its cost, but the achievement of scientific brains in putting together infinitely complex pieces of knowledge held by many men in different fields of science into a workable plan. And hardly less marvellous has been the capacity of industry to design, and of labor to operate, the machines and methods to do things never done before so that the brainchild of many minds came forth in physical shape and performed as it was supposed to do.

Both science and industry worked under the direction of the United States Army, which achieved a unique success in managing so diverse a problem in the advancement of knowledge in an amazingly short time. It is doubtful if such another combination could be got together in the world. What has been done is the greatest achievement of organized science in history. It was done under high pressure and without failure.

We are now prepared to obliterate more rapidly and completely every productive enterprise the Japanese have above ground in any city. We shall destroy their docks, their factories, and their communications. Let there be no mistake; we shall completely destroy Japan's power to make war.

'We have spent 2 billion dollars on the greatest scientific gamble in history and won. But the greatest marvel is not the size of the enterprise, its secrecy, nor its cost, but the achievement of scientific brains in putting together infinitely complex pieces of knowledge held by many men.'

It was to spare the Japanese people from utter destruction that the ultimatum of July 26 was issued at Potsdam. Their leaders promptly rejected that ultimatum. If they do not now accept our terms they may expect a rain of ruin from the air, the like of which has never been seen on this earth. Behind this air attack will follow sea and land forces in such numbers and power as they have not yet seen and with the fighting skill of which they are already well aware.

The Secretary of War, who has kept in personal touch with all phases of the project, will immediately make public a statement giving further details.

His statement will give facts concerning the sites at Oak Ridge near Knoxville, Tennessee, and at Richland near Pasco, Washington, and an installation near Santa Fe, New Mexico. Although the workers at the sites have been making materials to be used in producing the greatest destructive force in history they have not themselves been in danger beyond that of many other occupations, for the utmost care has been taken of their safety.

The fact that we can release atomic energy ushers in a new era in man's understanding of nature's forces. Atomic energy may in the future supplement the power that now comes from coal, oil, and falling water, but at present it cannot be produced on a basis to compete with them commercially. Before that comes there must be a long period of intensive research.

It has never been the habit of the scientists of this country or the policy of this Government to withhold from the world scientific knowledge. Normally, therefore, everything about the work with atomic energy would be made public.

But under present circumstances it is not intended to divulge the technical processes of production or all the military applications, pending further examination of possible methods of protecting us and the rest of the world from the danger of sudden destruction.

'The fact that we can release atomic energy ushers in a new era in man's understanding of nature's forces. Atomic energy may in the future supplement the power that now comes from coal, oil, and falling water, but at present it cannot be produced on a basis to compete with them commercially.'

I shall recommend that the Congress of the United States consider promptly the establishment of an appropriate commission to control the production and use of atomic power within the United States. I shall give further consideration and make further recommendations to the Congress as to how atomic power can become a powerful and forceful influence towards the maintenance of world peace.'

Cold War and Peace

The harmonious world post-World War II as envisioned by President Roosevelt was not to be. It took only months for strains to show between the Western powers and the Soviet Union.

Tensions simmered over co-administered Berlin and relations rapidly deteriorated to such a point that by late 1946, just over a year after hostilities had ended, Winston Churchill coined the term 'Iron Curtain', which he said the Soviets had drawn across Eastern Europe from the Baltic to the Adriatic.

In the following year the book *The Cold War* by award-winning American journalist Walter Lippmann (1889–1974) gave the world a new term for the sort of conflict that had now begun between the Western Bloc of the US, Britain, France and their allies, and the Eastern, of the Soviet Union and its satellite states including Poland, Czechoslovakia, Hungary and Bulgaria.

As early as 1947 the new terminology of 'Iron Curtain' and 'Cold War' was already in common usage. Over the years that followed the climate only worsened with such crises as the Korean War (1950–3) and Vietnam War (1955–75), 'hot' wars in which the opposing Western and Communist powers —and by 1949, this included China as well—engaged, and also the construction of the Berlin Wall, in 1961, which divided communist East from capitalist West Berlin.

For decades the United States and the Soviet Union engaged in a perilous game of brinkmanship, with knife-edge dramas such as the Cuban Missile Crisis (1962), when the world faced the very real threat of nuclear annihilation. It was mental trench warfare, fought also through the race for scientific supremacy, such as through the first Sputnik satellite launch in 1957 by the Soviets, and the United States putting the first man on the moon in 1969. Cultural weapons were used too; works of art, even operas, symphonies and poetry.

With both sides eventually armed with multiple-warhead missiles that could potentially end life on Earth, our lives were preserved only, we were told, by the doctrine of 'Mutually Assured Destruction' the bizarre and Strangelovean 'MAD'. This long-prevailing doctrine that nuclear war would be avoided because it would would destroy both sides and human civilization in the process led to Albert Einstein's famous quip: 'I know not with what weapons World War III will be fought, but World War IV will be fought with sticks and stones.' As weapon systems rapidly developed, however, even that was not adequate. Under this scenario, if World War III broke out, there would be no World War IV, ever, because life would be extinguished on Earth, with the possible exception of cockroaches.

Since then the world has seen the fall of the Berlin Wall, in 1989, and the collapse of the Soviet Union which followed. The MAD doctrine remains in force today, public concern with possible imminent nuclear destruction reduced only by other crises such as international terrorism and environmental and economic breakdown.

Some of these problems stem from competing economic and political systems, but most from simple misundertanding and miscommunication, fear and paranoia. The outcome, though, has been that since the 1940s, the human race has faced what amounts to an existential problem. The development of the immensely powerful hydrogen bomb with an explosive force equivalent in some instances to tens of millions of tonnes of TNT has meant humanity has effectively placed a gun to its own temple. The reasons for doing this are confused, unclear, and in no way correspond with the definitively self-destructive act of pulling the trigger. To end all life on Earth because we have different approaches to organising our economy? How absurd, even ridiculous, would be most people's normal reactions. But during the Cold War the human race sweated, coldly, with its finger on the trigger. The bad news, as Dr Helen Caldicott powerfully reminds us, is that nothing has changed: we still do so today.

William Faulkner

'I Decline To Accept the End of Man'

Acceptance speech for the 1949 Nobel Prize for Literature, Oslo, Norway, 10 December 1950.

Author William Faulkner receiving the US National Book Award in 1955.

Lauded as one of the great writers in English of the 20th century, William Faulkner (1897–1962) was born in the US state of Mississippi. After studies at the University of Mississippi, he struggled while writing fiction, which portrayed the decline of wealthy Southern families, marginalized whites and mistreated blacks. Yet, Faulkner's works, such as *The Sound and the Fury* (1929), *As I Lay Dying* (1930), and *Light in August* (1932), are all today regarded as modern literary classics.

Faulkner was awarded the Nobel Prize for Literature in 1949, at a time of global alarm about the peril of atomic warfare. In his acceptance speech he directly confronts such fears, and speaks about how human creativity can be a bulwark against a sense of meaninglessness in the face of looming extinction.

'I feel that this award was not made to me as a man, but to my life's work in the agony and sweat of the human spirit, not for glory and least of all for profit, but to create out of the materials of the human spirit something which did not exist before. So this award is only mine in trust. It will not be difficult to find a dedication for the money part of it commensurate with the purpose and significance of its origin. But I would like to do the same with the acclaim too, by using this moment as a pinnacle from which I might be listened to by the young men and women already dedicated to the same anguish and travail, among whom is already that one who will some day stand where I am standing.

Our tragedy today is a general and universal physical fear so long sustained by now that we can even bear it. There are no longer problems of the spirit. There is only the question: When will I be blown up? Because of this, the young man or woman writing today has forgotten the problems of the human heart in conflict with itself which alone can make good writing because only that is worth writing about, worth the agony and the sweat.

He must learn them again. He must teach himself that the basest of all things is to be afraid; and, teaching himself that, forget it forever, leaving no room in his workshop for anything but the old verities and truths of the heart, the universal truths lacking which any story is ephemeral and doomed—love and honour and pity and pride and compassion and sacrifice. Until he does so, he labours under a curse. He writes not of love but of lust, of defeats in which nobody loses anything of value, of victories without hope and, worst of all, without pity or compassion. His griefs grieve on no universal bones, leaving no scars. He writes not of the heart but of the glands.

Until he learns these things, he will write as though he stood among and watched the end of man. I decline to accept the end of man. It is easy enough to say that man is immortal simply because he will endure: that when the last ding-dong of doom has clanged and faded from the last worthless rock hanging tideless

'Our tragedy today is a general and universal physical fear so long sustained by now that we can even bear it. There are no longer problems of the spirit. There is only the question: When will I be blown up?'

in the last red and dying evening, that even then there will still be one more sound: that of his puny inexhaustible voice, still talking.

I refuse to accept this. I believe that man will not merely endure: he will prevail. He is immortal, not because he alone among creatures has an inexhaustible voice, but because he has a soul, a spirit capable of compassion and sacrifice and endurance.

The poet's, the writer's, duty is to write about these things. It is his privilege to help man endure by lifting his heart, by reminding him of the courage and honour and hope and pride and compassion and pity and sacrifice which have been the glory of his past. The poet's voice need not merely be the record of man, it can be one of the props, the pillars to help him endure and prevail.’

Bertrand Russell

'The Road Toward the Abyss'

Acceptance speech for the 1950 Nobel Prize for Literature, Oslo, Norway, 11 December 1950.

Bertrand Russell addressing an anti-nuclear rally in Trafalgar Square, London in 1961.

The British philosopher Bertrand Russell (1872–1970) once remarked: 'War does not determine who is right only who is left.' One of the 20th century's best-known philosophers, he was also a campaigner for peace, who took his beliefs beyond the lecture hall onto the streets. Russell rejected Christianity, was a sexual libertarian and pacifist and was imprisoned for his anti-war views.

Russell studied mathematics at Trinity College, Cambridge University, where he later lectured. He wrote several books, including *The Problems of Philosophy* (1912), which built on his faith in mathematical truths to posit a world-view constructed from the senses. *A History of Western Philosophy*, published in 1945, is among his best-known works. He was awarded the Nobel Prize for Literature in 1950.

When Russell accepted the 1950 Prize, he directly addressed, as Faulkner had, the overwhelming public concern of the day: the survival of the human race in the atomic age.

'Fear, at present, overshadows the world. The atom bomb and the bacterial bomb, wielded by the wicked communist or the wicked capitalist as the case may be, make Washington and the Kremlin tremble, and drive men further along the road toward the abyss. If matters are to improve, the first and essential step is to find a way of diminishing fear. The world at present is obsessed by the conflict of rival ideologies, and one of the apparent causes of conflict is the desire for the victory of our own ideology and the defeat of the other.

I do not think that the fundamental motive here has much to do with ideologies. I think the ideologies are merely a way of grouping people, and that the passions involved are merely those which always arise between rival groups. There are, of course, various reasons for hating communists.

First and foremost, we believe that they wish to take away our property. But so do burglars, and although we disapprove of burglars our attitude towards them is very different indeed from our attitude towards communists chiefly because they do not inspire the same degree of fear. Secondly, we hate the communists because they are irreligious. But the Chinese have been irreligious since the eleventh century, and we only began to hate them when they turned out Chiang Kai-shek. Thirdly, we hate the communists because they do not believe in democracy, but we consider this no reason for hating Franco. Fourthly, we hate them because they do not allow liberty; this we feel so strongly that we have decided to imitate them. It is obvious that none of these is the real ground for our hatred. We hate them because we fear them and they threaten us. If the Russians still adhered to the Greek Orthodox religion, if they had instituted parliamen-

'The atom bomb and the bacterial bomb, wielded by the wicked communist or the wicked capitalist as the case may be, make Washington and the Kremlin tremble, and drive men further along the road toward the abyss. If matters are to improve, the first and essential step is to find a way of diminishing fear.'

tary government, and if they had a completely free press which daily vituperated us, then—provided they still had armed forces as powerful as they have now—we should still hate them if they gave us ground for thinking them hostile.

There is, of course, the odium theologicum, and it can be a cause of enmity. But I think that this is an offshoot of herd feeling: the man who has a different theology feels strange, and whatever is strange must be dangerous. Ideologies, in fact, are one of the methods by which herds are created, and the psychology is much the same however the herd may have been generated.

You may have been feeling that I have allowed only for bad motives, or, at best, such as are ethically neutral. I am afraid they are, as a rule, more powerful than more altruistic motives, but I do not deny that altruistic motives exist, and may, on occasion, be effective. The agitation against slavery in England in the early 19th century was indubitably altruistic, and was thoroughly effective. Its altruism was proved by the fact that in 1833 British taxpayers paid many millions in compensation to Jamaican landowners for the liberation of their slaves, and also by the fact that at the Congress of Vienna the British Government was prepared to make important concessions with a view to inducing other nations to abandon the slave trade. This is an instance from the past, but present-day America has afforded instances equally remarkable. I will not, however, go into these, as I do not wish to become embarked in current controversies.

I do not think it can be questioned that sympathy is a genuine motive, and that some people at some times are made somewhat uncomfortable by the sufferings of some other people. It is sympathy that has produced the many humanitarian advances of the last 100 years. We are shocked when we hear stories of the ill-treatment of lunatics, and there are now quite a number of asylums in which they are not ill-treated. Prisoners in Western countries are not supposed to be tortured, and when they are, there is an outcry if the facts are discovered. We do not approve of treating orphans as they are treated in *Oliver Twist*. Protestant countries disapprove of cruelty to animals. In all these ways sympathy has been politically effective. If the fear of war were removed, its effectiveness would become much greater. Perhaps the best hope for the future of mankind is that ways will be found of increasing the scope and intensity of sympathy.

The time has come to sum up our discussion. Politics is concerned with herds rather than with individuals, and the passions which are important in politics are, therefore, those in which the various members of a given herd can feel alike. The broad instinctive mechanism upon which political edifices have to be built is one of co-operation within the herd and hostility towards other herds. The co-operation within the herd is never perfect. There are members who do not conform, who are, in the etymological sense, 'egregious', that is to say, outside the flock. These members are those who have fallen below, or risen above, the ordinary level. They are: idiots, criminals, prophets, and discoverers. A wise herd will learn to tolerate the eccentricity of those who rise above the average, and to treat with a minimum of ferocity those who fall below it.

'The time has come to sum up our discussion. Politics is concerned with herds rather than with individuals, and the passions which are important in politics are, therefore, those in which the various members of a given herd can feel alike.'

As regards relations to other herds, modern technique has produced a conflict between self-interest and instinct. In old days, when two tribes went to war, one of them exterminated the other, and annexed its territory. From the point of view of the victor, the whole operation was thoroughly satisfactory. The killing was not at all expensive, and the excitement was agreeable. It is not to be wondered at that, in such circumstances, war persisted.

Unfortunately, we still have the emotions appropriate to such primitive warfare, while the actual operations of war have changed completely. Killing an enemy in a modern war is a very expensive operation. If you consider how many Germans were killed in the late war, and how much the victors are paying in income tax, you can, by a sum in long division, discover the cost of a dead German, and you will find it considerable.

In the East, it is true, the enemies of the Germans have secured the ancient advantages of turning out the defeated population and occupying their lands. The Western victors, however, have secured no such advantages. It is obvious that modern war is not good business from a financial point of view. Although we won both the world wars, we should now be much richer if they had not occurred. If men were actuated by self-interest, which they are not—except in the case of a few saints, the whole human race would co-operate. There would be no more wars, no more armies, no more navies, no more atom bombs. There would not be armies of propagandists employed in poisoning the minds of Nation A against Nation B, and reciprocally of Nation B against Nation A. There would not be armies of officials at frontiers to prevent the entry of foreign books and foreign ideas, however excellent in themselves. There would not be customs barriers to ensure the existence of many small enterprises where one big enterprise would be more economic.

'Although we won both the world wars, we should now be much richer if they had not occurred. If men were actuated by self-interest, which they are not—except in the case of a few saints, the whole human race would co-operate. There would be no more wars ... no more atom bombs.'

All this would happen very quickly if men desired their own happiness as ardently as they desired the misery of their neighbours. But, you will tell me, what is the use of these utopian dreams? Moralists will see to it that we do not become wholly selfish, and until we do the millennium will be impossible.

I do not wish to seem to end upon a note of cynicism. I do not deny that there are better things than selfishness, and that some people achieve these things. I maintain, however, on the one hand, that there are few occasions upon which large bodies of men, such as politics is concerned with, can rise above selfishness, while, on the other hand, there are a very great many circumstances in which populations will fall below selfishness, if selfishness is interpreted as enlightened self-interest.

And among those occasions on which people fall below self-interest are most of the occasions on which they are convinced that they are acting from idealistic motives. Much that passes as idealism is disguised hatred or disguised love of power. When you see large masses of men swayed by what appear to be noble motives, it is as well to look below the surface and ask yourself what it is that makes these motives effective. It is partly because it is so easy to be taken in by a facade of nobility that a psychological inquiry, such as I have been attempting, is worth making. I would say, in conclusion, that if what I have said is right, the main thing needed to make the world happy is intelligence. And this, after all, is an optimistic conclusion, because intelligence is a thing that can be fostered by known methods of education.’

Bertrand Russell was active in Britain's Campaign for Nuclear Disarmament (CND) in the 1950s and 1960s. With seemingly undimmed energy, in his last years he wrote and published his three-volume *Autobiography* before his death in 1970.

Dwight D. Eisenhower

'A Trembling World'

Speech to the
UN General Assembly, New York City,
8 December 1953.

Dwight D. Eisenhower addresses a press conference in 1955.

Dwight David Eisenhower (1890–1969), or 'Ike', as he was more popularly known, was born in Texas. After graduating from the West Point Military Academy in 1915, he ascended the ranks of the US military to become Supreme Allied Commander of the 1944 D–Day landing in Normandy, France.

Six years later, with the Cold War at its most chilly, the Republican Party approached him to run for president. He won the 1952 election. As US President, he helped end the Korean War and attempted to reduce nuclear tensions between East and West, making peace overtures to the Soviets. The 'atoms for peace' speech, in which he proposes the world use the power of the atom for peaceful means rather than for racial suicide, is one of his best known.

'On 16 July 1945, the United States set off the world's first atomic explosion. Since that date in 1945, the United States of America has conducted 42 test explosions. Atomic bombs today are more than 25 times as powerful as the weapons with which the atomic age dawned, while hydrogen weapons are in the ranges of millions of tons of TNT equivalent.

Today, the United States' stockpile of atomic weapons, which, of course, increases daily, exceeds by many times the explosive equivalent of the total of all bombs and all shells that came from every plane and every gun in every theatre of war in all of the years of World War II.

A single air group, whether afloat or land-based, can now deliver to any reachable target a destructive cargo exceeding in power all the bombs that fell on Britain in all of World War II.

In size and variety, the development of atomic weapons has been no less remarkable. The development has been such that atomic weapons have virtually achieved conventional status within our armed services. In the United States, the Army, the Navy, the Air Force, and the Marine Corps are all capable of putting this weapon to military use.

But the dread secret, and the fearful engines of atomic might, are not ours alone. In the first place, the secret is possessed by our friends and allies, Great Britain and Canada, whose scientific genius made a tremendous contribution to our original discoveries, and the designs of atomic bombs.

The secret is also known by the Soviet Union.

The Soviet Union has informed us that, over recent years, it has devoted extensive resources to atomic weapons. During this period, the Soviet Union has exploded a series of atomic devices, including at least one involving thermo-nuclear reactions.

If at one time the United States possessed what might have been called a monopoly of atomic power, that monopoly ceased to exist several years ago. Therefore, although our earlier start has permitted us to accumulate what is today a great quantitative advantage, the atomic realities of today comprehend two facts of

'Today, the United States' stockpile of atomic weapons, which, of course, increases daily, exceeds by many times the explosive equivalent of the total of all bombs and all shells that came from every plane and every gun in every theatre of war in all of the years of World War II.'

even greater significance. First, the knowledge now possessed by several nations will eventually be shared by others—possibly all others.

Second, even a vast superiority in numbers of weapons, and a consequent capability of devastating retaliation, is no preventive, of itself, against the fearful material damage and toll of human lives that would be inflicted by surprise aggression.

The Free World, at least dimly aware of these facts, has naturally embarked on a large program of warning and defence systems. That program will be accelerated and expanded.

But let no one think that the expenditure of vast sums for weapons and systems of defence can guarantee absolute safety for the cities and citizens of any nation. The awful arithmetic of the atomic bomb does not permit of any such easy solution. Even against the most powerful defence, an aggressor in possession of the effective minimum number of atomic bombs for a surprise attack could probably place a sufficient number of his bombs on the chosen targets to cause hideous damage.

Should such an atomic attack be launched against the United States, our reactions would be swift and resolute. But for me to say that the defence capabilities of the United States are such that they could inflict terrible losses upon an aggressor—for me to say that the retaliation capabilities of the United States are so great that such an aggressor's land would be laid waste—all this, while fact, is not the true expression of the purpose and the hope of the United States.

To pause there would be to confirm the hopeless finality of a belief that two atomic colossi are doomed malevolently to eye each other indefinitely across a trembling world. To stop there would be to accept helplessly the probability of civilization destroyed—the annihilation of the irreplaceable heritage of mankind handed down to us generation from generation—and the condemnation of mankind to begin all over again the age-old struggle upward from savagery toward decency, and right, and justice.

'To stop there would be to accept helplessly the probability of civilization destroyed—the annihilation of the irreplaceable heritage of mankind handed down to us generation from generation—and the condemnation of mankind to begin all over again the age-old struggle upward from savagery toward decency.'

Surely no sane member of the human race could discover victory in such desolation. Could anyone wish his name to be coupled by history with such human degradation and destruction.

Occasional pages of history do record the faces of the "Great Destroyers" but the whole book of history reveals mankind's never-ending quest for peace, and mankind's God-given capacity to build.

It is with the book of history, and not with isolated pages, that the United States will ever wish to be identified. My country wants to be constructive, not destructive. It wants agreements, not wars, among nations. It wants itself to live in freedom, and in the confidence that the people of every other nation enjoy equally the right of choosing their own way of life.

So my country's purpose is to help us move out of the dark chamber of horrors into the light, to find a way by which the minds of men, the hopes of men, the souls of men everywhere, can move forward toward peace and happiness and well being... The United States would seek more than the mere reduction or elimination of atomic materials for military purposes. It is not enough to take this weapon out of the hands of the soldiers. It must be put into the hands of those who will know how to strip its military casing and adapt it to the arts of peace.

The United States knows that if the fearful trend of atomic military build-up can be reversed, this greatest of destructive forces can be developed into a great boon, for the benefit of all mankind.

The United States knows that peaceful power from atomic energy is no dream of the future. That capability, already proved, is here—now—today. Who can doubt, if the entire body of the world's scientists and engineers had adequate amounts of fissionable material with which to test and develop their ideas, that this capability would rapidly be transformed into universal, efficient, and economic usage...

Experts would be mobilized to apply atomic energy to the needs of agriculture, medicine, and other peaceful activities. A special purpose would be to provide abundant electrical energy in the power-starved areas of the world. Thus the contributing powers would be dedicating some of their strength to serve the needs rather than the fears of mankind.

The United States would be more than willing—it would be proud to take up with others "principally involved" in the development of plans whereby such peaceful use of atomic energy would be expedited... Against the dark background of the atomic bomb, the United States does not wish merely to present strength, but also the desire and the hope for peace.

The coming months will be fraught with fateful decisions. In this Assembly; in the capitals and military headquarters of the world; in the hearts of men everywhere, be they governors or governed, may they be the decisions which will lead this world out of fear and into peace.

To the making of these fateful decisions, the United States pledges before you—and therefore before the world—its determination to help solve the fearful atomic dilemma—to devote its entire heart and mind to find the way by which the miraculous inventiveness of man shall not be dedicated to his death, but consecrated to his life. ’

'The United States would be more than willing—it would be proud to take up with others "principally involved" in the development of plans whereby such peaceful use of atomic energy would be expedited... Against the dark background of the atomic bomb, the United States does not wish merely to present strength, but also the desire and the hope for peace.'

A Republican moderate, Eisenhower strove to uphold welfare, racially desegregated the US military, and in 1957 dispatched troops to Arkansas in the South to assure compliance with a court order on school desegregation to allow black and white children to attend the same schools. At the end of his second term in office, in his Farewell Address in January 1961, he issued his famous warning that the United States must 'guard against the acquisition of unwarranted influence by the military–industrial complex'.

John Foster Dulles

'Massive Retaliatory Power'

Speech on the Strategy of Massive Retaliation to the Council on Foreign Relations, Washington, DC, 12 January 1954.

John Foster Dulles, right, with French foreign minister Georges Bidault, centre, during a pre-Geneva conference in 1954.

The term 'nuclear brinkmanship' was originally applied to John Foster Dulles (1888–1959), secretary of state under President Dwight Eisenhower. His hard resistance to the US making concessions to communist countries—and the situations in which America and its citizens found themselves as a result—helped create the climate of unease and Cold War paranoia which characterized the 1950s.

Dulles was born in Washington, DC. He studied at Princeton University and the Sorbonne in Paris, France. He entered law but gradually gained a reputation in international relations, attending the Versailles Conference under President Woodrow Wilson and working with President Harry S. Truman, before being appointed Secretary of State under Eisenhower.

In this speech, made in the early period of Eisenhower's presidency, he articulates the doctrine that came to dominate the Cold War—that of massive retaliation. This meant that any strike against the United States would be met with overwhelming force, thus discouraging a strike in the first place. As such, massive retaliation became a central premise of the prevailing Cold War doctrine of Mutually Assured Destruction ('MAD').

'We live in a world where emergencies are always possible, and our survival may depend upon our capacity to meet emergencies. Let us pray that we shall always have that capacity. But, having said that, it is necessary also to say that emergency measures—however good for the emergency—do not necessarily make good permanent policies. Emergency measures are costly; they are superficial; and they imply that the enemy has the initiative. They cannot be depended on to serve our long-time interests.

This "long time" factor is of critical importance. The Soviet Communists are planning for what they call "an entire historical era", and we should do the same. They seek, through many types of manoeuvres, gradually to divide and weaken the free nations by overextending them in efforts which, as Lenin put it, are "beyond their strength, so that they come to practical bankruptcy". Then, said Lenin, "our victory is assured." Then, said Stalin, will be "the moment for the decisive blow."

'The Soviet Communists are planning for what they call "an entire historical era", and we should do the same. They seek, through many types of manoeuvres, gradually to divide and weaken the free nations by overextending them in efforts which, as Lenin put it, are "beyond their strength, so that they come to practical bankruptcy".'

In the face of this strategy, measures cannot be judged adequate merely because they ward off an immediate danger. It is essential to do this, but it is also essential to do so without exhausting ourselves.

When the Eisenhower administration applied this test, we felt that some transformations were needed. It is not sound military strategy permanently to commit US land forces to Asia to a degree that leaves us no strategic reserves. It is not sound economics, or good foreign policy to support permanently other

'A potential aggressor must know that he cannot always prescribe battle conditions that suit him. Otherwise, for example, a potential aggressor, who is glutted with manpower, might be tempted to attack in confidence that resistance would be confined to manpower.'

countries, for in the long run, that creates as much ill will as good will. Also, it is not sound to become permanently committed to military expenditures so vast that they lead to "practical bankruptcy".

Change was imperative to assure the stamina needed for permanent security. But it was equally imperative that change should be accompanied by understanding of our true purposes. Sudden and spectacular change had to be avoided. Otherwise, there might have been a panic among our friends and miscalculated aggression by our enemies.

We can, I believe, make a good report in these respects. We need allies and collective security. Our purpose is to make these relations more effective, less costly. This can be done by placing more reliance on deterrent power and less dependence on local defensive power.

This is accepted practice so far as local communities are concerned. We keep locks on our doors, but we do not have an armed guard in every home. We rely principally on a community security system so well equipped to punish any who break in and steal that, in fact, would-be aggressors are generally deterred. That is the modern way of getting maximum protection at a bearable cost. What the Eisenhower administration seeks is a similar international security system. We want, for ourselves and the other free nations, a maximum deterrent at a bearable cost.

Local defence will always be important. But there is no local defence which alone will contain the mighty landpower of the Communist world. Local defences must be reinforced by the further deterrent of massive retaliatory power. A potential aggressor must know that he cannot always prescribe battle conditions that suit him. Otherwise, for example, a potential aggressor, who is glutted with manpower, might be tempted to attack in confidence that resistance would be confined to manpower. He might be tempted to attack in places where his superiority was decisive.

The way to deter aggression is for the free community to be willing and able to respond vigorously at places and with means of its own choosing. So long as our basic policy concepts were unclear, our military leaders could not be selective in building our military power. If an enemy could pick his time and place and method of warfare—and if our policy was to remain the traditional one of meeting aggression by direct and local opposition—then we needed to be ready to fight in the Arctic and in the Tropics, in Asia, the Near East, and in Europe; by sea, by land, and by air; with old weapons and with new weapons. ’

Albert Schweitzer

'Let Us Dare To Face the Situation'

**Nobel Lecture on 'The Problem of Peace',
Oslo, Norway, 4 November 1954.**

Albert Schweitzer, humanitarian and Nobel Peace Prize winner during a ceremony naming a street after him in 1952.

The great humanitarian Albert Schweitzer (1875–1965) was born in Kayersberg, Alsace (then in Germany, now France) into a family of religious scholars and musicians. He studied philosophy and theology at the University of Strasbourg.

A gifted musician, he played the piano and organ from childhood, and gave his first recital at the age of nine. As a concert performer he was especially well known for his interpretations of Johann Sebastian Bach (1685–1750), and also wrote a biography of the illustrious composer.

Dr Schweitzer decided that his vocation was to be a medical missionary in Africa, and he and his wife travelled to French Equatorial Africa (now Gabon) where he worked with sufferers of leprosy and sleeping sickness, and also founded a hospital. His work was interrupted by World War I when the German-born Schweitzer and his wife were interned in a French camp. After the war, he returned to working with the sick in Africa, interspersing this with international concert tours to raise funds for his hospital.

When he received the Nobel Peace Prize in 1953, Schweitzer used the prize money to expand the hospital. In the following year, in the depths of the Cold War, he delivered the Nobel Lecture in Oslo.

'Let us dare to face the situation. Man has become superman. He is a superman because he not only has at his disposal innate physical forces, but also commands, thanks to scientific and technological advances, the latent forces of nature which he can now put to his own use.

To kill at a distance, man used to rely solely on his own physical strength; he used it to bend the bow and to release the arrow. The superman has progressed to the stage where, thanks to a device designed for the purpose, he can use the energy released by the combustion of a given combination of chemical products. This enables him to employ a much more effective projectile and to propel it over far greater distances.

'He requires such reason to put this vast power to solely reasonable and useful ends and not to destructive and murderous ones. Because he lacks it, the conquests of science and technology become a mortal danger to him rather than a blessing.'

However, the superman suffers from a fatal flaw. He has failed to rise to the level of superhuman reason which should match that of his superhuman strength. He requires such reason to put this vast power to solely reasonable and useful ends and not to destructive and murderous ones. Because he lacks it, the conquests of science and technology become a mortal danger to him rather than a blessing.

In this context is it not significant that the first great scientific discovery, the harnessing of the force resulting from the combustion of gunpowder, was seen at first only as a means of killing at a distance?

The conquest of the air, thanks to the internal-combustion engine, marked a decisive advance for humanity. Yet men grasped at once the opportunity it offered to kill and destroy from the skies. This invention underlined a fact which had hitherto been steadfastly denied: the more the superman gains in strength, the poorer he becomes. To avoid exposing himself completely to the destruction unleashed from the skies, he is obliged to seek refuge underground like a hunted animal. At the same time he must resign himself to abetting the unprecedented destruction of cultural values.

A new stage was reached with the discovery and subsequent utilisation of the vast forces liberated by the splitting of the atom. After a time, it was found that the destructive potential of a bomb armed with such was incalculable, and that even large-scale tests could unleash catastrophes threatening the very existence of the human race. Only now has the full horror of our position become obvious. No longer can we evade the question of the future of mankind.

'What really matters is that we should all of us realize that we are guilty of inhumanity. The horror of this realization should shake us out of our lethargy so that we can direct our hopes and our intentions to the coming of an era in which war will have no place.'

But the essential fact which we should acknowledge in our conscience, and which we should have acknowledged a long time ago, is that we are becoming inhuman to the extent that we become supermen. We have learned to tolerate the facts of war: that men are killed en masse—some 20 million in the Second World War [many historians now believe it was double that number]—that whole cities and their inhabitants are annihilated by the atomic bomb, that men are turned into living torches by incendiary bombs.

We learn of these things from the radio or newspapers and we judge them according to whether they signify success for the group of peoples to which we belong, or for our enemies. When we do admit to ourselves that such acts are the results of inhuman conduct, our admission is accompanied by the thought that the very fact of war itself leaves us no option but to accept them. In resigning ourselves to our fate without a struggle, we are guilty of inhumanity.

What really matters is that we should all of us realize that we are guilty of inhumanity. The horror of this realization should shake us out of our lethargy so that we can direct our hopes and our intentions to the coming of an era in which war will have no place.

This hope and this will can have but one aim: to attain, through a change in spirit, that superior reason which will dissuade us from misusing the power at our disposal.

The first to have the courage to advance purely ethical arguments against war and to stress the necessity for reason governed by an ethical will was the great humanist Erasmus of Rotterdam in his *Querela Pacis* (*The Complaint of Peace*), which appeared in 1517. In this book he depicts Peace on stage seeking an audience.

Erasmus found few adherents to his way of thinking. To expect the affirmation of an ethical necessity to point the way to peace was considered a utopian ideal. Kant shared this opinion. In his essay on Perpetual Peace, which appeared in 1795, and in other publications in which he touches upon the problem of peace, he states his belief that peace will come only with the increasing authority of an international code of law, in accordance with which an international court of arbitration would settle disputes between nations. This authority, he maintains, should be based entirely on the increasing respect which in time, and for purely practical motives, men will hold for the law as such.

Kant is unremitting in his insistence that the idea of a league of nations cannot be hoped for as the outcome of ethical argument, but only as the result of the perfecting of law. He believes that this process of perfecting will come of itself. In his opinion, 'nature, that great artist' will lead men, very gradually, it is true, and over a very long period of time, through the march of history and the misery of wars, to agree on an international code of law which will guarantee perpetual peace.

A plan for a league of nations having powers of arbitration was first formulated with some precision by Sully, the friend and minister of Henry IV. It was given detailed treatment by the Abbé Castel de Saint-Pierre in three works, the most important of which bears the title *Projet de paix perpétuelle entre les souverains chrétiens* [*Plan for Perpetual Peace between Christian Sovereigns*]. Kant was aware of the views it developed, probably from an extract which Rousseau published in 1761.

'Today we can judge the efficacy of international institutions by the experience we have had with the League of Nations in Geneva and with the United Nations. Such institutions can render important services by offering to mediate conflicts at their very inception.'

Today we can judge the efficacy of international institutions by the experience we have had with the League of Nations in Geneva and with the United Nations. Such institutions can render important services by offering to mediate conflicts at their very inception, by taking the initiative in setting up international projects, and by other actions of a similar nature, depending on the circumstances.

One of the League of Nations' most important achievements was the creation in 1922 of an internationally valid passport for the benefit of those who became stateless as a consequence of war. What a position those people would have been in if this travel document had not been devised through Nansen's initiative! What would have been the fate of displaced persons after 1945 if the United Nations had not existed!

Nevertheless these two institutions have been unable to bring about peace. Their efforts were doomed to fail since they were obliged to undertake them in a world in which there was no prevailing spirit directed toward peace. And being only legal institutions, they were unable to create such a spirit. The ethical spirit alone has the power to generate it. Kant deceived himself in thinking that he could dispense with it in his search for peace. We must follow the road on which he turned his back.

What is more, we just cannot wait the extremely long time he deemed necessary for this movement toward peace to mature. War today means annihilation, a fact that Kant did not foresee…

May the men who hold the destiny of peoples in their hands, studiously avoid anything that might cause the present situation to deteriorate and become even more dangerous. May they take to heart the words of the Apostle Paul: "If it be possible, as much as lieth in you, live peaceably with all men." These words are valid not only for individuals, but for nations as well. May these nations, in their efforts to maintain peace, do their utmost to give the spirit time to grow and to act.’

In addition to the 1952 Nobel Peace Prize, Schweitzer was awarded a multitude of other honours, including the Goethe Prize, and election to the Academie Française. He also found time to continue writing and publishing: his major works include *Civilization and Ethics* (1923) and *From My African Notebook* (1936).

John F. Kennedy

'Terror Is Not a New Weapon'

Address to the UN General Assembly, following the death of UN Secretary-General Dag Hammarskjöld, 25 September 1961.

John F Kennedy making a State of the Union Address in January 1962, with Lyndon B. Johnson in the background.

John F. Kennedy (1917–63) features prominently among those who are considered the finest political orators of the 20th century. Elected to the US presidency in 1960, Kennedy came to office at a time when the global nuclear plight had never been more perilous, with the Americans and Soviets effectively in a Mexican stand-off, each armed to the teeth with weapons that each boasted could end life as humankind knew it.

Kennedy broached the problem head on, remarking, in the speech that follows, 'Mankind must put an end to war, or war will put an end to mankind'. Yet, commenting on Soviet leader Nikita Khrushchev (1894–1971) during the Cuban Missile Crisis, Kennedy reportedly remarked that 'the other fellow just blinked' after the Soviets backed down.

The son of politician Joseph P. Kennedy (1888–1969), the Massachusetts-born and Harvard-educated John was a decorated World War II hero before being elected to the US House of Representatives in 1946.

Charismatic and youthfully energetic, with his attractive and stylish wife Jacqueline (née Lee Bouvier) and young family by his side, 'JFK', as he became more popularly known, presented the ideal president for a new decade. The problems he faced were manifest and complex, however: a hair-trigger nuclear stand-off, poverty in the developing world as well as at home, the conflict in Indochina and the burgeoning movement for black equal rights, all commanded his attention from the outset.

Kennedy delivered many fine speeches during his albeit brief three-year presidency, but perhaps none finer than the one he gave to the UN General Assembly, following the death of the Swedish statesman and UN Secretary-General Dag Hammarskjöld (1905–61).

The son of a former Swedish prime minister, Hjalmar Hammarskjöld, Dag excelled at school and university, and played a key role in the Marshall Plan that helped revive the economies of postwar Europe. He became a Swedish delegate to the UN in 1949, and four years later was elected secretary-general by an overwhelming majority.

Known as a lover of the arts, including poetry and painting, he proved a very popular secretary-general, even though his tenure included testing times with trouble spots including Korea, Vietnam and the Suez. Re-elected to the position in 1957, Hammarskjöld's deepest crisis occurred in Africa in 1961, when Katanga seceded from the newly independent Republic of the Congo (today Democratic Republic of the Congo), which had only gained its independence from Belgium the year before. Hammarskjöld died in a plane crash on the night of 17 September 1961, while on his way to meet with Moise Tshombe (1919–69), leader of Katanga, following the outbreak of fighting between his people and UN peacekeeping forces. Fifteen other people perished with Hammarskjöld in the crash.

President Kennedy addressed the UN General Assembly just over a week after Hammarskjöld's death.

'We meet in an hour of grief and challenge. Dag Hammarskjöld is dead. But the United Nations lives. His tragedy is deep in our hearts, but the task for which he died is at the top of our agenda. A noble servant of peace is gone. But the quest for peace lies before us.

The problem is not the death of one man—the problem is the life of this organization. It will either grow to meet the challenges of our age, or it will be gone with the wind, without influence, without force, without respect. Were we to let it die, to enfeeble its vigour, to cripple its powers, we would condemn our future.

For in the development of this organization rests the only true alternative to war—and war appeals no longer as a rational alternative. Unconditional war can no longer lead to unconditional victory. It can no longer serve to settle disputes. It can no longer concern the Great Powers alone. For a nuclear disaster, spread by wind and water and fear, could well engulf the great and the small, the rich and the poor, the committed and the uncommitted alike. Mankind must put an end to war, or war will put an end to mankind.

So let us here resolve that Dag Hammarskjöld did not live, or die, in vain. Let us call a truce to terror. Let us invoke the blessings of peace. And as we build an international capacity to keep peace, let us join in dismantling the national capacity to wage war.

This will require new strength and new roles for the United Nations. For disarmament without checks is but a shadow, and a community without law is but a shell. Already the United Nations has become both the measure and the vehicle of man's most generous impulses. Already it has provided—in the Middle East, in Asia, in Africa this year in the Congo—a means of holding man's violence within bounds.

But the great question which confronted this body in 1945 is still before us: whether man's cherished hopes for progress and peace are to be destroyed by terror and disruption, whether the "foul winds of war" can be tamed in time to see the cooling winds of reason, and whether the pledges of our charter are to be fulfilled or defied—pledges to secure peace, progress, human rights and world law...

'Dag Hammarskjöld is dead. But the United Nations lives. His tragedy is deep in our hearts, but the task for which he died is at the top of our agenda. A noble servant of peace is gone. But the quest for peace lies before us.'

Men no longer debate whether armaments are a symptom or a cause of tension. The mere existence of modern weapons—ten million times more powerful than any that the world has ever seen, and only minutes away from any target on Earth—is a source of horror, and discord and distrust. Men no longer maintain that disarmament must await the settlement of all disputes—for disarmament must be a part of any permanent settlement. And men may no longer pretend that the quest for disarmament is a sign of weakness, for in a spiralling arms race, a nation's security may well be shrinking even as its arms increase.

For 15 years, this organization has sought the reduction and the destruction of arms. Now that goal is no longer a dream, it is a practical matter of life or death. The risks inherent in disarmament pale in comparison to the risks inherent in an unlimited arms race... It is therefore our intention to challenge the Soviet Union, not to an arms race, but to a peace race—to advance together, step by step, stage by stage, until general and complete disarmament has been achieved...

Terror is not a new weapon. Throughout history it has been used by those who could not prevail, either by persuasion or example. But inevitably they fail, either because men are not afraid to die for a life worth living, or because the terrorists themselves came to realize that free men cannot be frightened by threats, and that aggression would meet its own response. And it is in the light of that history that every nation today should know, be he friend or foe, that the United States has both the will and the weapons to join free men in standing up to their responsibilities.

'Terror is not a new weapon. Throughout history it has been used by those who could not prevail, either by persuasion or example. But inevitably they fail.'

But I come here today to look across this world of threats to a world of peace. In that search we cannot expect any final triumph—for new problems will always arise. We cannot expect that all nations will adopt like systems—for conformity is the jailer of freedom, and the enemy of growth. Nor can we expect to reach our goal by contrivance, by fiat, or even by the wishes of all.

But however close we sometimes seem to that dark and final abyss, let no man of peace and freedom despair. For he does not stand alone. If we all can persevere, if we can in every land and office, look beyond our own shores and ambitions, then surely the age will dawn in which the strong are just and the weak secure and the peace preserved.

Ladies and gentlemen of this Assembly, the decision is ours. Never have the nations of the world had so much to lose, or so much to gain. Together we shall save our planet, or together we shall perish in its flames. Save it we can—and save it we must—and then shall we earn the eternal thanks of mankind, and, as peacemakers, the eternal blessing of God.'

Kennedy was destined to die violently himself, assassinated on a visit to Dallas, Texas, on 22 November 1963. Conspiracy theories have abounded about his murder ever since.

There are also a number of theories regarding the death of Dag Hammarskjöld. In August 1998, Reuters reported that Archbishop Desmond Tutu had stated that the South African Truth and Reconciliation Commission had uncovered 'documents discussing the sabotage of the aircraft in which the UN Secretary-General Dag Hammarskjöld died on the night of September 17–18 1961'.

The documents had been traced to a front company for the South African military, and included references to the US CIA and Britain's MI5. In one document, the South African military and MI5 agreed that the secretary-general should be 'removed', while another outlined plans to plant explosives in the undercarriage of Hammarskjöld's aircraft.

The revelations add weight to London newspaper reports from the time of Hammarskjöld's death that British intelligence was involved in a plot to murder him as part of an ongoing conflict over diamond-rich Katanga.

Dag Hammarskjöld was posthumously awarded the Nobel Peace Prize in 1961.

Helen Caldicott

'It's More Dangerous Now Than It Was at the Height of the Cold War'

Public lecture at the First Congregational Church of Long Beach, Los Angeles, California, 12 October 2008.

Anti-nuclear campaigner and environmentalist Helen Caldicott, in 1982.

Named by the Smithsonian Institute as one of the most influential women of the 20th century, Dr Helen Caldicott (1938–) continues with her anti-nuclear environmental activism into the 21st century.

Born in Melbourne, Australia, Caldicott gained her medical degree from the University of Adelaide in 1961. She founded the Cystic Fibrosis Clinic at the Adelaide Children's Hospital in 1975. Caldicott moved to the United States, where she was an instructor in Pediatrics at Harvard Medical School. She resigned in 1980 to work full-time on the prevention of nuclear war, and has devoted herself ever since to a passionate international campaign to educate people everywhere about the medical hazards of the nuclear age and on ways to stop environmental destruction.

She has received 19 honorary doctoral degrees, and many prizes and awards, including the Lannan Foundation's 2003 Prize for Cultural Freedom. She was personally nominated for the Nobel Peace Prize by US scientist and Nobel Prize winner Linus Pauling (1901–94). Caldicott currently divides her time between Australia and the United States, where she lectures.

In this speech, made in October 2008, in the dying days of President George W. Bush's administration, she reminds her audience that the nuclear risk to humanity posed by the Cold War has by no means passed, and indeed is worse than ever, with Russia's possession of a real-life Strangelovean 'Doomsday Machine'. She also pours scorn on the US anti-missile 'Star Wars' programme, initiated more than two decades ago by Ronald Reagan's administration, stating that it heightens international tensions—and will never work.

'There is no possible physical way that missile defence will ever work. I mean, just briefly, Russia's missiles are MIRVed. MIRVing means Multiple Independent Re-Entry Vehicles. So they might have eight bombs on one missile. They launch the rocket, the missile goes into space, the "bus" continues—these are Pentagon terms—with its "passengers", which are the hydrogen bombs, and then out of that single target come eight more targets.

And so America launches an anti-ballistic missile, with a "kill vehicle" that homes in only on the specks of light and reflection of light as these bombs hurtle through space. One missile will never hit eight—A. B, you can confuse the kill vehicle by putting balloons amongst the hydrogen bombs and then the kill vehicle doesn't even know what's going on... add lots of what they call chaff, or aluminium pieces, and it's totally confused.

And every test they've done, with only one target, and one kill vehicle, and the target sending out radio signals saying "here I am, here I am"—never worked! None of them have ever worked. None of them. But they have spent 110 billion dollars of your money on this aimless, stupid, ridiculous project, which is provocative because Russia says, "oh yeah, you're building a missile defence system, well we'll just super-saturate it and build more missiles." So does China.

The psychology behind this is aimless but it's stupid. I don't understand the men in the White House at the moment... I don't understand some of the men in the Pentagon, and I do think there's a bell-shaped curve of men.

On one end are beautiful, lovely men like every one of you here who would never hurt a fly. In the middle are men who would go from nought to 100 miles an hour in three seconds and that's why they want these crazy cars. Who would play video games... you walk through airports and you see them all the time... and who would go to war and who would many of them come back absolutely devastated, as we're seeing. And then on the other end I think there's a small minority of men whose reptilian mid-brain has a toxic reaction to testosterone...

I know that a couple of miles from here is an ammunition base almost certainly housing nuclear weapons. Did you know that? Did you? Well they say you're not allowed to know on account of national security, but in fact they're your weapons. You paid for them. This is your democracy and you have an absolute right to know. Do you know they drive nuclear weapons around in Winnebagos? On the highways, with submachine guns on the dashboard? Do you know the ships coming in to San Diego, the nuclear-powered ships, have nuclear weapons on board? Probably transporting them from the ships to the ammunition depot. Find out what is going on at that depot. Insist. Demand, and the military has no right to keep you in ignorance. Because they're your weapons and it's your life.

Do you know what would happen if one of them exploded? I'll tell you. By accident. They're a thing called 'broken arrows'... they drop them sometimes... they have accidents with them, their safety catches go off. Just near here, right here in Los Angeles, it would explode with the heat inside the centre of the sun and dig a hole three-quarters of a mile wide and eight hundred feet deep, turning millions of tons of rock into radioactive fallout. Then five miles... and you are within that radius... five miles in all directions, every person is vaporized.

'Right here in Los Angeles, it would explode with the heat inside the centre of the sun and dig a hole three-quarters of a mile wide and eight hundred feet deep, turning millions of tons of rock into radioactive fallout. Then five miles... and you are within that radius... five miles in all directions, every person is vaporized.'

In Hiroshima, which was a tiny little firecracker of a bomb, a little boy was reaching up to catch a red dragonfly on his hand against the blue sky, and there was a blinding flash—and he disappeared. And if you go to the Hiroshima museum there's a shadow on the pavement of that little boy. Never before have we been about to vaporize our fellow human beings. A woman was running with her baby and she and the baby have been converted to a charcoal statue.

Twenty miles from here in all directions, everyone's lethally burnt. Winds of 500 miles an hour a hurricane's a hundred—suck people out of buildings turning them into missiles travelling at a hundred miles an hour... shards of glass like pop corn fly through the air, decapitating people. Then the whole area would be engulfed in a firestorm and there's a lot to burn in houses now... plastic and wood... and the fire would consume everything, a raging firestorm, so if you are in a shelter you would be asphyxiated.

And then if all bombs are used in the arsenal, a huge cloud of toxic black smoke would rise up and cover the Earth with a cloud so thick it blots out the sun for maybe four or five years creating a nuclear winter, and the end of most life on earth, except for cockroaches…

Of the 30,000 hydrogen bombs in the world, Russia and America own 97 per cent of them, so who are the real rogue nations? Russia's got you targeted with 40 H–Bombs on New York alone. And almost certainly LA would have 40 to 60 H–Bombs. Because Russia's got two and a half thousand weapons she can launch and land in half an hour, and such a redundancy as there are only 240 cities in the northern hemisphere. Such a redundancy everything's targeted—universities, factories, everything that you hold most dear.

And you have 5,500 hydrogen bombs to drop on Russia, and since the Cold War ended, you have now targeted China. Fancy that, for god's sake.

And America's got a policy, which you might not know, to fight and win a nuclear war against Russia. How do you win it? You send over a missile, you decapitate Moscow and kill Putin so he can't press his button. Then quickly you launch all your missiles and land two hydrogen bombs on each missile silo and you kill the missiles. Millions of people dying, this is called collateral damage, it's really irrelevant to the Pentagon.

'America's got a policy, which you might not know, to fight and win a nuclear war against Russia. How do you win it? You send over a missile, you decapitate Moscow and kill Putin so he can't press his button. Then quickly you launch all your missiles and land two hydrogen bombs on each missile silo and you kill the missiles. Millions of people dying, this is called collateral damage, it's really irrelevant to the Pentagon.'

Now the Russians are a little paranoid, and they've got a missile called the Dead Hand, and if Putin is decapitated they launch the Dead Hand which sends a signal to all their missiles to launch, with no human input.

That's the situation we live in, right this minute.

And the Russian early warning systems have ceased to work, because they haven't afforded to be able to keep them up. And they are clinically paranoid. You don't threaten clinically paranoid patients because they'll do something really dangerous.

On 9–11 you got to the second highest stage of nuclear alert. Five—four—three—two, and the last one is they turn the keys in the locks and off they go. Why? Because no-one knew what was happening.

As the international situation becomes more and more anxiety-making, and fear prevails, ecologically, economically, so we enter a period of an unknown territory… with these bombs it's more dangerous now than it was at the height of the Cold War when we were all so frightened… we've forgotten, it's the elephant in the sitting room that's never talked about.'

The Battle of the Sexes

Although the pages of history as conventionally written bear a preponderance of male names, the female force in history, art and literature goes back to ancient times. The Greek poet Sappho (c.610–570BCE), the British Warrior Queen Boudicca (died 60CE), the mediaeval French leader Joan of Arc (c.1412–31), and the Restoration playwright and poet Aphra Behn (c.1640–89), all made their mark on history.

The French Revolution of 1789 fostered myriad new notions about equality and freedom that were argued over by peoples around the world, and feminist writer Mary Wollstonecraft's A *Vindication of the Rights of Women* (1792) was a clarion call for equality of the sexes in a time when women were denied voting and property rights and other fundamental civil liberties.

The philosophers Karl Marx (1818–83) and John Stuart Mill (1806–73) argued for equality of the sexes, and the 19th century saw women striving ever more purposefully in many parts of the world for equality, their campaign expressed initially in pressing for the right to vote, and for other rights in subsequent waves of feminist activity.

The Suffragette movement of the early 20th century, spearheaded by Emmeline Pankhurst (1858–1928) and her daughter Christobel (1880–1958), campaigned to deliver votes for women in Britain and the United States (long after they had gained the vote in New Zealand and Australia), eventually achieving their objective in the post-World War I era in both countries.

Women recruited to war industries during World War II gained access to income and freedoms they had previously not known, and although the 1950s saw a concerted effort to return them to the kitchen, a rising feminist consciousness articulated by authors such as Betty Friedan (1921–2006), Gloria Steinem (1934–), Germaine Greer (1939–) and Kate Millett (1934–) soon led to dissent, protest rallies and ultimately new laws against sexual discrimination.

As they made their mark on the public debate through books, the media, and public appearances, the 'war of the sexes' was rejoined with new vigour, with decades-long battles fought over key issues such as contraception, abortion, property rights, equal pay, and the degrading depiction of women in advertising. Feminism became a central intellectual battleground of the 20th century, and remains so into the 21st, with considerable gains in the West at least. While very few would suggest total sexual equality has been achieved anywhere, the rights enjoyed by women in many countries now stand in marked contrast to their situation of decades and centuries past.

Susan B. Anthony

'A Hateful Oligarchy of Sex'

Speech to the jury at her trial for voting in the 1872 US presidential election, at Canandaigua, New York, 17 June 1873.

American suffragette Susan B. Anthony, circa 1898.

A lifelong campaigner for suffrage, Susan Brownell Anthony (1820–1906) was born in Massachusetts into an activist Quaker family. From an early age she developed a strong sense of social justice and zeal for change, initially through the Temperance movement. She taught for 15 years before devoting herself entirely to social activism, becoming involved in the anti-slavery movement, and the women's rights movement of the 1850s.

Despite being abused and attacked at rallies, she toured the United States for many years, in particular speaking out for women's right to vote. In the 1872 presidential election she was arrested for voting in Rochester, New York, along with several other women. At her trial in the nearby town of Canandaigua the following year, she was convicted and fined US $100. When she refused to pay it, the presiding judge decided against imprisoning her.

'Friends and fellow citizens, I stand before you tonight under indictment for the alleged crime of having voted at the last presidential election, without having a lawful right to vote. It shall be my work this evening to prove to you that in thus voting, I not only committed no crime, but, instead, simply exercised my citizen's rights, guaranteed to me and all United States citizens by the National Constitution, beyond the power of any state to deny.

The preamble of the Federal Constitution says: "We, the people of the United States, in order to form a more perfect union, establish justice, insure domestic tranquillity, provide for the common defense, promote the general welfare, and secure the blessings of liberty to ourselves and our posterity, do ordain and establish this Constitution for the United States of America."

It was we, the people; not we, the white male citizens; nor yet we, the male citizens; but we, the whole people, who formed the Union. And we formed it, not to give the blessings of liberty, but to secure them; not to the half of ourselves and the half of our posterity, but to the whole people—women as well as men. And it is a downright mockery to talk to women of their enjoyment of the blessings of liberty while they are denied the use of the only means of securing them provided by this democratic-republican government—the ballot.

For any state to make sex a qualification that must ever result in the disfranchisement of one entire half of the people, is to pass a bill of attainder, or, an ex post facto law, and is therefore a violation of the supreme law of the land. By it the blessings of liberty are forever withheld from women and their female posterity.

To them this government has no just powers derived from the consent of the governed. To them this government is not a democracy. It is not a republic. It is an odious aristocracy; a hateful oligarchy of sex; the most hateful aristocracy ever established on the face of the globe; an oligarchy of wealth, where the rich

'It is a downright mockery to talk to women of their enjoyment of the blessings of liberty while they are denied the use of the only means of securing them provided by this democratic-republican government—the ballot.'

govern the poor. An oligarchy of learning, where the educated govern the ignorant, or even an oligarchy of race, where the Saxon rules the African, might be endured; but this oligarchy of sex, which makes father, brothers, husband, sons, the oligarchs over the mother and sisters, the wife and daughters, of every household—which ordains all men sovereigns, all women subjects, carries dissension, discord, and rebellion into every home of the nation.

Webster, Worcester, and Bouvier all define a citizen to be a person in the United States, entitled to vote and hold office. The only question left to be settled now is: Are women persons? And I hardly believe any of our opponents will have the hardihood to say they are not. Being persons, then, women are citizens; and no state has a right to make any law, or to enforce any old law, that shall abridge their privileges or immunities. Hence, every discrimination against women in the constitutions and laws of the several states is today null and void, precisely as is every one against Negroes. ’

She continued to campaign for the rest of her life for suffrage and women's rights, including financial, property and educational rights, achieving an important milestone in 1900 when the University of Rochester agreed to admit women. She died in 1906. American women finally gained the vote in 1920—nearly 50 years after her trial for voting in Rochester.

Emmeline Pankhurst

'Our Civil War'

Fundraising Speech at Hartford, Connecticut, 13 November 1913.

British suffragette Emmeline Pankhurst at an open-air rally in 1908.

Born Emmeline Goulden (1858–1928), the great British suffragist married lawyer Richard Pankhurst, who was himself a strong advocate of women's rights. The Pankhursts initiated a vigorous campaign for the vote for British women, founding the Women's Franchise League.

After the setback of Richard's death in 1898, Emmeline and her daughters Christobel and Sylvia redoubled their efforts, forming the Women's Social and Political Union in 1903. They began a campaign of escalating civil disobedience including chaining themselves to fences and posts, resisting police and embarking on hunger strikes.

Suffragettes were jailed on many occasions and refused food in prison, sometimes being force-fed. Emmeline Pankhurst took responsibility for the bombing of the country house of the chancellor of the exchequer, David Lloyd George, and was jailed repeatedly under the so-called 'Cat and Mouse Act' where a suffragette could be released from prison to recover from the effects of a hunger strike, and then be re-imprisoned.

Following is part of a renowned speech that Pankhurst delivered in Hartford, Connecticut, on a tour of the United States in 1913. (Another section of this speech was published in Alan J. Whiticker's *Speeches That Shaped The Modern World,* also published by New Holland.) In this section she reflects upon a number of key areas of discrimination against women of the era.

'Now, I want to say to you who think women cannot succeed, we have brought the government of England to this position, that it has to face this alternative: either women are to be killed or women are to have the vote. I ask American men in this meeting, what would you say if in your state you were faced with that alternative, that you must either kill them or give them their citizenship—women, many of whom you respect, women whom you know have lived useful lives, women whom you know, even if you do not know them personally, are animated with the highest motives, women who are in pursuit of liberty and the power to do useful public service?

Well, there is only one answer to that alternative; there is only one way out of it, unless you are prepared to put back civilization two or three generations, you must give those women the vote. Now that is the outcome of our civil war.

You won your freedom in America when you had the revolution, by bloodshed, by sacrificing human life. You won the civil war by the sacrifice of human life when you decided to emancipate the negro. You have left it to women in your land, the men of all civilized countries have left it to women, to work out their own salvation. That is the way in which we women of England are doing. Human life for us is sacred, but we say if any life is to be sacrificed it shall be ours; we won't do it ourselves, but we will put the enemy in the position where they will have to choose between giving us freedom or giving us death.

Now whether you approve of us or whether you do not, you must see that we have brought the question of women's suffrage into a position where it is of first rate importance, where it can be ignored no longer. Even the most hardened politician will hesitate to take upon himself directly the responsibility of sacrificing the lives of women of undoubted honour, of undoubted earnestness of purpose. That is the political situation as I lay it before you today.

Now then, let me say something about what has brought it about because you must realize that only the very strongest of motives would lead women to do what we have done. Life is sweet to all of us. Every human being loves life and loves to enjoy the good things and the happiness that life gives: and yet we have a state of things in England that has made not two or three women but thousands of women quite prepared to face these terrible situations that I have been trying without any kind of passion or exaggeration to lay before you.

'Well, there is only one answer to that alternative; there is only one way out of it, unless you are prepared to put back civilization two or three generations, you must give those women the vote. Now that is the outcome of our civil war.'

Well, I might spend two or three nights dealing with the industrial situation as it affects women, with the legal position of women, with the social position of women. I want very briefly to say a few words about all. First of all there is the condition of the working woman. One of the things which gives strength to our agitation is that the women who are taking an active part in it are not the poorest women, are not the overworked women; they are the women who are held to be fortunate, the women who have no special personal grievance of their own. Those women have taken up this fight for their own sake, it is true, because they wish to be free, but chiefly for the sake of the women less fortunate than themselves.

The industrial workers of Great Britain have an average wage, mind you, not a minimum wage, an average wage, of less than two dollars a week. Think what would happen in any country if the men in industry of that country had to subsist on a wage like that. Thousands upon thousands of these women—because there are over 5 million wage earners in my country—thousands of these women have dependants; they are women with children dependent upon them, deserted wives with children dependent on them, or wives with sick husbands; they are unmarried mothers, or they are unmarried women who have old parents or younger brothers and sisters, or sick relatives dependent upon them.

Their average income, taking the highly skilled woman teacher and averaging her wage with the unskilled home worker, the average income is less than two dollars a week. There you have in itself an explanation of an uprising of a very determined kind to secure better conditions; and when you know that the government is the largest employer of all the employers and sets a horribly bad example to the private employer in the wages that it pays to women, there you have another explanation. Constant economies are being affected in government departments by the substitution of women's labour for men's, and there is always a reduction in wages whenever women are employed. That is the industrial situation. To speak of the sweated home-worker would take too long, but there are women, women even with dependants, only able to earn three or four shillings a week, thousands of them, and having to pay with the increased cost of living, exorbitant rents in our great cities for single rooms, so that you get several families in one room: they cannot afford even to have a room for themselves. So much for the industrial situation.

Then there is the legal situation. The marriage laws of our country are bringing hundreds and hundreds of women into the militant ranks because we cannot get reform, the kind of reform that women want, of our marriage laws. First of all, a girl is held marriageable by English law, at the age of twelve years. When I was on trial they produced a little girl as a witness, a little girl who had found something in the neighbourhood of the house of the chancellor of the exchequer [David Lloyd George], which was destroyed by some women, and this little girl was produced as a witness. It was said that it was a terrible thing to bring a little girl of twelve years of age and put her in the witness box in a court of law. I agreed, but I pointed out to the judge and the jury that one of the reasons why women were in revolt was because that little girl, whose head just appeared over the top of the witness box, was considered old enough by the laws of her country to take upon herself the terrible responsibilities of wifehood and motherhood, and women could not get it altered, no politicians would listen to us, when we asked to have the marriage law altered in that particular.

'The marriage laws of our country are bringing hundreds and hundreds of women into the militant ranks because we cannot get reform, the kind of reform that women want, of our marriage laws. First of all, a girl is held marriageable by English law, at the age of twelve years.'

Then, the position of the wife. It is very frequently said that every woman who wants a vote, wants a vote because she has been disappointed, because she has not been chosen to be a wife. Well, I can assure you that if most women made a study of the laws before they decided to get married, a great many women would seriously consider whether it was worthwhile, whether the price was not too heavy, because, according to English law, a woman may toil all her life for her husband and her family, she may work in her husband's business, she may help him to build up the family income, and if he chooses at the end of a long life to take every penny of the money that woman has helped to earn away from her and her children, he can do it, and she has no redress. She may at the end of a long, hard life find herself and her children absolutely penniless because her husband has chosen to will the money away from her. So that you see when you look at it from the legal point of view, it is not such a very, very great gain to become a wife in my country. There are a great many risks that go along with it.

Then take her as a mother. If the child of two parents has any property inherited from relatives, and that child dies before it is of age to make a will, or without making a will, the only person who inherits the property of that child is the child's father; the mother does not exist as her child's heir at all; and during the father's lifetime she not only cannot inherit from her child but she has no voice whatever in deciding the life of her child. Her husband can give the child away to be educated somewhere else or he can bring whomever he pleases into the house to educate the child. He decides absolutely the conditions in which that child is to live; he decides how it is to be educated; he can even decide what religion it is to profess, and the mother's consent is not obtained to any of these decisions. Women are trying to alter it, have tried for generations, but they cannot because the legislatures have no time to listen to the opinions and the desires of people who have no votes.

Well then, when it comes to the question of how people are to get out of marriage, if they are unhappy, under the laws of divorce, the English law of divorce is the most scandalous divorce law in the civilized world. There may be a few states in America, and I believe in Canada, where the same law obtains, but the English divorce law is in itself such a stigma upon women, such a degradation to women, such an invitation to immorality on the part of the married man, that I think that divorce law in itself would justify a rebellion on the part of the women.

You get registered in law unequal standards of morals in marriage, and a married man is encouraged by law to think that he can make as many lapses as he thinks fit in marital fidelity; whereas, if one act of infidelity is proved against her the husband can get rid of her by divorce, can take her children away from her and make her an outcast.

'You get registered in law unequal standards of morals in marriage, and a married man is encouraged by law to think that he can make as many lapses as he thinks fit in marital fidelity; whereas, if one act of infidelity is proved against her the husband can get rid of her by divorce.'

Women who have been clamouring for an equal divorce law for generations cannot get any attention. Well now, we have had a royal commission on divorce and we have had a report, but there is no security for women that they are to have justice under a new law so long as men are chosen by men to legislate and those men are likely to register the moral opinions of men, not the moral opinions of women, in legislation.

We have to look facts in the face. Part of the militant movement for woman suffrage has had that effect, that women have learned to look facts in the face; they have got rid of sentimentalities; they are looking at actual facts: and when anti-suffragists talk about chivalry, and when they talk about putting women on pedestals and guarding them from all the difficulties and dangers of life, we look to the facts in life as we see them and we say: 'Women have every reason to distrust that kind of thing, every reason to be dissatisfied; we want to know the truth however bad it is, and we face that truth because it is only through knowing the truth that you ever will get to anything better.'

We are determined to have these things faced and cleared up, and it is absolutely ridiculous to say to women that they can safely trust their interests in the hands of men who have already registered in the legislation of their country a standard of morals so unequal for both sexes as we find on the statute books of England today.

When the divorce commission sat, evidence was given by all kinds of people, and women had the experience of reading in the newspapers the evidence of the man who had been chosen by other men to preside over the divorce court, the judge whose duty it was to decide what was legal cruelty and decide whether women were to continue to be bound to their husbands or not. What did he say? I am glad to think that he is not in a position to give effect to his ideas any more; he now adorns the House of Lords: but he was still judge of the divorce court when he said, that in his opinion the wise wife was the woman who closed her eyes to the moral failings of her husband; and that was the man, women in this meeting, who had for years decided what was legal cruelty and what women were to endure or what they were not to endure in that relationship of husband and wife.

'Once you cease to listen to politicians, once you cease to allow yourself to look at the facts of life through men's spectacles but look at them through your own, every day that passes you are having fresh illustrations of the need there is for women to refuse to wait any longer for their enfranchisement...'

Well, can you wonder that all these things make us more militant? It seems to me that once you look at things from the woman's point of view, once you cease to listen to politicians, once you cease to allow yourself to look at the facts of life through men's spectacles but look at them through your own, every day that passes you are having fresh illustrations of the need there is for women to refuse to wait any longer for their enfranchisement...

People have said: "Why does Mrs Pankhurst come to America? Has she come to America to rouse American women to be militant?" No, I have not come to America to arouse American women to be militant. I believe that American women, as their earnestness increases, as they realize the need for the enfranchisement of their sex, will find out for themselves the best way to secure that object. Each nation must work out its own salvation, and so the American women will find their own way and use their own methods capably.

Other people have said: "What right has Mrs Pankhurst to come to America and ask for American dollars?" Well, I think I have the right that all oppressed people have to ask for practical sympathy of others freer than themselves. Your right to send to France and ask for help was never questioned. You did it, and you got that help. Men of all nationalities have come to America, and they have not gone away empty-handed, because American sympathy has been extended to struggling peoples all over the world.

In England, if you could understand it, there is the most pathetic and the most courageous fight going on, because you find the people whom you have been accustomed to look upon as weak and reliant, the people you have always thought leaned upon other people for protection, have stood up and are fighting for themselves.

Women have found a new kind of self-respect, a new kind of energy, a new kind of strength: and I think that of all oppressed peoples who might claim your sympathy and support, women who are fighting this fight unknown in the history of humanity before, fighting this fight in the 20th century for greater powers of self-development, self-expression and self-government, might very well attract the sympathy and the practical help of American people.

There hasn't been a victory the women of America have won that we have not rejoiced in. I think as we have read month by month of the new states that have been added to the list of fully enfranchised states, perhaps we who know how hard the fight is, have rejoiced even more than American women themselves.

I have heard cheers ring out in a meeting in London when the news of some new state being added to the list was given, cheers louder and more enthusiastic than I have ever heard for any victory in an American meeting. It is very true that those who are fighting a hard battle, those who are sacrificing greatly in order to win a victory, appreciate victories and are more enthusiastic when victories are won. We have rejoiced wholeheartedly in your victories. We feel that those victories have been easier perhaps because of the hard times that we were having, because out of our militant movement in the storm centre of the suffrage movement have gone waves that have helped to rouse women all over the world. You could only explain the strange phenomena in that way.

Ten years ago there was hardly any woman suffrage movement at all. Now even in China and Japan, in India, in Turkey, everywhere women are rising up and asking for these larger opportunities, which modern conditions demand that women should have: and we women think that we have helped. Well, if we have helped at all, if, as has been said from the chair tonight, we have even helped to rouse suffrage enthusiasm in Connecticut, can you blame me very much if I come and tell you of the desperate struggle we are having, of how the government is trying to break us down in every possible way, even by involving us in lawsuits, and trying to frighten our subscribers by threatening to prosecute even people who help us by subscribing money? Can you wonder I come over to America? Have you read about American dollars that have been given the Irish law-breakers?

So here am I. I come in the intervals of prison appearance: I come after having been four times imprisoned under the "Cat and Mouse Act", probably going back to be rearrested as soon as I set my foot on British soil. I come to ask you to help to win this fight. If we win it, this hardest of all fights, then, to be sure, in the future it is going to be made easier for women all over the world to win their fight when their time comes.’

The Pankhursts suspended their campaign the following year, after the outbreak of World War I, and helped recruit women into the war effort. Their long struggle finally bore its first fruit in 1918 with Britain's granting of the vote to women over the age of 30, and final victory in 1928 with equality of franchise. Emmeline Pankhurst lived to see it, but died a few months later.

Virginia Woolf

'You Have Won Rooms of Your Own'

Speech to the National Society for Women's Service, London, 21 January 1931.

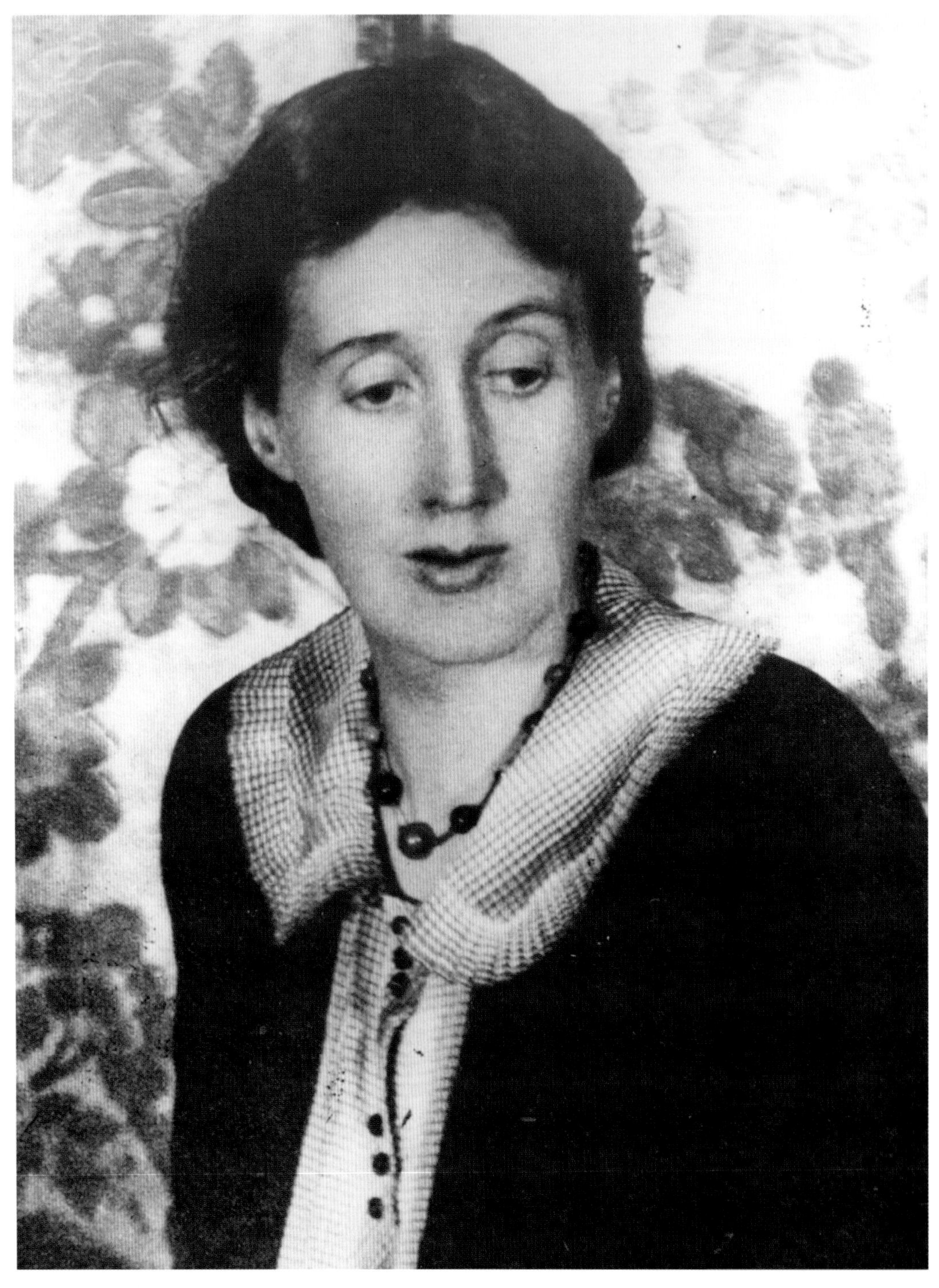

Writer Virginia Woolf, a member of the Bloomsbury Group, in 1927.

The feminist commitment, poetic sensitivity and fearless literary innovation of Virginia Woolf (1882–1941) all help to enshrine her among the finest authors of the past century.

Born in London into an aristocratic literary and artistic family, she suffered a nervous breakdown at the age of 22 following the death of her father.

She later moved into a house in Bloomsbury in London with her artist sister Vanessa and their two brothers, and instituted a weekly get-together where like-minded people could discuss literature, art and politics: thus the Bloomsbury Group was born, its members including economist John Maynard Keynes (1883–1946) and historian Lytton Strachey (1880–1932).

In 1912, she married the political author Leonard Woolf (1880–1969). Her publishing debut came with the shipboard novel *The Voyage Out* (1915), but she is best known for *Mrs Dalloway* (1925), *To The Lighthouse* (1927) and the feminist essay *A Room of One's Own* (1929), some of the ideas of which resonate in this speech.

‘When your secretary invited me to come here, she told me that your society is concerned with the employment of women, and she suggested that I might tell you something about my own professional experiences. It is true I am a woman; it is true I am employed; but what professional experiences have I had? It is difficult to say.

My profession is literature; and in that profession there are fewer experiences for women than in any other, with the exception of the stage—fewer, I mean, that are peculiar to women. For the road was cut many years ago—by Fanny Burney, by Aphra Behn, by Harriet Martineau, by Jane Austen, by George Eliot—many famous women, and many more unknown and forgotten, have been before me, making the path smooth, and regulating my steps.

Thus, when I came to write, there were very few material obstacles in my way. Writing was a reputable and harmless occupation. The family peace was not broken by the scratching of a pen. No demand was made upon the family purse. For10 and sixpence one can buy paper enough to write all the plays of Shakespeare—if one has a mind that way. Pianos and models, Paris, Vienna and Berlin, masters and mistresses, are not needed by a writer. The cheapness of writing paper is, of course, the reason why women have succeeded as writers before they have succeeded in the other professions.

But to tell you my story—it is a simple one. You have only got to figure to yourselves a girl in a bedroom with a pen in her hand. She had only to move that pen from left to right, from 10 o'clock to one. Then it occurred to her to do what is simple and cheap enough after all—to slip a few of those pages into an envelope, fix a penny stamp in the corner, and drop the envelope into the red box at the corner. It was thus that I became a journalist; and my effort was rewarded on the first day of the following month—a very glorious day it was for me—by a letter from an editor containing a cheque for one pound 10 shillings and sixpence.

But to show you how little I deserve to be called a professional woman, how little I know of the struggles and difficulties of such lives, I have to admit that instead of spending that sum

'But to show you how little I deserve to be called a professional woman, how little I know of the struggles and difficulties of such lives, I have to admit that instead of spending that sum upon bread and butter, rent, shoes and stockings, or butcher's bills, I went out and bought a cat—a beautiful cat.'

upon bread and butter, rent, shoes and stockings, or butcher's bills, I went out and bought a cat—a beautiful cat, a Persian cat, which very soon involved me in bitter disputes with my neighbours.

What could be easier than to write articles and to buy Persian cats with the profits? But wait a moment. Articles have to be about something. Mine, I seem to remember, was about a novel by a famous man. And while I was writing this review, I discovered that if I were going to review books I should need to do battle with a certain phantom. And the phantom was a woman, and when I came to know her better I called her after the heroine of a famous poem, *The Angel in the House*.

It was she who used to come between me and my paper when I was writing reviews. It was she who bothered me and wasted my time and so tormented me that at last I killed her. You who come of a younger and happier generation may not have heard of her—you may not know what I mean by the Angel in the House. I will describe her as shortly as I can.

She was intensely sympathetic. She was immensely charming. She was utterly unselfish. She excelled in the difficult arts of family life. She sacrificed herself daily. If there was chicken, she took the leg; if there was a draught she sat in it—in short she was so constituted that she never had a mind or a wish of her own, but preferred to sympathize always with the minds and wishes of others. Above all—I need not say it—she was pure. Her purity was supposed to be her chief beauty—her blushes, her great grace. In those days—the last of Queen Victoria—every house had its Angel. And when I came to write I encountered her with the very first words.

The shadow of her wings fell on my page; I heard the rustling of her skirts in the room. Directly, that is to say, I took my pen in my hand to review that novel by a famous man, she slipped behind me and whispered: "My dear, you are a young woman. You are writing about a book that has been written by a man. Be sympathetic; be tender; flatter; deceive; use all the arts and wiles of our sex. Never let anybody guess that you have a mind of your own. Above all, be pure."

And she made as if to guide my pen. I now record the one act for which I take some credit to myself, though the credit rightly belongs to some excellent ancestors of mine who left me a certain sum of money—shall we say five hundred pounds a year?—so that it was not necessary for me to depend solely on charm for my living. I turned upon her and caught her by the throat. I did my best to kill her.

My excuse, if I were to be had up in a court of law, would be that I acted in self-defence. Had I not killed her she would have killed me. She would have plucked the heart out of my writing. For, as I found, directly I put pen to paper, you cannot review even a novel without having a mind of your own, without expressing what you think to be the truth about human relations, morality, sex. And all these questions, according to the Angel of the House, cannot be dealt with freely and openly by women; they must charm, they must conciliate, they must—to put it bluntly—tell lies if they are to succeed. Thus, whenever I felt the shadow of her wing or the radiance of her halo upon my page, I took up the inkpot and flung it at her. She died hard. Her fictitious nature was of great assistance to her. It is far harder to kill a phantom than a reality. She was always creeping back when I thought I had despatched her. Though I flatter myself that I killed her in the end, the struggle was severe; it took much time that had better have been spent upon learning Greek grammar; or in roaming the world in search of adventures. But it was a real experience; it was an experience that was bound to befall all women writers at that time. Killing the Angel in the House was part of the occupation of a woman writer.

But to continue my story. The Angel was dead; what then remained? You may say that what remained was a simple and common object—a young woman in a bedroom with an inkpot. In other words, now that she had rid herself of falsehood, that young woman had only to be herself. Ah, but what is "herself"? I mean, what is a woman? I assure you, I do not know. I do not believe that you know. I do not believe that anybody can know until she has expressed herself in all the arts and professions open to human skill. That indeed is one of the reasons why I have come here out of respect for you, who are in process of showing us by your experiments what a woman is, who are in process of providing us, by your failures and successes, with that extremely important piece of information.

But to continue the story of my professional experiences. I made one pound 10 and six by my first review; and I bought a Persian cat with the proceeds. Then I grew ambitious. A Persian cat is all very well, I said; but a Persian cat is not enough. I must have a motor car. And it was thus that I became a novelist—for it is a very strange thing that people will give you a motor car if you will tell them a story. It is a still stranger thing that there is nothing so delightful in the world as telling stories. It is far pleasanter than writing reviews of famous novels. And yet, if I am to obey your secretary and tell you my professional experiences as a novelist, I must tell you about a very strange experience that befell me as a novelist. And to understand it you must try first to imagine a novelist's state of mind.

I hope I am not giving away professional secrets if I say that a novelist's chief desire is to be as unconscious as possible. He has to induce in himself a state of perpetual lethargy. He wants life to proceed with the utmost quiet and regularity. He wants to see the same faces, to read the same books, to do the same things day after day, month after month, while he is writing, so that nothing may break the illusion in which he is living—so that nothing may disturb or disquiet the mysterious nosings about, feelings round, darts, dashes and sudden discoveries of that very shy and illusive spirit, the imagination. I suspect that this state is the same both for men and women. Be that as it may, I want you to imagine me writing a novel in a state of trance.

I want you to figure to yourselves a girl sitting with a pen in her hand, which for minutes, and indeed for hours, she never dips into the inkpot. The image that comes to my mind when I think of this girl is the image of a fisherman lying sunk in dreams on the verge of a deep lake with a rod held out over the water. She

'Then I grew ambitious. A Persian cat is all very well, I said; but a Persian cat is not enough. I must have a motor car. And it was thus that I became a novelist—for it is a very strange thing that people will give you a motor car if you will tell them a story.'

'You have won rooms of your own in the house hitherto exclusively owned by men. You are able, though not without great labour and effort, to pay the rent. You are earning your five hundred pounds a year. But this freedom is only a beginning—the room is your own, but it is still bare. It has to be furnished; it has to be decorated; it has to be shared.'

was letting her imagination sweep unchecked round every rock and cranny of the world that lies submerged in the depths of our unconscious being.

Now came the experience, the experience that I believe to be far commoner with women writers than with men. The line raced through the girl's fingers. Her imagination had rushed away. It had sought the pools, the depths, the dark places where the largest fish slumber. And then there was a smash. There was an explosion. There was foam and confusion. The imagination had dashed itself against something hard. The girl was roused from her dream. She was indeed in a state of the most acute and difficult distress. To speak without figure she had thought of something, something about the body, about the passions which it was unfitting for her as a woman to say. Men, her reason told her, would be shocked. The consciousness of what men will say of a woman who speaks the truth about her passions had r oused her from her artist's state of unconsciousness. She could write no more. The trance was over. Her imagination could work no longer.

This I believe to be a very common experience with women writers—they are impeded by the extreme conventionality of the other sex. For though men sensibly allow themselves great freedom in these respects, I doubt that they realize or can control the extreme severity with which they condemn such freedom in women.

These then were two very genuine experiences of my own. These were two of the adventures of my professional life. The first—killing the Angel in the House—I think I solved. She died. But the second, telling the truth about my own experiences as a body, I do not think I solved. I doubt that any woman has solved it yet. The obstacles against her are still immensely powerful, and yet they are very difficult to define. Outwardly, what is simpler than to write books? Outwardly, what obstacles are there for a woman rather than for a man? Inwardly, I think, the case is very different; she has still many ghosts to fight, many prejudices to overcome. Indeed it will be a long time still, I think, before a woman can sit down to write a book without finding a phantom to be slain, a rock to be dashed against. And if this is so in literature, the freest of all professions for women, how is it in the new professions which you are now for the first time entering?

Those are the questions that I should like, had I time, to ask you. And indeed, if I have laid stress upon these professional experiences of mine, it is because I believe that they are, though in different forms, yours also. Even when the path is nominally open—when there is nothing to prevent a woman from being a doctor, a lawyer, a civil servant—there are many phantoms and obstacles, as I believe, looming in her way. To discuss and define them is I think of great value and importance; for thus only can the labour be shared, the difficulties be solved.

But besides this, it is necessary also to discuss the ends and the aims for which we are fighting, for which we are doing battle with these formidable obstacles. Those aims cannot be taken for granted; they must be perpetually questioned and examined. The whole position, as I see it, here in this hall surrounded by women practising for the first time in history I know not how many different professions, is one of extraordinary interest and importance.

You have won rooms of your own in the house hitherto exclusively owned by men. You are able, though not without great labour and effort, to pay the rent. You are earning your five hundred pounds a year. But this freedom is only a beginning—the room is your own, but it is still bare. It has to be furnished; it has to be decorated; it has to be shared. How are you going to furnish it, how are you going to decorate it? With whom are you going to share it, and upon what terms?

These, I think are questions of the utmost importance and interest. For the first time in history you are able to ask them; for the first time you are able to decide for yourselves what the answers should be. Willingly would I stay and discuss those questions and answers, but not tonight. My time is up, and I must cease.'

It is a tragic fact that such a vital and sympathetic mind as Virginia Woolf's endured lifelong problems. Returning from visiting Blitz-ravaged London in 1941, and suffering from depression, she drowned herself near her country house in Sussex.

Jessie Street

'Equal Pay To Men and Women'

Broadcast on the Australian Broadcasting Commission's National Program, 17 April 1944.

Jessie Street at the United Women's Conference in San Fransisco, 19 May 1945.

Jessie Street (1889–1970) was born in India and grew up on her family's property near Grafton in New South Wales, Australia. She was schooled in Britain before returning to Australia where she graduated from the University of Sydney in 1911. She married barrister Kenneth Street (1890–1972), who later rose to become chief justice of New South Wales.

In the 1930s, she headed the Australian Federation of Women Voters, an organization striving for equality of the sexes and an end to all forms of discrimination against women.

This is a radio address she made towards the end of World War II on the future of those women who had enjoyed new liberties working during the war years. She makes a plea for equal pay for those women who chose to stay in the workforce.

‘There is a good deal of talk just now about what they are going to do after the war with the women: Must they be made to return to the home? Are they going to take them out of the factory, the office, off the land?

To me, this sort of discussion is very disquieting. It makes me think we've already forgotten the reasons why we're fighting this war. Aren't we fighting for liberty, for democracy and to eradicate Fascism and Nazism in every form? Surely we don't mean liberty and democracy for men only? Indeed, I hope women will enjoy the liberty which they have helped to win and be permitted to choose what they want to do.

Do you remember that one of the first things the Nazis did when they came to power was to put women out of the professions, out of the factories? They barred the doors of the universities to all but a few women and they severely limited women's opportunities for any kind of higher education; by these methods the Nazis forced women back to the home—back to the kitchen. I can't help thinking that if any attempt is made here after the war to force women back to the home, it will be proof that fascism still has strong roots in Australia.

‘Do you remember that one of the first things the Nazis did when they came to power was to put women out of the professions, out of the factories? They barred the doors of the universities to all but a few women and they severely limited women's opportunities for any kind of higher education; by these methods the Nazis forced women back to the home.’

Women should not be forced to return to the home, but they should be free to return there if they wish to. I don't like what's implied in the suggestion that women will have to be forced back into the home—that's a slight not only on home life, but also on the work of bearing and rearing children, don't you agree? The greatest happiness for many women is to care for a home and to raise a family. The trouble in the past has been that society has failed to make it possible for all the women who wanted to have homes and raise families to do so.

And while we're on the subject of women in the home, I think that this life could be made attractive to many more women by

'I believe that in a democratic, free society women should be at liberty to choose whether they will take up home life or work outside the home; that men and women should receive equal pay and equal opportunity; that home life should be made less of a tie and the burden of raising a family be lightened.'

developing amenities and customs that render home less of a prison than it is to many women with young families. Just think of the prospects of family life, as lived under present conditions, to a clever, energetic, bright young girl.

Soon after marriage there will be a baby, and from then on she cannot move unencumbered. The more babies, the harder she has to work and the greater her restrictions. If we want more women to choose home life, we must make home life less hard. But how can we do this? Well, we can have creches and kindergartens and supervised playgrounds where children can be left in safe surroundings.

Then we must change many of our conventions. Why should a woman do all the work in the home? Why can't we, for example, have community kitchens and laundries? If a woman wants to work outside the home, why shouldn't she? Let her be free to choose. There's just as much and more reason to believe that the best interests of her family and of society will be served by giving a woman a free choice than by expecting her to adhere to a lot of worn-out conventions.

Anyway, the contribution that women can make to public life through the professions or in industry is important. Women in the past have been very much hampered by their inexperience in these spheres. They haven't had the opportunity to qualify for representative positions or positions of control and direction. In other words, because of the lack of opportunity to gain experience they're denied the opportunity of exerting any influence in framing policies or directing public affairs.

I am pretty sure that many women will remain in industry after the war, for we shall be in need of more skilled hands rather than less. Remember, we couldn't exert a full war effort until women were absorbed into industry; therefore, how can we exert a full peace program without making use of their services? Everyone knows how short we are of houses and hospitals and offices, of furniture, of bathroom and kitchen fittings, of curtains, wallpaper, clothing, foodstuffs, in fact, hundreds of commodities. Can you imagine the tremendous amount of work that will be required? Not only have we to make up the deficiency of the war years, but we must provide all these amenities on a much larger scale after the war. There were large numbers of people before the war who had no homes, not even enough to eat; hospital accommodation was inadequate, and so on.

Although all these could have been provided for a few million pounds, we believed we could not afford to better these conditions. It took a total war to show us what we could do with our own resources. If we can raise money for war we can raise it for peace, surely. It would be inexcusable in the future to condemn people to live under the conditions so many endured before the war.

Why is there so much opposition to women remaining in industry? The secret isn't far to seek. It's simply that they got paid less—they are cheap labour, certainly not, as so many have alleged, because they're weaker or less efficient. Unfortunately, because their labour is cheaper, women not only threaten the wage standards of men workers, but they also threaten the standard of living of all workers. The obvious and just way to avoid this is to give equal pay to men and women.

To put this in a nutshell, I believe that in a democratic, free society women should be at liberty to choose whether they will take up home life or work outside the home; that men and women should receive equal pay and equal opportunity; that home life should be made less of a tie and the burden of raising a family be lightened. If we can face these peacetime problems with the spirit of determination and conciliation with which we're facing our war problems, we may hope to solve them.'

After the war Jessie Street became the sole female advisor in the Australian delegation to the UN Conference in San Francisco. In co-operation with women from other nations, she ensured the word "sex" appeared in the clause "without distinction as to race, sex, language or religion" in the UN Charter. In later years she took a leading role in the international peace movement, and worked for Aboriginal rights. She died in Sydney in 1970.

Claudia (Lady Bird) Johnson

'Let Eleanor Roosevelt Teach Us All'

Tribute to the Eleanor Roosevelt Memorial Foundation, New York City, 9 April 1964.

Claudia (Lady Bird) Johnson speaking at the
US Democratic National Convention in 1960.

Claudia Johnson (née Taylor, 1912–2007), the woman who stood by US President Lyndon B. Johnson's side during his turbulent administration in the 1960s, was born into a well-off Texas business family. Claudia gained the nickname 'Lady Bird' in childhood as she had a love of nature. She studied the classics, and gained a degree in arts and journalism from the University of Texas.

At the age of 21 she met Lyndon Johnson, and they married a year later. She gave birth to two children in the years that followed, and helped her husband campaign for the US Senate. In 1960, Lyndon Johnson became vice-president under President John F. Kennedy. Following Kennedy's assassination in 1963, Johnson became president and Lady Bird the first lady.

Like Eleanor Roosevelt, several decades earlier, Lady Bird Johnson was active in social issues, including her husband's educational initiatives and war on poverty. In this speech, Lady Bird reflects on the life of Eleanor Roosevelt, the liberal and social activist wife of President Franklin D. Roosevelt.

'I met Eleanor Roosevelt first in print and admired her. I met her later in person and loved her. As she did to many very young and very timid Congressional wives, she extended her hand and hospitality to me... and Washington was warmer.

I saw her last when she came to my home on February 12, 1962, the day the Commission on the Status of Women was organized under her chairmanship and her inspiration. She was 78. I have often thought how much she made those years count for her country.

"Nobody," said Marcus Aurelius, "is either the better or the worse for being praised." We are engaged in an idle ceremony, which would have brought no comfort to Eleanor Roosevelt, if we come here merely to praise her great qualities and achievements. She does not need our praise.

All of us are familiar with people who are the partisans of departed virtue, but are afraid to defend an unpopular truth today. Mrs Roosevelt never stood with this timid company. Her conscience was her counsellor, and she followed its commands with unfaltering courage. Nor did she really understand what people meant when they praised her for taking so many risks. She would have taken the greatest risk of all if she had remained silent in the presence of wrong. She would have risked the integrity of her soul.

A rabbi of the Jewish community in Berlin under the Hitler regime once said: "The most important thing I learned is that bigotry and hatred are not the most urgent problems. The most urgent, the most disgraceful, the most shameful, and the most tragic problem—is silence."

Eleanor Roosevelt taught us that sometimes silence is the greatest sin. Do you remember what Dr Samuel Johnson said about courage? "Unless a man has that virtue, he has no security for preserving any other." Mrs Roosevelt knew what those words meant. She lived their meaning every day of her life. Courage sustained by compassion—that was the watchword of her entire career.

Always she thought not of abstract rights, but of living wrongs. I watched her at close range one day when she spent two hours helping the 75th Congressional Club give a benefit luncheon

'She thought of the suffering individual, not of a theoretical principle. She saw an unemployed father, and so she helped him. She saw a neglected Negro child, and so she educated him. She saw dictators hurling the world into war, and so she worked unflinchingly for peace.'

to buy a wheelchair for a crippled boy. Only one person was involved. Where else do you start, but with one person?

She thought of the suffering individual, not of a theoretical principle. She saw an unemployed father, and so she helped him. She saw a neglected Negro child, and so she educated him. She saw dictators hurling the world into war, and so she worked unflinchingly for peace. She saw the United Nations divided by the conflict of ideology and power, and so she became the prophet of the Universal Declaration of Human Rights.

Are we ready to fight similar battles against new foes in our own day? If not, our grief is an empty thing, and the spirit of Eleanor Roosevelt is not among us.

President Wilson used to say that some people in Washington grow in office, while others merely swell. Mrs Roosevelt steadily grew under the compulsions and inspirations of her great office. But, it is perhaps the ultimate tribute to Mrs Roosevelt that she reached true greatness after the shock of her bereavement when she went bravely forward in a new career as a spokesman for America and a servant of world peace. In the White House she was the First Lady in the land, but after the White House she became, as Ambassador Stevenson has reminded us, the First Lady in the world. Great was her goodness, and it was her goodness that made her so great.

Let us today earnestly resolve to build the true foundation for Eleanor Roosevelt's memory—to pluck out prejudice from our lives, to remove fear and hate where it exists, and to create a world unafraid to work out its destiny in peace. Eleanor Roosevelt has already made her own splendid and incomparable contribution to that foundation. Let us go and do likewise, within the measure of our faith and the limits of our ability. Let Eleanor Roosevelt teach us all how to turn the arts of compassion into the victories of democracy.'

Lyndon B. Johnson did not re-contest the presidency in 1968, and died five years later. Lady Bird continued on in public life through her foundation of the National Wildflower Research Center in 1982, and serving on the board of the National Geographic Society.

Betty Friedan

'The "Sex Plus" Doctrine'

Testimony before the US Senate Judiciary Committee, Washington, DC, 21 August 1970.

American feminist and author Betty Friedan in 1970.

Renowned for her landmark book, *The Feminine Mystique*, Betty Friedan (1921–2006) was a pioneer of the 'second wave' of feminism of the 1960s and 70s. Born in the US state of Illinois, she graduated from Smith College and undertook postgraduate studies in psychology at the Univerity of Berkeley, California. She worked as a university lecturer and as a journalist.

Married in the late 1940s, she experienced the frustration of the idealized 'perfect homemaker' wife of conservative 1950s America, and believed that suburban married life was a trap for women, denying them freedom and opportunity, and sapping their emotional and psychological wellbeing.

Publication of *The Feminine Mystique* in 1963 created a sensation, the book becoming an international best-seller with sales approaching 3 million. It effectively launched a second wave of feminism, paving the way for other campaigning feminists such as Gloria Steinem and Germaine Greer.

Believing the position of women would be improved through fundamental changes such as equal pay and equality of job opportunity, Friedan founded the National Organization for Women (NOW) in 1966, to agitate for change. The body became one of the most important feminist organizations of the past few decades, with membership of half a million.

In 1970 she publicly opposed the appointment proposed by President Richard Nixon of the arch-conservative anti-desegregationist Judge G. Harrold Carswell (1919–92) to the US Supreme Court.

'I am here to testify before this committee to oppose Judge Carswell's appointment to Supreme Court Justice on the basis of his proven insensitivity to the problems of the 53 per cent of United States citizens who are women, and specifically on the basis of his explicit discrimination in a circuit court decision in 1969 against working mothers.

I speak in my capacity as national president of the National Organization for Women, which has led the exploding new movement in this country for "full equality for women in truly equal partnership with men", and which was organized in 1966 to take action to break through discrimination against women in employment, education, government and in all fields of American life.

On October 13, 1969, in the Fifth Circuit Court of Appeals, Judge Carswell was party to a most unusual judiciary action which would permit employers, in defiance of the law of the land as embodied in Title VII of the 1964 Civil Rights Act, to refuse to hire women who have children.

The case involved Mrs Ida Phillips, who was refused employment by Martin Marietta Corporation as an aircraft assembler because she had pre-school aged children, although the company said it would hire a man with pre-school aged children. This case was considered a clear-cut violation of the law which forbids job discrimination on the grounds of sex as well as race.

The EEOC [Equal Employment Opportunity Commission], empowered to administer Title

VII, filed an amicus brief on behalf of Mrs Phillips; an earlier opinion of the Fifth Circuit filed in May upholding the company was considered such a clear violation of the Civil Rights Act by Chief Judge John Brown that he vacated the opinion and asked to convene the full court to consider the case.

Judge Carswell voted to deny a rehearing of the case, an action which in effect would have permitted employers to fire the 4.1 million working mothers in the US today who have children under six. They comprise 38.9 per cent of the nearly 10.6 million mothers in the labor force today.

In his dissent to this ruling in which Judge Carswell claimed no sex discrimination was involved, Chief Judge Brown said: "The case is simple. A woman with pre-school aged children may not be employed, a man with pre-school children may. The distinguishing factor seems to be motherhood versus fatherhood. The question then arises: Is this sex related? To the simple query, the answer is just as simple: Nobody—and this includes judges, Solomonic or life-tenured—has yet seen a male mother. A mother, to over-simplify the simplest biology, must then be a woman. It is the fact of the person being a mother—i.e., a woman—not the age of the children, which denies employment opportunity to a woman which is open to men."

'In his pernicious action, Judge Carswell not only flaunted the Civil Rights Act, designed to end the job discrimination which denied women, along with other minority groups, equal opportunity in employment, but specifically defied the policy of this administration to encourage women in poverty ... to work.'

It is important for this committee to understand the dangerous insensitivity of Judge Carswell to sex discrimination, when the desire and indeed the necessity of women to take a fully equal place in American society has already emerged as one of the most explosive issues in the 1970s, entailing many new problems which will ultimately have to be decided by the Supreme Court.

According to government figures, over 25 per cent of mothers who have children under six are in the labor force today. Over 85 per cent of them work for economic reasons. Over half a million are widowed, divorced or separated. Their incomes are vitally important to their children. Perhaps even more important, as a portent of the future, is the fact that there has been an astronomical increase in the last three decades in the number of working mothers.

Between 1950 and the most recent compilation of government statistics, the number of working mothers in the United States nearly doubled. For every mother of children who worked in 1940, 10 mothers are working today, an increase from slightly over 1.5 million to nearly 11 million.

In his pernicious action, Judge Carswell not only flaunted the Civil Rights Act, designed to end the job discrimination which denied women, along with other minority groups, equal opportunity in employment, but specifically defied the policy of this administration to encourage women in poverty, who have children, to work by expanding day-care centres, rather than having them depend on the current mediaeval welfare system which perpetuates the cycle of poverty from generation to generation. Mothers and children today comprise 80 per cent of the welfare load in major cities.

'To countenance outright sexism, not only in words, but by judicial flaunting of the law in an appointee to the Supreme Court in 1970, when American women—not in the hundreds or thousands but in the millions—are finally beginning to assert their human rights, is unconscionable.'

Judge Carswell justified discrimination against such women by a peculiar doctrine of "sex plus", which claimed that discrimination which did not apply to all women but only to women who did not meet special standards—standards not applied to men—was not sex discrimination.

In his dissent, Chief Judge Brown said, "the sex-plus rule in this case sows the seed for future discrimination against black workers through making them meet extra standards not imposed on whites".

The "sex plus" doctrine would also penalize the very women who most need jobs.

Chief Judge Brown said, "Even if the 'sex plus' rule is not expanded, in its application to mothers of pre-school children, it will deal a serious blow to the objectives of Title VII. If the law against sex discrimination means anything, it must protect employment opportunities for those groups of women who most need jobs because of economic necessity. Working mothers of pre-schoolers are such a group. Studies show that, as compared to women with older children or no children, these mothers of pre-school children were much more likely to have gone to work because of pressing need... because of financial necessity and because their husbands are unable to work. Frequently, these women are a key or only source of income for their families. Sixty-eight per cent of working women do not have husbands present in the household, and two-thirds of these women are raising children in poverty. Moreover, a barrier to jobs for mothers of pre-schoolers tends to harm non-white mothers more than white mothers."

I am not a lawyer, but the wording of Title VII of the Civil Rights Act so clearly conveys its intention to provide equal job opportunity to all oppressed groups, including women—who today in America earn on the average less than half the earnings of men—that only outright sex discrimination or sexism, as we new feminists call it, can explain Judge Carswell's ruling.

Human rights are indivisible, and I, and those for whom I speak, would oppose equally the appointment to the Supreme Court of a racist judge who had been totally blind to the humanity of black men and women since 1948, as the appointment of a sexist judge totally blind to the humanity of women in 1969.

To countenance outright sexism, not only in words, but by judicial flaunting of the law in an appointee to the Supreme Court in 1970, when American women—not in the hundreds or thousands but in the millions—are finally beginning to assert their human rights, is unconscionable.

I trust that you gentlemen of the committee do not share Judge Carswell's inability to see women as human beings, too. I will, however, put these questions to you.

How would you feel if in the event you were not re-elected, you applied for a job at some company or law firm or university, and were told you weren't eligible because you had a child? How would you feel if your sons were told explicitly or implicitly that they could not get or keep certain jobs if they had children?

Then how do you feel about appointing to the Supreme Court a man who has said your daughters may not hold a job if they have children?

The economic misery and psychological conflicts entailed for untold numbers of American women, and their children and husbands, by Judge Carswell's denial of the protection of a law that was enacted for their benefit suggest only a faint hint of the harm that would be done in appointing such a sexually backward judge to the Supreme Court.

For during the next decade I can assure you that the emerging revolution of the no-longer-quite-so-silent majority will pose many pressing new problems to our society, problems which will inevitably come before the courts and which indeed will probably preoccupy the Supreme Court of the 1970s as did questions arising from the civil rights movement in the 1960s…

Here are a few existing instances of discrimination against women, that are or will be before the courts:

1. In New York City, male, but not female, teachers are paid for their time spent on jury duty.

2. In Syracuse, New York, male, but not female, teachers are paid for athletic coaching.

3. In Syracuse, an employer wants to challenge the rule that forbids her to hire female employees at night in violation of New York State restrictive laws.

4. In Pennsylvania, a woman has requested help in obtaining a tax deduction for household help necessary for her to work.

5. In Arizona, a female law professor is fighting a rule that forbids her to be hired by the same university that employs her husband in another department.

6. In California, a wife is challenging a community property law which makes it obligatory for a husband to control their joint property.

7. And all over the country the EEOC regulation, which made it illegal to have separate want ads for males and females, has not been followed by most newspapers.

The Honourable Shirley Chisholm, a national board member of NOW, has summed it all up in her statement that she has been more discriminated against as a woman than as a black.

It would show enormous contempt for every woman of this country and contempt for every black American, as well as contempt for the Supreme Court itself, if you confirm Judge Carswell's appointment.'

Conservative senators rallied to Judge Carswell's defence, though the most memorable statement by one right-wing senator amounted to damnation with faint praise: "Even if he is mediocre, there are a lot of mediocre judges and people and lawyers. They are entitled to a little representation, aren't they, and a little chance?"

Judge Carswell did not gain appointment to the Supreme Court. Nixon had failed, and Friedan and her fellow feminists had won.

'The economic misery and psychological conflicts entailed for untold numbers of American women, and their children and husbands, by Judge Carswell's denial of the protection of a law that was enacted for their benefit suggest only a faint hint of the harm that would be done in appointing such a sexually backward judge to the Supreme Court.'

Jane Fonda

'Our Task Is To Bring Back Balance'

Speech at the 3rd Annual Women & Power Conference, New York City, 13 September 2004.

Jane Fonda meets Vice Premier Nguyen Duy Trinh in Hanoi in 1972.

Jane Fonda (1937–) found worldwide fame not only as an Oscar-winning actor, but for her feminism and social activism. She was born in New York City to screen legend Henry Fonda (1905–82) and socialite Frances Seymour Brokaw, and in her late teens joined Lee Strasberg's famed Actors Studio. She gained an Academy Award for her performance in the thriller *Klute* (1971), and a second Oscar for *Coming Home* (1978). Among the five other films for which she received Academy Award nominations were the classic *They Shoot Horses, Don't They?* (1969), and *On Golden Pond* (1981), in which she co-starred alongside her father and Katharine Hepburn (1907–2003).

Despite her success, Fonda's left-liberal political views and committed social activism often saw her having to deal with a different kind of public attention, and she became the subject of heated controversy after her 1972 visit to the North Vietnamese capital of Hanoi, then being bombed by American aircraft during the Vietnam War. In the following speech, made in 2004, she reflects upon the feminist movement and her own attitudes towards the cause, and recounts two memorable incidents from her 1972 visit to Hanoi.

'When my daughter read the brochure for this conference, she said, "Oh, mom, it's so New Age. Yoga, meditation. Inner peace. I thought it was going to be political. The elections are two months away." Well, I understand her reaction. I would have had that reaction when I was 35. Or 45. Or 55.

I realized that if I was going to become an effective agent for change, I had some healing to do. And that things that we consider New Age, like music and dance and painting and drama therapy and prayer and laughter can be part of the healing process. I know that it was while I was laughing when I first saw Eve Ensler perform *The Vagina Monologues* that my feminism slipped out of my head and took up residence in my body. Where it has lived ever since ... Embodied at last.

Up until then I had been a feminist in the sense that I supported women. I brought gender issues into my movie roles. I helped women make their bodies strong. I read all the books. I thought I had it in my heart and my body. I didn't. I didn't. I didn't. It was too scary. It was like stepping off a cliff without knowing if there was a trampoline down below to catch me. It meant re-arranging my cellular structure. It meant doing life differently. And I was too scared. Women have internalized patriarchy's tokens in various ways, but for me I silenced my true authentic voice all my life to keep a man. Because God forbid I should be without a man. Preferably an alpha male. Because without that, what would validate me?

And I needed to try to be perfect because I knew that if I wasn't perfect, I would never be loved. And as I sat on the panel yesterday, my sense of imperfection became focussed on my body. I hated my body. It started around the beginning of adolescence. Before then I had been too busy climbing trees and wrestling with boys to worry about being perfect. What was more important than perfect was strong and brave. But then suddenly the wrestling became about sex and being popular and being right and good and perfect and fitting in. And then I became an actress in an imaged-focused profession. And being competitive, I said, "Well, damn. If I'm supposed to be perfect, I'll show them." Which of course pitted me against other women and against myself. Because as Carl Jung said, perfection is for the gods. Completeness is what we mortals must strive for. Perfection is the curse of patriarchy. It makes us hate ourselves. And you can't be embodied if you hate your body. So one of the things we have to do is help our girls to get angry. Angry. Not at their own bodies, but at the paradigm that does this to us, to all of us. Let us usher perfection to the door and learn that good enough is good enough.

There's a theory of behavioural change called social inoculation. Maybe some of you have daughters. Social inoculation. It means politicizing the problem. Let me tell you a story that explains this. In one of the ghettos of Chicago, young girls weren't going to school any more. And community organizers weren't going to school any more and they found out they didn't have the right Nike Jordan shoes. So the organizers did something differently. They invited all the boys going to school into the community centre and they took a Nike Jordan shoe and they dissected it. They cut off one layer of the rubber and they said "See this? This is not a god. This was made in Korea." People were paid slave wages to make this, robbing your mothers and fathers of jobs. And he cut off another slice. And so it went. Deconstructing the Nike Jordan sneaker so the boys would understand the false god that they had been worshipping. We need to name the problem so that our girls can say, "It's not me and we're going to get mad."

'Because as Carl Jung said, perfection is for the gods. Completeness is what we mortals must strive for. Perfection is the curse of patriarchy. It makes us hate ourselves. And you can't be embodied if you hate your body. So one of the things we have to do is help our girls to get angry. Angry. Not at their own bodies, but at the paradigm that does this to us, to all of us.'

We also have to stop looking over our shoulder to see who is the expert with the plan. We're the experts if we allow ourselves to listen to what Marion Woodman calls our feminine consciousness, but this has been muted in a lot of us by the power-centred male belief centre called patriarchy. I don't like that word. The first night Eve spoke about the old and new paradigm and never said the word. I guess I'm too... it's so rhetorical. It makes people's eyes glaze over. It did for me. The first time I ever heard Gloria Steinem use it back in the 70s, I thought, "Oh, my God, what that means is men are bad and we have to replace patriarchy with matriarchy." Of course, given the way women are different than men, maybe a dose of matriarchy wouldn't be bad, maybe balancing things out. My favourite ex-husband Ted Turner—maybe some of you saw him say it on *Charlie Rose*. Men, we had our chance and we blew it. We have to turn it over to women now...

I never told these stories in a context like this, but I'm going to tell you two stories. I went to Hanoi in 1972 in July. And I was there while my government was bombing the country that had received me as a guest. And I was in a lot of air raids. And I was taken into a lot of air raid shelters. And I noticed that every time I would go into a shelter, including one which was in a hospital because I had a broken foot, so I was with patients in an air raid shelter during a bombing raid. And the Vietnamese people would look at me and ask the interpreter—probably they thought I was Russian—who was this white woman. And when the interpreter would say American, they would get all excited and they would smile at me.

And I would search their eyes for anger. I wanted to see anger. It would have made it easier if I could have seen what I know what I would have in my eyes if I were them. But I never did. Ever. And one day I had been taken several hours south of Hanoi to visit what had been the textile capital of North Vietnam that was razed to the ground and we were in the car and suddenly the driver and my interpreter said, "Quick, get out!" All along the road there are these manholes that hold one person and you jump in them and you pull kind of a straw lid over to protect you from shrapnel if there's a raid. I couldn't even hear bombs coming... I was running down the street to get into one of these holes and suddenly I was grabbed from behind by a young girl. She was clearly a schoolgirl because she had a bunch of books tied with a rubber belt hanging over her shoulder and she grabbed me by the hand and ran with me in front of this peasant hut. And she pulled the straw thatch off the top of the hole and jumped in and pulled me in afterward. These are small holes. These are meant for one small Vietnamese person. She and I got in the hole and she pulled the lid over and the bombs started dropping and causing the ground to shake and I'm thinking, this is not happening. I'm going to wake up. I'm not in a bomb hole with a Vietnamese girl whom I don't know. I could feel her breath on my cheek. I could feel her eyelash on my cheek. It was so small that we were crammed together.

'She and I got in the hole and she pulled the lid over and the bombs started dropping and causing the ground to shake and I'm thinking, this is not happening. I'm going to wake up. I'm not in a bomb hole with a Vietnamese girl whom I don't know.'

Pretty soon the bombing stopped. It turned out it was not that close. She crawled out and I got out and I started to cry and I just said to her, "I'm so sorry. I'm so sorry. I'm so sorry." And she started to talk to me in Vietnamese. And the translator came over.

She must have been 15, 14. And she looked me straight in the eye and she said, "Don't be sorry for us. We know why we're fighting. It's you who don't know."

Well, it couldn't have been staged. It was impossible for it to have been staged. And I thought this young girl who says to me it's you—you have to cry for your own people because we know why we're fighting. And I'm thinking this must be a country of saints or something. Nobody gets angry.

Several days later I'm asked to go see a production of a play—a travelling troop of Vietnamese actors is performing. It's Arthur Miller's play, *All My Sons*. They want me as an American to critique it to say if the capitalists are really the way they look. Two-toned saddle shoes and a polka dot tie and I was like, OK, that will work. It's a story about a factory owner who makes parts for bombers during the Second World War. He finds out that his factory is making faulty parts for the bombers, which could cause an airplane crash, but he doesn't say anything because he doesn't want to lose his government contract. One of his sons is a pilot and dies in an airplane crash. The other son accuses—attacks his father for putting greed and self-interest ahead of what was right.

Well, I watched the play and I kept thinking why are they… why are they… there's a war going on. Why are they performing *All My Sons*, a Vietnamese travelling troop of actors in North Vietnam. And I asked the director, "Why are you doing this?" And he said, "We are a small country. We cannot afford to hate you. We have to teach our people there are good Americans and there are bad Americans. So that they will not hate Americans because one day when this war ends, we will have to be friends."

When you come back home from a thing like that and people talk about enemy, you think, "Wait a minute. Will we ever have a government here that will go to such sophisticated lengths to help our people not hate a country that is bombing them?"… Their government taught them to love and to separate good from evil. That to me is a lesson that I will never ever forget.

So there's a dual journey to be taken. There's an inner journey and an outer journey and there's no conceptual model for the vision that we're working for. There's no road map for the politics of love. It's never happened.

Women have never yet had a chance in all of history to make a revolution. But if we're going to lead, we have to become the change that we seek. We have to incubate it in our bodies and embody it. When you think about it all the most impactful teachers, healers, activists are always people who embody their politics…

Throughout history many of the most patriarchal regimes and institutions—Hitler, Pinochet, the Vatican, Bush, have been the most opposed to women controlling their reproduction. The life of the foetus is only the most recent strategy. In other countries at other times it's been national security, upholding the national culture. There have been many strategies.

But we have to understand reproduction and sexuality are keys to women's empowerment. Child-bearing and child-rearing is a—they're complex undertakings that can't be decided by a medical doctor or by policy makers or aging bishops. Celibate on top of it. Because that makes a woman an object. It dismisses her knowledge about her own body and her own life. And instead of enhancing her dignity and self-respect it belittles and disempowers her. Robbed of her reproductive health and contraceptive decision-making, a woman loses an essential element of what it means to be human. We have to hold this reproductive choice as a basic human right.

I want to talk about men for a minute. Because it's important—one of the things as I've been through three marriages now and I'm writing my memoirs so I thought deeply about the marriages and my husbands and my father and I feel it has made me love them even more because I have come to realize that patriarchy is toxic to men as well as women. We don't see

'Throughout history many of the most patriarchal regimes and institutions—Hitler, Pinochet, the Vatican, Bush, have been the most opposed to women controlling their reproduction. The life of the foetus is only the most recent strategy. In other countries at other times it's been national security, upholding the national culture. There have been many strategies.'

it so clearly because in some ways it privileges them and it's kind of—well, men will be men. That's the way things are... But it's why men split off from their emotions. Why the empathy gene is plucked from their hearts. Why there's a bifurcation from between their head and their heart.

The system that undermines the notion of masculinity, what it means to be a real man, is a poison that runs deep and crosses generations. Fathers learn the steps to the non-relational dance of patriarchy at their father's knees and their fathers probably learned it at the grandfather's knees. So the toxins continue generation after generation until now. We have to change the steps of the dance for ourselves and for our children...

'The system that undermines the notion of masculinity, what it means to be a real man, is a poison that runs deep and crosses generations. Fathers learn the steps to the non-relational dance of patriarchy at their father's knees and their fathers probably learned it at the grandfather's knees. So the toxins continue generation after generation until now.'

So our task is to bring back the balance. In ourselves, in our families, our communities, and in the world. It's so hard because patriarchy has been around so long that we just think that's life. It's ordained. An argument can be made that there was a time in history when it was necessary to build civilizations out of societies that were hunter-gatherers. Somebody has to be in charge. But you can also make an argument that that paradigm has—it's not only outlived its usefulness. It's become—it's destroying everything. It's destroying balance. It's destroying nature. It's destroying men. It's destroying women. So our task is to bring back balance.'

Luísa Dias Diogo

'Where Women Have No Rights There Are No Human Rights'

Speech to the 'Women For A Better World' Congress, Madrid, 7 March 2007.

Mozambique Prime Minister Luísa Dias Diogo at the World Economic Forum in Davos on 30 January, 2009.

Hailed as a visionary leader, Luísa Dias Diogo (1958–) became Mozambique's prime minister in 2004. A year later she was named by Forbes among the world's 100 most powerful women.

Diogo was born in Magoe in Mozambique, and studied arts and economics, gaining a master's degree from the University of London. She married one of Mozambique's leading attorneys, and has three children. Entering politics, she served in a wide variety of roles, including as National Budget Director and Minister of Planning and Finance before becoming Prime Minister of Mozambique.

In this speech, made in Madrid, she outlines significant advances that have been made towards sexual equality in African countries.

'The meeting which begins today coincides with the celebration on 8 March of International Women's Day, a symbol of homage and of solidarity with all the world's women, through various public actions and demonstrations constituting and continuing to make history in the fight for women's human rights.

March 8 is not just a day to claim and demand, but also one to celebrate the successes we have achieved, which strengthen and inspire us to confront tomorrow's challenges. The motto of International Women's Day is "Ending impunity for violence against women and girls", confirming the efforts which have been made worldwide to eliminate any form of discrimination against women and girls.

I would like to emphasize that in Mozambique awareness is constantly increasing of the need to combat all forms of violence, specifically domestic violence and the sexual abuse of minors. We are engaged in debate on a draft bill against domestic violence, involving civil society and, in parallel, action is under way to respond to cases of such violence.

Your Majesty [Queen Sofia of Spain], Ladies and Gentlemen, where women have no rights there are no human rights. We note with satisfaction that African governments successfully adopted action plans for the application of the Beijing Platform and approved the protocol of the Charter of African Human and People's Rights on the Rights of Women in Africa and the Solemn Declaration on Gender Equality in Africa. The practical application of these instruments has led us to create legislation on gender equality so that women are represented in significant realms of government and are able to access health services, and girls are able to receive primary education.

In relation to the participation of women in political leadership, we can refer with great pride to the case of the Right Honourable Ellen Johnson-Sirleaf, President of Liberia, who is here with us. She is an illustrious woman, an outstanding daughter of mother Africa, and we would like to congratulate her very specially. At the same time, the Speaker of the Pan-African Parliament is a notable woman, the honourable Gertrude Mongella. In our region, in southern Africa, we have two Vice-Presidents, in Zimbabwe and in South Africa, my beloved sisters Joyce Mujuru and Phumzile Mlambo. In the field of activity on gender, Mozambique has been involved in a drive to enhance girls' access to education, and I wish to highlight the following results:

'In the field of women's status and their ratio in all legislative and executive bodies at the level of the public administration, great efforts have been made to ensure that gender balance. The Mozambique Parliament is one example of that, 36 per cent of its 250 members are women, making our chamber a point of reference not just in Africa but worldwide.'

a significant reduction of gender disparity in all indicators relative to access, frequency and completion of education; increased numbers of women in training and primary teacher courses (64 per cent in 2006), and the preparation of new school texts which include feminine models.

Access to healthcare is a right of women and one of the priorities of African governments. In 2005, African Union member states approved the continental sexual and reproductive health policy, designed to reduce maternal, neonatal and infant mortality. The following year, African Union Health Ministers drew up the plan for the operation of that policy. National policy on health and sexual and reproductive rights began to be implemented in Mozambique, its results reflected in cuts in maternal mortality rates, from 900 to 408 per 100,000 live births; in fact, in addition to the maternal deaths, many women are left with after-effects like fistulas, urinary incontinence or sterility. There was also a reduction in infant mortality, from 147 to 124 per thousand live births, and a significant improvement in family planning and maternal-infant health indicators.

Despite everything, these successes are threatened by the challenge of the prevalence of the AIDS virus in our country, affecting 16.2 per cent of the population.

Your Majesty, Ladies and Gentlemen, this New Economic Partnership for Africa's Development (NEPAD) assigns special importance to women's full participation in national development agendas. In this context, particular attention is given to access to information and financial resources, indispensable conditions for women's involvement in the fight against poverty and to secure their economic empowerment. We have to reach the Millennium Development Goals, which form a component of gender equality and the empowerment of women in the world in which we live.

In Mozambique, the results of empowerment are visible and yet insufficient. In the field of women's status and their ratio in all legislative and executive bodies at the level of the public administration, great efforts have been made to ensure that gender balance. The Mozambique Parliament is one example of that, 36 per cent of its 250 members are women, making our chamber a point of reference not just in Africa but worldwide. We know that Rwanda is well ahead, and I must congratulate them for that.

Apart from the prime minister, 26 per cent of our Executive comprises women ministers and deputy-ministers. We have progressed, because all these ministers and deputy-ministers hold portfolios with power, such as Justice, Foreign Affairs, Labour, etcetera. We have also made great strides forward at the provincial level, with two provincial governors and a considerable number of women in various district administrations and in the Mozambican judicial system. These apparently modest data assume great scope when it is remembered that, until quite recently, in our society women occupied a secondary position.

Considerable successes have been won in other spheres of society such as the law, the economy and social affairs, the result of uniting the forces of government, civil society and communities to promote and give more power to women. So in August 2004, our Parliament passed the Family Act, according to the Republic's Constitution, adapted to the remaining instruments of international law, of course with respect for the culture and identity of the Mozambican people, eliminating the base provisions underlying inequality in the treatment of family relations. There remains, however, a long path to the attainment of the objectives set.’

Independence and the Dream of Change

Global conflict dominated the first half of the 20th century. By the time it was over, the cities, factories and farms—the economies of most of the European powers as well as Japan—lay in ruins. Colonies in Africa and Asia sought to regain their independence from their now-weakened European masters, who in previous centuries had invaded their lands and looted their wealth and produce for the greater glory of rulers in Lisbon and Madrid, Paris and London.

Asia, Africa and Central and South America produced abundant raw materials for the developed world—oil and rubber, gold and silver, iron and copper, diamonds, rubies and sapphires, coffee, tea, spices, and of course, chocolate. Cheap and easy access to these would not be given up easily by the Western powers; and in many instances, not without a fight.

The Indian independence movement was among the first to seek to make inroads, against the resolve of imperial Britain, in a series of non-violent actions in the 1920s and 1930s under the stewardship of Mohandas ('Mahatma') Gandhi (1869-1948).

There were rumblings elsewhere in Asia too, notably in Vietnam, where the French were ousted by the Japanese, who were in turn defeated by the US and the troops of Ho Chi Minh (1890–1969), the Viet Minh.

After the defeat of the Japanese, Ho Chi Minh declared Vietnam an independent republic, only to see the French return and try to reassert their authority; and, later, his old friends the Americans, re-ordering their pieces in the global Cold War chess game, become enemies of Vietnamese independence. In Indonesia the Dutch tossed out by the Japanese similarly attempted to reassert themselves, but were met with determined opposition from the nationalists of Dr Soekarno.

In Africa, rumblings also began for independence from the European nations that had long ago spread down into West Africa, taking so many colonial bites out of the coastline of the continent, and dividing up the remainder on green baize tables in smoke-filled rooms in chilly distant capitals.

In South America, the United States sought to create a postcolonial imperium via the promotion and support of tinpot dictators, and in planning, staging, aiding and abetting actions such as the abortive Bay of Pigs 're-invasion' of Cuba in 1961, the violent overthrow of the democratically-elected government of Salvadore Allende in Chile in 1973, and the Reagan administration's clandestine efforts to undermine the left-wing government of Nicaragua during the 1980s.

Meanwhile in the Western world, a different kind of independence was increasingly in vogue: the so-called Swinging 60s brought new music and modes of hair and dress to the cities of Europe, the United States and most major cities of the world, and they brought a dream too, at the least, of a fairer and more equitable world. This was voiced in songs of protest by Bob Dylan (1941–) and Joan Baez (1941–), in poetry by Allen Ginsberg (1926–97), and in the speeches of black leaders such as Martin Luther King, Jr (1929-1968), and Malcolm X (1925–65), who all in their own manner helped spearhead the struggle for change.

The dream that Dr King declared to the heavens was one which many dared to share in the heady 1960s, and it was powerful enough to survive the harsher, meaner decades that followed, kept alive into the new millennium in the words and deeds of Corazon Aquino (1933–), Nelson Mandela (1918-), Aung San Suu Kyi (1945–) and Barack Obama (1961–).

Ho Chi Minh

'We Have Wrested Our Independence'

Declaration of the Independence of the Democratic Republic of Vietnam, Ba Dinh Square, Hanoi, 2 September 1945.

Vietnamese Communist revolutionary and statesman Ho Chi in 1964.

The revolutionary leader known to the world as Ho Chi Minh was born Nguyen Tat Thanh in 1890, but in his lifetime went by many other names. He was born in a village in central Vietnam, and worked as a teacher and merchant seaman before settling in Paris, France, soon after World War I. A founder of the French Communist Party, he spent four decades as a communist activist in France, China and Hong Kong, along with stints in the Soviet Union. He returned to Vietnam in 1941, founded the Viet Minh armed resistance to the Japanese occupation, and became President of the Democratic Republic of Vietnam at the end of World War II.

'All men are created equal. They are endowed by their Creator with certain unalienable Rights; among these are Life, Liberty, and the pursuit of Happiness.'

This immortal statement was made in the Declaration of Independence of the United States of America in 1776. In a broader sense, this means: All the peoples on the earth are equal from birth, all the peoples have a right to live, to be happy and free.

The Declaration of the French Revolution made in 1791 on the Rights of Man and the citizen also states: "All men are born free and with equal rights, and must always remain free and have equal rights."

These are undeniable truths. Nevertheless, for more than 80 years, the French imperialists, abusing the standard of Liberty, Equality, and Fraternity, have violated our fatherland and oppressed our fellow citizens. They have acted contrary to the ideals of humanity and justice.

In the field of politics, they have deprived our people of every democratic liberty. They have enforced inhuman laws; they have set up three distinct political regimes in the North, the Centre, and the South of Vietnam in order to wreck our national unity and prevent our people from being united. They have built more prisons than schools. They have mercilessly slain our patriots; they have drowned our uprisings in rivers of blood. They have fettered public opinion; they have practiced obscurantism against our people.

To weaken our race they have forced us to use opium and alcohol. In the field of economics, they have fleeced us to the backbone, impoverished our people and devastated our land. They have robbed us of our rice fields, our mines, our forests, and our raw materials. They have monopolized the issuing of bank notes and the export trade. They have invented numerous unjustifiable taxes and reduced our people, especially our peasantry, to a state of extreme poverty. They have hampered the prospering of our national bourgeoisie; they have mercilessly exploited our workers.

In the autumn of 1940, when the Japanese fascists violated Indochina's territory to establish new bases in their fight against the Allies, the French imperialists went down on their bended knees and handed over our country to them. Thus, from that date, our people were subjected to the double yoke of the French and the Japanese. Their sufferings and miseries increased. The result was that, from the end of last year to the beginning of this year, from Quang Tri Province to the North of Vietnam, more than 2 million of our fellow citizens died from starvation.

On 9 March [1945], the French troops were disarmed by the Japanese. The French colonialists either fled or surrendered, showing that not only were they incapable of "protecting" us, but that, in the span of five years, they had twice sold our country to the Japanese.

On several occasions before March 9, the Viet Minh League urged the French to ally themselves with it against the Japanese. Instead of agreeing to this proposal, the French colonialists so intensified their terrorist activities against the Viet Minh members, that before fleeing they massacred a great number of our political prisoners detained at Yen Bay and Cao Bang.

Notwithstanding all this, our fellow citizens have always manifested toward the French a tolerant and humane attitude. Even after the Japanese putsch of March, 1945, the Viet Minh League helped many Frenchmen to cross the frontier, rescued some of them from Japanese jails, and protected French lives and property.

From the autumn of 1940, our country had in fact ceased to be a French colony and had become a Japanese possession. After the Japanese had surrendered to the Allies, our whole people rose to regain our national sovereignty and to found the Democratic Republic of Vietnam.

The truth is that we have wrested our independence from the Japanese and not from the French. The French have fled, the Japanese have capitulated, Emperor Bao Dai has abdicated. Our people have broken the chains which for nearly a century have fettered them, and have won independence for the fatherland. Our people at the same time have overthrown the monarchic regime that has reigned supreme for dozens of centuries. In its place has been established the present Democratic Republic.

'The French have fled, the Japanese have capitulated, Emperor Bao Dai has abdicated. Our people have broken the chains which for nearly a century have fettered them, and have won independence for the fatherland.'

For these reasons, we, members of the Provisional Government, representing the whole Vietnamese people, declare that from now on we break off all relations of a colonial character with France; we repeal all the international obligations that France has so far subscribed to on behalf of Vietnam, and we abolish all the special rights the French have unlawfully acquired in our fatherland.

The whole Vietnamese people, animated by a common purpose, are determined to fight to the bitter end against any attempt by the French colonialists to reconquer their country.

We are convinced that the Allied nations, which at Teheran and San Francisco have acknowledged the principles of self-determination and equality of nations, will not refuse to acknowledge the independence of Vietnam.

A people who have courageously opposed French domination for more than 80 years, a people who have fought side by side with the Allies against the fascists during these last years, such a people must be free and independent.

For these reasons, we, members of the Provisional Government of the Democratic Republic of Vietnam, solemnly declare to the world that Vietnam has the right to be a free and independent country—and in fact it is so already. The entire Vietnamese people are determined to mobilize all their physical and mental strength, to sacrifice their lives and property in order to safe guard their independence and liberty.'

The French returned to their former colony and fighting broke out again. The Viet Minh fought a guerrilla campaign, culminating in French defeat in the battle of Dien Bien Phu in 1954. The United States intervened, and the country was subsequently divided into the communist North, with its capital in Hanoi, and the US-supported South, with its capital in Saigon under a Geneva agreement of 1954. This was intended to be a temporary division until elections in 1956, which, if they had been conducted fairly, there is little doubt Ho would have won. The American role in the South, however, at first as aid and military advisors, escalated into a commitment of hundreds of thousands of combatants during in the 1960s. The US presence was still massive in 1969 at the time of Ho Chi Minh's death, although the Tet Offensive of 1968 had shown their grip was weakening. Six years after Ho's death, the Americans left in defeat, and Saigon was renamed Ho Chi Minh City in his honour.

Thirty years after the Hanoi proclamation of Ho Chi Minh, Vietnam was again an independent unified republic.

Jawaharlal Nehru

'Tryst with Destiny'

The Indian leader's speech as India gained its independence from Britain, midnight 15 August 1947.

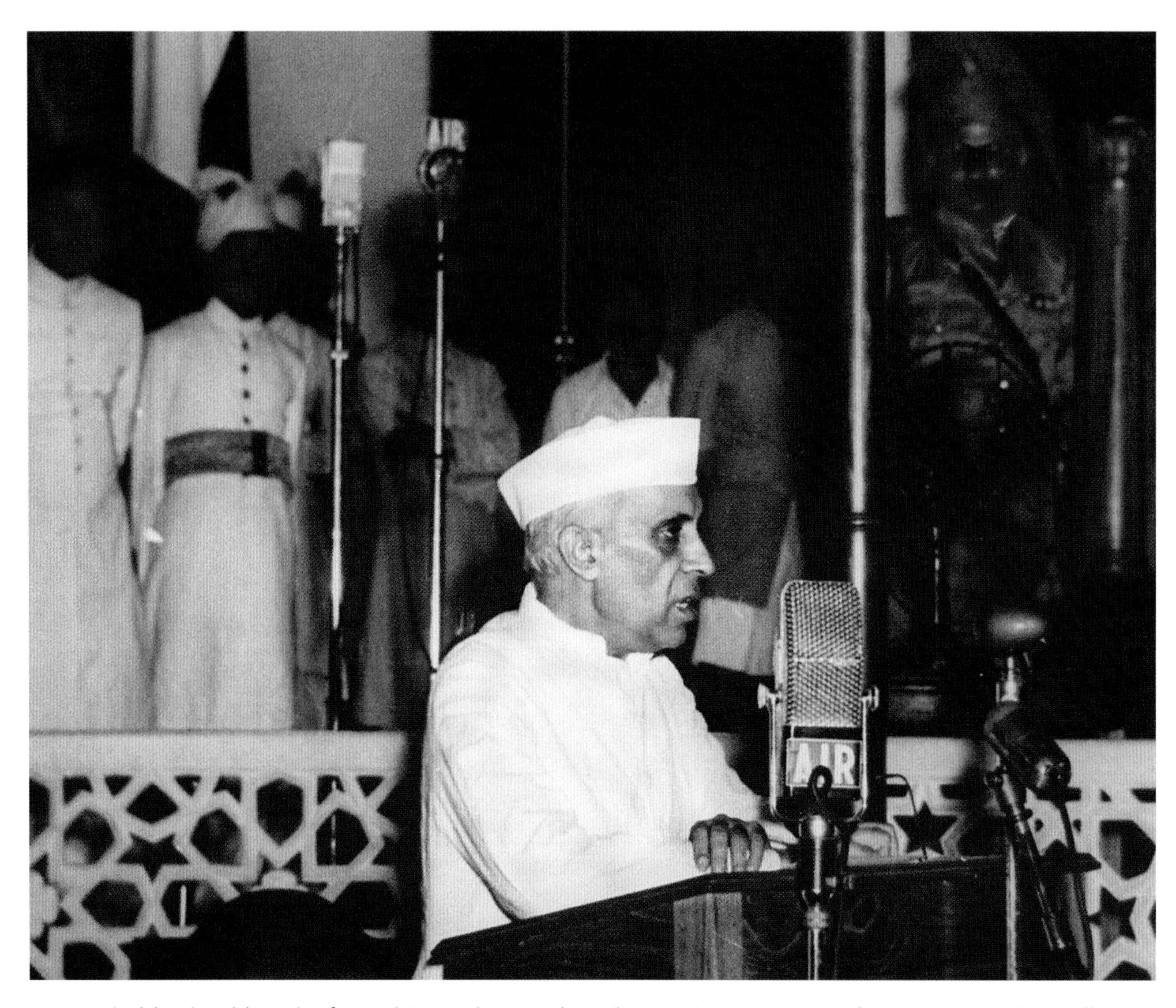

Jawaharlal Nehru delivers his famous 'Tryst with Destiny' speech on 15 August 1947 at Parliament House in New Delhi.

India's founding Prime Minister Jawaharlal Nehru (1889–1964) was one of the renowned statesmen of the 20th century. The son of a lawyer, he was educated at Harrow in England and Cambridge University. After graduating, he was admitted to the bar there before returning to India, where he met the Indian independence and civil rights leader Mohandas ('Mahatma') Gandhi soon after the end of World War I.

Perhaps the single most influential political figure of the last century, Gandhi garnered enormous popular backing for his cause, and gained global recognition through his renunciation of violence. The thinker and activist developed and implemented his own philosophy of non-violent dissent, and came to be known as the Mahatma ('Great Soul').

Born in the north-western Indian state of Gujurat, like Nehru he studied law in England. He was offered a legal position in South Africa, and during the two decades he spent there experienced first-hand virulent racist treatment at the hands of the ruling white minority towards the non-white majority. It was there that he began to campaign against discrimination and unfair treatment by the authorities.

Returning to India in 1915, Gandhi urged the native independence movement to follow his philosophy of non-violent resistance to British rule. His campaign included strikes, Indian officials resigning from colonial posts, parents withdrawing children from schools and streets being blocked by sit-ins.

When the authorities responded with violence, Gandhi instructed his followers to stand their ground and turn the other cheek. His belief was that in the end the British would realize that violence was useless and accede to Indian demands.

Although Nehru did not, at first, wholeheartedly embrace Gandhi's philosophy of non-violence, the pair worked side by side for three decades, until they achieved the British withdrawal from India. Like Gandhi, Nehru was repeatedly imprisoned, spending close to a decade behind bars during this time.

Exhausted and financially depleted after the war, Britain came to accept the inevitability of Indian independence, but at the terrible cost of the partition of India. Nehru made the following very famous speech in August 1947.

'Long years ago we made a tryst with destiny, and now the time comes when we shall redeem our pledge, not wholly or in full measure, but very substantially. At the stroke of the midnight hour, when the world sleeps, India will awake to life and freedom. A moment comes, which comes but rarely in history, when we step out from the old to the new, when an age ends, and when the soul of the nation, long suppressed, finds utterance. It is fitting that at this solemn moment we take the pledge of dedication to the service of India and her people and to the still larger cause

'The service of India means the service of the millions who suffer. It means the ending of poverty and ignorance and disease and inequality of opportunity. The ambition of the greatest man of our generation has been to wipe every tear from every eye. That may be beyond us, but as long as there are tears and suffering, so long our work will not be over.'

of humanity. At the dawn of history India started on her unending quest, and trackless centuries are filled with her striving and the grandeur of her success and her failures. Through good and ill fortune alike she has never lost sight of that quest or forgotten the ideals which gave her strength. We end today a period of ill fortune and India discovers herself again. The achievement we celebrate today is but a step, an opening of opportunity, to the greater triumphs and achievements that await us. Are we brave enough and wise enough to grasp this opportunity and accept the challenge of the future?

Freedom and power bring responsibility. The responsibility rests upon this Assembly, a sovereign body representing the sovereign people of India. Before the birth of freedom we have endured all the pains of labour and our hearts are heavy with the memory of the sorrow. Some of those pains continue even now. Nevertheless, the past is over and it is the future that beckons to us now.

That future is not one of ease or resting but of incessant striving so that we might fulfil the pledges we have so often taken and the one we shall take today. The service of India means the service of the millions who suffer. It means the ending of poverty and ignorance and disease and inequality of opportunity. The ambition of the greatest man of our generation has been to wipe every tear from every eye. That may be beyond us, but as long as there are tears and suffering, so long our work will not be over.

And so we have to labour and to work, and work hard to give reality to our dreams. Those dreams are for India, but they are also for the world, for all the nations and peoples are too closely knit together today for any one of them to imagine that it can live apart. Peace has been said to be indivisible; so is freedom, so is prosperity now, and so also a disaster in this One World that can no longer be split into isolated fragments.

To the people of India, whose representatives we are, we make an appeal to join us with faith and confidence in this great adventure. This is no time for petty and destructive criticism, no time for ill will or blaming others. We have to build the noble mansion of free India where all her children may dwell. ’

A few months after Indian independence, Gandhi was assassinated by a political extremist, Nathuram Godse, a fellow Hindu who disagreed with the partitioning of India and the creation of the state of Pakistan for India's Muslim minority.

Philosopher, revolutionary and holy man in roughly equal parts, Gandhi showed that a different way of approaching human conflict and a conviction that violence only begets violence. His abiding influence can be seen in struggles as diverse as the US civil rights movement under Martin Luther King, Jr, the massed demonstrations and sit-ins against the Vietnam War, the Filipino popular struggle against dictator Ferdinand E. Marcos (1917–89), the Burmese pro-democracy movement, and the final peaceful victory of

Nelson Mandela's African National Congress over the racially discriminatory system of apartheid.

Revered by many of his fellow Indians, Nehru held the prime ministership until his death in 1964. He became one of the world's leading statesmen, prominent in the Non-Alignment Movement, and familiar to people everywhere in his signature Nehru jacket. Two years after his death, his daughter Indira Gandhi (1917–84, who acquired that surname through her marriage to Feroze Gandhi) became prime minister. She served two terms in office.

Martin Luther King Jr

'Always Fight With Love'

Sermon on 'The Birth of a New Nation', Dexter Avenue Baptist Church Montgomery, Alabama 7 April 1957.

Dr Martin Luther King Jr preaching from the pulpit circa 1960 at the Ebenezer Baptist Church in Atlanta, Georgia.

The visionary and charismatic leader of the US black civil rights movement of the 1950s and 1960s, Martin Luther King Jr was born in 1929 in the American South, in Atlanta, Georgia. He studied theology and gained a doctorate, before becoming a Baptist minister, preaching to a congregation in Birmingham, Alabama.

At the time, America's black population were treated very much as second-class citizens, suffering prejudice and discrimination on an everyday basis. At enormous personal risk, Dr King organized a boycott of the city's segregated buses in 1955–6, and was vindicated when the US Supreme Court ruled segregation unconstitutional.

Though he was harassed by state and local authorities, imprisoned on numerous occasions and assaulted and abused by racist opponents, Dr King became the focal point of a Gandhian-style non-violent protest movement in America against racial prejudice, disadvantage and poverty.

In the following sermon at the Dexter Avenue Baptist Church in Montgomery Alabama, today a national monument, he recounts his attendance at the then recent independence celebrations in Ghana—the first black African nation to free itself from colonialism—and exhorts his congregation to themselves follow Ghana's lead and strive for change through non-violent means.

'I want to preach this morning from the subject: "The Birth of a New Nation." And I would like to use as a basis for our thinking together a story that has long since been stencilled on the mental sheets of succeeding generations. It is the story of the Exodus, the story of the flight of the Hebrew people from the bondage of Egypt, through the wilderness, and finally, to the Promised Land.

It's a beautiful story. I had the privilege the other night of seeing the story in movie terms in New York City, entitled *The Ten Commandments*, and I came to see it in all of its beauty—the struggle of Moses, the struggle of his devoted followers as they sought to get out of Egypt. And they finally moved on to the wilderness and toward the promised land. This is something of the story of every people struggling for freedom. It is the first story of man's explicit quest for freedom. And it demonstrates the stages that seem to inevitably follow the quest for freedom.

Prior to March the 6th, 1957, there existed a country known as the Gold Coast. This country was a colony of the British Empire. And this country was situated in that vast continent known as Africa. I'm sure you know a great deal about Africa, that continent with some 200 million people. And it extends and covers a great deal of territory. There are many familiar names associated with Africa that you would probably remember, and there are some countries in Africa that many people never realize. For instance, Egypt is in Africa. And there is that vast area of North Africa with Egypt and Ethiopia, with Tunisia and Algeria and Morocco and Libya. Then you might move to South Africa and you think of that extensive territory known as the Union of South Africa. There is that capital city Johannesburg that you read so much about these

'You also know that for years and for centuries, Africa has been one of the most exploited continents in the history of the world. It's been the "Dark Continent". It's been the continent that has suffered all of the pain and the affliction that could be mustered up by other nations.'

days. Then there is central Africa with places like Rhodesia and the Belgian Congo. And then there is East Africa with places like Kenya and Tanganyika, and places like Uganda and other very powerful countries right there. And then you move over to West Africa where you find the French West Africa and Nigeria, and Liberia and Sierra Leone and places like that. And it is in this spot, in this section of Africa, that we find the Gold Coast, there in West Africa.

You also know that for years and for centuries, Africa has been one of the most exploited continents in the history of the world. It's been the "Dark Continent". It's been the continent that has suffered all of the pain and the affliction that could be mustered up by other nations. And it is that continent which has experienced slavery, which has experienced all of the lowest standards that we can think about that have been brought into being by the exploitation inflicted upon it by other nations. And this country, the Gold Coast, was a part of this extensive continent known as Africa.

It's a little country there in West Africa about 91,000 miles in area, with a population of about 5 million people, a little more than four and a half million. And it stands there with its capital city Accra.

For years the Gold Coast was exploited and dominated and trampled over. The first European settlers came in there about 1444, the Portuguese, and they started legitimate trade with the people in the Gold Coast; they started dealing with them with their gold, and in turn they gave them guns and ammunition and gunpowder and that type of thing. Well, pretty soon America was discovered a few years later in the 1400s, and then the British West Indies. And all of these growing discoveries brought about the slave trade. You remember it started in America in 1619.

And there was a big scramble for power in Africa. With the growth of the slave trade there came into Africa, into the Gold Coast in particular, not only the Portuguese but also the Swedes and the Danes and the Dutch and the British. And all of these nations competed with each other to win the power of the Gold Coast so that they could exploit these people for commercial reasons and sell them into slavery.

Finally, in 1850, Britain won out and she gained possession of the total territorial expansion of the Gold Coast. From 1850 to 1957, March 6th, the Gold Coast was a colony of the British Empire. And as a colony she suffered all of the injustices, all of the exploitation, all of the humiliation that comes as a result of colonialism.

But like all slavery, like all domination, like all exploitation, it came to the point that the people got tired of it. And that seems to be the long story of history. There seems to be a throbbing desire, there seems to be an internal desire for freedom within the soul of every man. And it's there—it might not break forth in the beginning, but eventually it breaks out, for men realize that freedom is something basic.

To rob a man of his freedom is to take from him the essential basis of his manhood. To take from him his freedom is to rob him of something of God's image. To paraphrase the words of Shakespeare's *Othello*:

Who steals my purse steals trash; 't is something, nothing;
'T was mine, 't is his, has been slave to thousands;
But he that filches from me my freedom
Robs me of that which not enriches him
But makes me poor indeed.

There is something in the soul that cries out for freedom. There is something deep down within the very soul of man that reaches out for Canaan. Men cannot be satisfied with Egypt. They try to adjust to it for awhile. Many men have vested interests in Egypt, and they are slow to leave. Egypt makes it profitable to them; some people profit by Egypt. The vast majority, the masses of people, never profit by Egypt, and they are never content with it. And eventually they rise up and begin to cry out for Canaan's land.

And so these people got tired. It had a long history—as far back as 1844, the chiefs themselves of the Gold Coast rose up and came together and revolted against the British Empire and the other powers that were in existence at that time dominating the Gold Coast. They revolted, saying that they wanted to govern themselves. But these powers clamped down on them, and the British said that we will not let you go.

About 1909, a young man was born on the 12th of September. History didn't know at that time what that young man had in his mind. His mother and father, illiterate, not a part of the powerful tribal life of Africa, not chiefs at all, but humble people. And that boy grew up. He went to school at Atchimoto for a while in Africa, and then he finished there with honours and decided to work his way to America. And he landed to America one day with about 50 dollars in his pocket in terms of pounds, getting ready to get an education.

And he went down to Pennsylvania, to Lincoln University. He started studying there, and he started reading the great insights of the philosophers, he started reading the great insights of the ages. And he finished there and took his theological degree there and preached awhile around Philadelphia and other areas as he was in the country. And went over to the University of Pennsylvania and took up a masters there in philosophy and sociology. All the years that he stood in America, he was poor, he had to work hard. He says in his autobiography how he worked as a bellhop in hotels, as a dishwasher, and during the summer how he worked as a waiter trying to struggle through school.

[Then he said] "I want to go back home. I want to go back to West Africa, the land of my people, my native land, for there is some work to be done there." He got a ship and went to London and stopped for a while by London School of Economics and picked up another degree there. Then while in London, he came,

'But like all slavery, like all domination, like all exploitation, it came to the point that the people got tired of it. And that seems to be the long story of history. There seems to be a throbbing desire, there seems to be an internal desire for freedom within the soul of every man.'

he started thinking about Pan-Africanism and the problem of how to free his people from colonialism, for as he said, he always realized that colonialism was made for domination and for exploitation. It was made to keep a certain group down and exploit that group economically for the advantage of another. And he studied and thought about all of this and one day he decided to go back to Africa.

He got to Africa and he was immediately elected the executive secretary of the United Party of the Gold Coast. And he worked hard and he started getting a following. And the people in this party, the old, the people who had had their hands on the plough for a long time, thought he was pushing a little too fast and they got a little jealous of his influence. So finally he had to break from the United Party of the Gold Coast, and in 1949 he organized the Convention People's Party. It was this party that started out working for the independence of the Gold Coast. He started out in a humble way urging his people to unite for freedom and urging the officials of the British Empire to give them freedom. They were slow to respond, but the masses of people were with him, and they had united to become the most powerful and influential party that had ever been organized in that section of Africa.

'Nkrumah himself was finally placed in jail for several years because he was a seditious man, he was an agitator. He was imprisoned on the basis of sedition. And he was placed there to stay in prison for many years, but he had inspired some people outside of prison.'

He started writing, and his companions with him and many of them started writing so much that the officials got afraid and they put them in jail. And Nkrumah himself was finally placed in jail for several years because he was a seditious man, he was an agitator. He was imprisoned on the basis of sedition. And he was placed there to stay in prison for many years, but he had inspired some people outside of prison. They got together just a few months after he'd been in prison and elected him the prime minister while he was in prison.

For a while the British officials tried to keep him there, and Gbedemah says, one of his close associates, the minister of finance, Mr Gbedemah, said that that night the people were getting ready to go down to the jail and get him out.

But Gbedemah said, "This isn't the way, we can't do it like this; violence will break out and we will defeat our purpose." But the British Empire saw that they had better let him out, and in a few hours Kwame Nkrumah was out of jail, the Prime Minister of the Gold Coast. He was placed there for 15 years but he only served eight or nine months, and now he comes out the Prime Minister of the Gold Coast.

This was the struggling that had been going on for years. It was now coming to the point that this little nation was moving toward its independence. Then came the continual agitation, the continual resistance, so that the British Empire saw that it could no longer rule the Gold Coast. And they agreed that on the 6th of March, 1957, they would release this nation. This nation would no longer be a colony of the British Empire, but this nation would be a sovereign nation within the British Commonwealth. All of this was because of the persistent protest, the continual agitation, on the part of Prime Minister Kwame Nkrumah and the other leaders who worked along with him and the masses of people who were willing to follow. So that day finally came. It was a great day. The week ahead was a great week. They had been preparing for this day for many years and now it was here. People coming in from all over the world. They had started getting in by the second of March. Seventy nations represented had come to say to this new nation, "We greet you and we give you our moral support. We hope for you God's guidance as you move now into the realm of independence." From America itself more than a hundred persons. And the press, the diplomatic guests, and the prime minister's guests.

And oh, it was a beautiful experience to see some of the leading persons on the scene of civil rights in America on hand to say, "Greetings to you," as this new nation was born. Look over, to my right is Adam Powell, to my left is Charles Diggs, to my right again is Ralph Bunche. To the other side is Her Majesty's First Minister of Jamaica, Manning, Ambassador Jones of Liberia. All of these people from America, Mordecai Johnson, Horace Mann Bond, all of these people just going over to say, "We want to greet you and we want you to know that you have our moral support as you grow." Then you look out and see the vice-president of the United States; you see A. Philip Randolph; you see all of the people who have stood in the forefront of the struggle for civil rights over the years coming over to Africa to say we bid you godspeed. This was a great day not only for Nkrumah but for the whole of the Gold Coast.

Then came Tuesday... That night we walked into the closing of Parliament—the closing of the old Parliament, the old Parliament which was presided over by the British Empire, the old Parliament which designated colonialism and imperialism. Now that Parliament is closing. That was a great sight and a great picture and a great scene. We sat there that night, just about 500 able to get in there. People, thousands and thousands of people waiting outside, just about five hundred in there, and we were fortunate enough to be sitting there at that moment as guests of the Prime Minister. And at that hour we noticed Prime Minister Nkrumah walking in with all of his ministers, with his justices of the Supreme Court of the Gold Coast, and with all of the people of the Convention People's Party, the leaders of that party. Nkrumah came up to make his closing speech to the old Gold Coast. There was something old now passing away.

'The thing that impressed me more than anything else that night was the fact that when Nkrumah walked in and his other ministers who had been in prison with him, they didn't come in with the crowns and all of the garments of kings, but they walked in with prison caps and the coats that they had lived with for all of the months that they had been in prison.'

The thing that impressed me more than anything else that night was the fact that when Nkrumah walked in and his other ministers who had been in prison with him, they didn't come in with the crowns and all of the garments of kings, but they walked in with prison caps and the coats that they had lived with for all of the months that they had been in prison. Nkrumah stood up and made his closing speech to Parliament with the little cap that he wore in prison for several months and the coat that he wore in prison for several months, and all of his ministers round about him. That was a great hour. An old Parliament passing away.

'And I stood there thinking about so many things. Before I knew it I started weeping; I was crying for joy. And I knew about all of the struggles, and all of the pain, and all of the agony that these people had gone through for this moment.'

And then at twelve o'clock that night we walked out. As we walked out we noticed all over the polo grounds almost a half-a-million people. They had waited for this hour and this moment for years. As we walked out of the door and looked at that beautiful building, we looked up to the top of it and there was a little flag that had been flowing around the sky for many years. It was the Union Jack flag of the Gold Coast, the British flag, you see. But at twelve o'clock that night we saw a little flag coming down, and another flag went up. The old Union Jack flag came down, and the new flag of Ghana went up. This was a new nation now, a new nation being born.

And when Prime Minister Nkrumah stood up before his people out in the polo ground and said, "We are no longer a British colony. We are a free, sovereign people," all over that vast throng of people we could see tears. And I stood there thinking about so many things. Before I knew it I started weeping; I was crying for joy. And I knew about all of the struggles, and all of the pain, and all of the agony that these people had gone through for this moment.

And after Nkrumah had made that final speech, it was about 12.30 now and we walked away. And we could hear little children six years old and old people 80 and 90 years old walking the streets of Accra crying, "Freedom! Freedom!" They couldn't say it in the sense that we say it—many of them don't speak English too well—but they had their accents and it could ring out, "Free-doom!" They were crying it in a sense that they had never heard it before, and I could hear that old Negro spiritual once more crying out:

Free at last! Free at last!
Great God Almighty, I'm free at last!

They were experiencing that in their very souls. And everywhere we turned, we could hear it ringing out from the housetops; we could hear it from every corner, every nook and crook of the community: "Freedom! Freedom!" This was the birth of a new nation. This was the breaking aloose from Egypt.

Wednesday morning the official opening of Parliament was held. There again we were able to get on the inside. There Nkrumah made his new speech. And now the Prime Minister of the Gold Coast with no superior, with all of the power that Macmillan of England has, with all of the power that Nehru of India has—now a free nation, now the prime minister of a sovereign nation.

The Duchess of Kent walked in; the Duchess of Kent, who represented the Queen of England, no longer had authority now. She was just a passing visitor now. The night before she was the official leader and spokesman for the Queen, thereby the power behind the throne of the Gold Coast. But now it's Ghana—it's a new nation now, and she's just an official visitor like M.L. King and Ralph Bunche and Coretta King and everybody else, because this is a new nation. A new Ghana has come into being. And now Nkrumah stands the leader of that great nation. And when he drives out, the people standing around the streets of the city after Parliament is open cry out, "All hail, Nkrumah!" The name of Nkrumah crowning around the whole city, everybody crying this name, because they knew he had suffered for them, he had sacrificed for them, he'd gone to jail for them. This was the birth of a new nation.

This nation was now out of Egypt and has crossed the Red Sea. Now it will confront its wilderness. Like any breaking aloose from Egypt, there is a wilderness ahead. There is a problem of adjustment. Nkrumah realizes that. There is always this wilderness standing before you. For instance, it's a one-crop country, cocoa mainly; 60 per cent of the cocoa of the world comes from the Gold Coast, or from Ghana.

In order to make the economic system more stable it will be necessary to industrialize. Cocoa is too fluctuating to base a whole economy on that, so there is the necessity of industrializing. Nkrumah said to me that one of the first things that he will do is to work toward industrialization. And also he plans to work toward the whole problem of increasing the cultural standards of the community. Still 90 per cent of the people are illiterate, and it is necessary to lift the whole cultural standard of the community in order to make it possible to stand up in the free world.

Yes, there is a wilderness ahead, though it is my hope that even people from America will go to Africa as immigrants, right there to the Gold Coast, and lend their technical assistance, for there is great need and there are rich opportunities there. Right now is the time that American Negroes can lend their technical assistance to a growing new nation. I was very happy to see already people who have moved in and making good. The son of the late president of Bennett College, Dr Jones, is there, who started an insurance company and making good, going to the top. A doctor from Brooklyn, New York had just come in that week and his wife is also a dentist, and they are living there now, going in there and working and the people love them. There will be hundreds and thousands of people, I'm sure, going over to make for the growth of this new nation. And Nkrumah made it very clear to me that he would welcome any persons coming there as immigrants to live there.

Now don't think that because they have 5 million people the nation can't grow, that that's a small nation to be overlooked. Never forget the fact that when America was born in 1776, when it received its independence from the British Empire, there were fewer, less than 4 million people in America, and today it's more than 160 million. So never underestimate a people because it's small now. America was smaller than Ghana when it was born.

There is a great day ahead. The future is on its side. It's going now through the wilderness. But the Promised Land is ahead.

Now I want to take just a few more minutes as I close to say three or four things that this reminds us of and things that it says to us—things that we must never forget as we ourselves find ourselves breaking aloose from an evil Egypt, trying to move through the wilderness toward the Promised Land of cultural integration. Ghana has something to say to us. It says to us first

'Never forget the fact that when America was born in 1776, when it received its independence from the British Empire, there were fewer, less than 4 million people in America, and today it's more than 160 million. So never underestimate a people because it's small now. America was smaller than Ghana when it was born.'

that the oppressor never voluntarily gives freedom to the oppressed. You have to work for it. And if Nkrumah and the people of the Gold Coast had not stood up persistently, revolting against the system, it would still be a colony of the British Empire. Freedom is never given to anybody, for the oppressor has you in domination because he plans to keep you there, and he never voluntarily gives it up. And that is where the strong resistance comes—privileged classes never give up their privileges without strong resistance.

So don't go out this morning with any illusions. Don't go back into your homes and around Montgomery thinking that the Montgomery City Commission and that all of the forces in the leadership of the South will eventually work out this thing for Negroes. It's going to work out; it's going to roll in on the wheels of inevitability. If we wait for it to work itself out, it will never be worked out.

Freedom only comes through persistent revolt, through persistent agitation, through persistently rising up against the system of evil. The bus protest is just the beginning. Buses are integrated in Montgomery, but that is just the beginning. And don't sit down and do nothing now because the buses are integrated, because if you stop now we will be in the dungeons of segregation and discrimination for another hundred years, and our children and our children's children will suffer all of the bondage that we have lived under for years. It never comes voluntarily.

We've got to keep on keeping on in order to gain freedom. It never comes like that. It would be fortunate if the people in power had sense enough to go on and give up, but they don't do it like that. It is not done voluntarily, but it is done through the pressure that comes about from people who are oppressed.

If there had not been a Gandhi in India with all of his noble followers, India would have never been free. If there had not been an Nkrumah and his followers in Ghana, Ghana would still be a British colony. If there had not been abolitionists in America, both Negro and white, we might still stand today in the dungeons of slavery. And then because there have been, in every period, there are always those people in every period of human history who don't mind getting their necks cut off, who don't mind being persecuted and discriminated and kicked about, because they know that freedom is never given out, but it comes through the persistent and the continual agitation and revolt on the part of those who are caught in the system. Ghana teaches us that.

'If Nkrumah and the people of the Gold Coast had not stood up persistently, revolting against the system, it would still be a colony of the British Empire. Freedom is never given to anybody, for the oppressor has you in domination because he plans to keep you there.'

It says to us another thing. It reminds us of the fact that a nation or a people can break aloose from oppression without violence. Nkrumah says in the first two pages of his autobiography, which was published on the 6th of March—a great book which you ought to read—he said that he had studied the social systems of social philosophers and he started studying the life of Gandhi and his techniques. And he said that in the beginning he could not see how they could ever get aloose from colonialism without armed revolt, without armies and ammunition, rising up. Then he says after he continued to study Gandhi and continued to study this technique, he came to see that the only way was through non-violent positive action. And he called his program "positive action". And it's a beautiful thing, isn't it? That here is a nation that is now free and it is free without rising up with arms and with ammunition; it is free through non-violent means. Because of that the British Empire will not have the bitterness for Ghana that she has for China, so to speak. Because of that, when the British Empire leaves Ghana, she leaves with a different attitude than she would have left with if she had been driven out by armies. We've got to revolt in such a way that after revolt is over we can live with people as their brothers and their sisters. Our aim must never be to defeat them or humiliate them.

On the night of the State Ball, standing up talking with some people, Mordecai Johnson called my attention to the fact that Prime Minister Kwame Nkrumah was there dancing with the Duchess of Kent. And I said, "Isn't this something? Here it is the once-serf, the once-slave, now dancing with the lord on an equal plane." And that is done because there is no bitterness. These two nations will be able to live together and work together because the breaking aloose was through nonviolence and not through violence.

'The aftermath of nonviolence is the creation of the beloved community. The aftermath of nonviolence is redemption. The aftermath of nonviolence is reconciliation. The aftermaths of violence are emptiness and bitterness. This is the thing I'm concerned about. Let us fight passionately and unrelentingly for the goals of justice and peace.'

The aftermath of nonviolence is the creation of the beloved community. The aftermath of nonviolence is redemption. The aftermath of nonviolence is reconciliation. The aftermaths of violence are emptiness and bitterness. This is the thing I'm concerned about. Let us fight passionately and unrelentingly for the goals of justice and peace, but let's be sure that our hands are clean in this struggle. Let us never fight with falsehood and violence and hate and malice, but always fight with love, so that when the day comes that the walls of segregation have completely crumbled in Montgomery that we will be able to live with people as their brothers and sisters.'

Dubbed 'the father of African nationalism', Kwame Nkrumah (1909–1972) became one of Africa's most celebrated figures. He long cherished a desire to free and unite the entire continent, famously speaking out for a 'United States of Africa':

'This mid-20th century is Africa's. This decade is the decade of African independence. Forward then to independence—to independence now! Tomorrow—the United States of Africa.'

He ruled independent Ghana for nearly a decade until he was deposed by the military while on an overseas visit in 1966, and died in exile.

Martin Luther King Jr, was named *Time* magazine's Man of the Year in 1964, and in the same year was awarded the Nobel Peace Prize, its youngest-ever recipient at 35.

On 4 April 1968, while in Memphis, Tennessee, to speak in support of striking garbage workers, he was shot while on the balcony of his motel room. A single bullet struck him in the head, and he was pronounced dead in hospital just over an hour later. A white man named James Earl Ray (1928–98) was arrested a few weeks later, and confessed to the murder. He subsequently changed his story, saying he had been set up by a US intelligence agent, but was sentenced to life imprisonment, and died in jail. Although a murder conspiracy was widely suspected involving right-wing forces, including the FBI which had been harassing King, nothing was ever proven.

The baton for peaceful change passed to King's widow Coretta Scott King (1926–2006), who worked for black rights up to her own death, and a young clergyman who was with King in Memphis when he was murdered, the Reverend Jesse Jackson (1941–). Himself a powerful orator and at one time a US presidential contender, Jackson continued King's work campaigning, among other things, to raise the living standards of African Americans.

In November 2008 the baton was passed again to another highly articulate African American, Barack Obama, when he was elected president of the United States. His campaign slogan was 'Change we can believe in'.

Lyndon B. Johnson

'We Shall Overcome'

Speech to US Congress, Washington, DC, following lethal racial violence in Selma, Alabama, 15 March 1965.

Lyndon B. Johnson holding a White House press conference in 1966.

Lyndon B. Johnson took the presidential oath of office aboard Air Force One, as the presidential aircraft flew the body of assassinated president John F. Kennedy back to Washington, DC, on the fateful 22 November 1963. The following year the Southerner Johnson won the presidency in his own right, defeating the ultra-conservative Republican Barry Goldwater (1909–98).

Johnson was born in Texas, and as a young man worked as a schoolteacher. He was elected as a congressman for the Democratic Party in 1937 and served in the US Navy during World War II. 'LBJ', as he became known, was elected to the US Senate in 1953 before contesting the Democratic nomination in 1960, losing to Kennedy who then chose him as his running mate.

Pledging himself against poverty and intent on creating the 'Great Society', he revealed himself as perhaps more of a liberal progressive than Kennedy had been, with the Civil Rights bill passing in the year after he took over the presidency. A serious outbreak of police violence in the city of Selma in the southern state of Alabama in 1965 prompted further decisive action from Johnson.

On Sunday 7 March, around 600 people had started a 80-kilometre walk from the city of Selma to the Alabama state capital, Montgomery, demonstrating for voting rights, and against police violence.

As they crossed a bridge on the outskirts of Selma, they were set upon by state troopers and deputies armed with clubs and tear gas. Images of the brutal assault on peaceful protesters captured by press photographers on that 'Bloody Sunday' went across the United States and around the world, and helped galvanize support for the civil rights movement and bring about change.

'I speak tonight for the dignity of man and the destiny of Democracy. I urge every member of both parties, Americans of all religions and of all colours, from every section of this country, to join me in that cause.

At times, history and fate meet at a single time in a single place to shape a turning point in man's unending search for freedom. So it was at Lexington and Concord. So it was a century ago at Appomattox. So it was last week in Selma, Alabama. There, long suffering men and women peacefully protested the denial of their rights as Americans. Many of them were brutally assaulted. One good man—a man of God—was killed. There is no cause for pride in what has happened in Selma. There is no cause for self-satisfaction in the long denial of equal rights of millions of Americans.

But there is cause for hope and for faith in our Democracy in what is happening here tonight. For the cries of pain and the hymns and protests of oppressed people have summoned into convocation all the majesty of this great government—the government of the greatest nation on earth. Our mission is at once the oldest and the most basic of this country—to right wrong, to do justice, to serve man. In our time we have come to live with the moments of great crises. Our lives have been marked with debate about great issues, issues of war and peace, issues of prosperity and depression.

But rarely in any time does an issue lay bare the secret heart of America itself. Rarely are we met with a challenge, not to our growth or abundance, or our welfare or our security, but rather to the values and the purposes and the meaning of our beloved nation. The issue of equal rights for American Negroes is such an issue. And should we defeat every enemy, and should we double our wealth and conquer the stars, and still be unequal to this issue, then we will have failed as a people and as a nation. For, with a country as with a person, "what is a man profited if he shall gain the whole world, and lose his own soul?"

There is no Negro problem. There is no Southern problem. There is no Northern problem. There is only an American problem. And we are met here tonight as Americans, not as Democrats or Republicans; we're met here as Americans to solve that problem. This was the first nation in the history of the world to be founded with a purpose.

The great phrases of that purpose still sound in every American heart, North and South: "All men are created equal." "Government by consent of the governed." "Give me liberty or give me death."

And those are not just clever words, and those are not just empty theories. In their name Americans have fought and died for two centuries and tonight around the world they stand there as guardians of our liberty risking their lives. Those words are promised to every citizen that he shall share in the dignity of man. This dignity cannot be found in a man's possessions. It cannot be found in his power or in his position. It really rests on his right to be treated as a man equal in opportunity to all others. It says that he shall share in freedom. He shall choose his leaders, educate his children, provide for his family according to his ability and his merits as a human being...

'There is no Negro problem. There is no Southern problem. There is no Northern problem. There is only an American problem. And we are met here tonight as Americans, not as Democrats or Republicans; we're met here as Americans to solve that problem.'

What happened in Selma is part of a far larger movement which reaches into every section and state of America. It is the effort of American Negroes to secure for themselves the full blessings of American life. Their cause must be our cause too. Because it's not just Negroes, but really it's all of us, who must overcome the crippling legacy of bigotry and injustice. And we shall overcome.

As a man whose roots go deeply into Southern soil, I know how agonising racial feelings are. I know how difficult it is to reshape the attitudes and the structure of our society. But a century has passed—more than 100 years—since the Negro was freed. And he is not fully free tonight. It was more than 100 years ago that Abraham Lincoln—a great President of another party—signed the Emancipation Proclamation. But emancipation is a proclamation and not a fact.

A century has passed—more than 100 years—since equality was promised, and yet the Negro is not equal. A century has passed since the day of promise, and the promise is unkept. The time

'This great rich, restless country can offer opportunity and education and hope to all—all, black and white, North and South, sharecropper and city dweller. These are the enemies: poverty, ignorance, disease. They are our enemies, not our fellow man, not our neighbour. And these enemies too—poverty, disease and ignorance—we shall overcome.'

of justice has now come, and I tell you that I believe sincerely that no force can hold it back. It is right in the eyes of man and God that it should come, and when it does, I think that day will brighten the lives of every American. For Negroes are not the only victims. How many white children have gone uneducated? How many white families have lived in stark poverty? How many white lives have been scarred by fear, because we wasted energy and our substance to maintain the barriers of hatred and terror?

And so I say to all of you here and to all in the nation tonight that those who appeal to you to hold on to the past do so at the cost of denying you your future. This great rich, restless country can offer opportunity and education and hope to all—all, black and white, North and South, sharecropper and city dweller. These are the enemies: poverty, ignorance, disease. They are our enemies, not our fellow man, not our neighbour.

And these enemies too—poverty, disease and ignorance—we shall overcome.

Now let none of us in any section look with prideful righteousness on the troubles in another section or the problems of our neighbours. There is really no part of America where the promise of equality has been fully kept. In Buffalo as well as in Birmingham, in Philadelphia as well as Selma, Americans are struggling for the fruits of freedom.

This is one nation. What happens in Selma and Cincinnati is a matter of legitimate concern to every American. But let each of us look within our own hearts and our own communities and let each of us put our shoulder to the wheel to root out injustice wherever it exists. As we meet here in this peaceful historic chamber tonight, men from the South, some of whom were at Iwo Jima, men from the North who have carried Old Glory to the far corners of the world and who brought it back without a stain on it, men from the east and from the west are all fighting together without regard to religion or colour or region in Vietnam.

Men from every region fought for us across the world 20 years ago. And now in these common dangers, in these common sacrifices, the South made its contribution of honour and gallantry no less than any other region in the great republic.

And in some instances, a great many of them, more. And I have not the slightest doubt that good men from everywhere in this country, from the Great Lakes to the Gulf of Mexico, from the Golden Gate to the harbours along the Atlantic, will rally now together in this cause to vindicate the freedom of all Americans. For all of us owe this duty and I believe that all of us will respond to it.

Your president makes that request of every American.

The real hero of this struggle is the American Negro. His actions and protests, his courage to risk safety, and even to risk his life, have awakened the conscience of this nation. His demonstrations have been designed to call attention to injustice, designed to provoke change;

designed to stir reform. He has been called upon to make good the promise of America. And who among us can say that we would have made the same progress were it not for his persistent bravery and his faith in American democracy? For at the real heart of the battle for equality is a deep-seated belief in the democratic process. Equality depends, not on the force of arms or tear gas, but depends upon the force of moral right—not on recourse to violence, but on respect for law and order.

There have been many pressures upon your President and there will be others as the days come and go. But I pledge to you tonight that we intend to fight this battle where it should be fought—in the courts, and in the Congress, and the hearts of men. We must preserve the right of free speech and the right of free assembly. But the right of free speech does not carry with it—as has been said—the right to holler fire in a crowded theatre.

We must preserve the right to free assembly. But free assembly does not carry with it the right to block public thoroughfares to traffic. We do have a right to protest. And a right to march under conditions that do not infringe the Constitutional rights of our neighbours. And I intend to protect all those rights as long as I am permitted to serve in this office.

We will guard against violence, knowing it strikes from our hands the very weapons which we seek—progress, obedience to law, and belief in American values. In Selma, as elsewhere, we seek and pray for peace. We seek order, we seek unity, but we will not accept the peace of stifled rights or the order imposed by fear, or the unity that stifles protest—for peace cannot be purchased at the cost of liberty...

All Americans must have the privileges of citizenship, regardless of race, and they are going to have those privileges of citizenship regardless of race. But I would like to caution you and remind you that to exercise these privileges takes much more than just legal rights. It requires a trained mind and a healthy body. It requires a decent home and the chance to find a job and the opportunity to escape from the clutches of poverty.

Of course people cannot contribute to the nation if they are never taught to read or write; if their bodies are stunted from hunger; if their sickness goes untended; if their life is spent in hopeless poverty, just drawing a welfare check.

So we want to open the gates to opportunity. But we're also going to give all our people, black and white, the help that they need to walk through those gates. My first job after college was as a teacher in Cotulla, Texas, in a small Mexican-American school. Few of them could speak English and I couldn't speak much Spanish. My students were poor and they often came to class without breakfast and hungry. And they knew even in their youth the pain of prejudice. They never seemed to know why people disliked them, but they knew it was so because I saw it in their eyes.

I often walked home late in the afternoon after the classes were finished wishing there was more that I could do. But all I knew

'For at the real heart of the battle for equality is a deep-seated belief in the democratic process. Equality depends, not on the force of arms or tear gas, but depends upon the force of moral right—not on recourse to violence, but on respect for law and order.'

'This is the richest, most powerful country which ever occupied this globe. The might of past empires is little compared to ours. But I do not want to be the president who built empires, or sought grandeur, or extended dominion. I want to be the President who educated young children to the wonders of their world.'

was to teach them the little that I knew, hoping that I might help them against the hardships that lay ahead. And somehow you never forget what poverty and hatred can do when you see its scars on the hopeful face of a young child.

I never thought then, in 1928, that I would be standing here in 1965. It never even occurred to me in my fondest dreams that I might have the chance to help the sons and daughters of those students, and to help people like them all over this country. But now I do have that chance. And I'll let you in on a secret—I mean to use it. And I hope that you will use it with me.

This is the richest, most powerful country which ever occupied this globe. The might of past empires is little compared to ours. But I do not want to be the president who built empires, or sought grandeur, or extended dominion.

I want to be the President who educated young children to the wonders of their world. I want to be the President who helped to feed the hungry and to prepare them to be taxpayers instead of tax eaters. I want to be the President who helped the poor to find their own way and who protected the right of every citizen to vote in every election. I want to be the President who helped to end hatred among his fellow men and who promoted love among the people of all races, all regions and all parties. I want to be the President who helped to end war among the brothers of this earth.

And so, at the request of your beloved Speaker and the Senator from Montana, the Majority Leader, the Senator from Illinois, the Minority Leader, Mr McCullock and other members of both parties, I came here tonight, not as President Roosevelt came down one time in person to veto a bonus bill; not as President Truman came down one time to urge passage of a railroad bill, but I came down here to ask you to share this task with me. And to share it with the people that we both work for.

I want this to be the Congress—Republicans and Democrats alike—which did all these things for all these people. Beyond this great chamber—out yonder—in 50 states are the people that we serve. Who can tell what deep and unspoken hopes are in their hearts tonight as they sit there and listen? We all can guess, from our own lives, how difficult they often find their own pursuit of happiness, how many problems each little family has. They look most of all to themselves for their future, but I think that they also look to each of us.

Above the pyramid on the Great Seal of the United States it says in Latin, "God has favoured our undertaking." God will not favour everything that we do. It is rather our duty to divine His will. But I cannot help but believe that He truly understands and that He really favours the undertaking that we begin here tonight.'

Despite his civil rights initiatives at home, it was a struggle far from America's shores, the war in Vietnam, which dogged Johnson's presidency. The postcolonial conflict he had inherited consumed him, as it did the lives of the tens of thousands of Americans who fought there, and the Vietnamese who died in millions. Johnson escalated the war, and at one point about 500,000 American troops were committed, but the stunning Viet Cong and North Vietnamese Tet Offensive of early 1968 brought home that military force could not defeat the Vietnamese resolve for a unified, independent nation.

A beaten Johnson announced he would not seek a second term in the November 1968 presidential elections. The shootings that same year of Martin Luther King Jr and John Kennedy's younger brother and presidential contender Robert F. ('Bobby') Kennedy (1925–68) shattered the liberal dream of change in the United States for a generation.

Instead the Republican Richard Nixon entered the White House, and before being forced out of office in the wake of the Watergate Scandal of 1972, he had massively extended the bombing campaign in Indochina. He mercilessly bombarded Cambodia and Laos with bombs, and even ordered the saturation B52 bombing of civilians in Hanoi in 1972, the so-called 'Christmas Bombing' campaign, an outrage which was only brought to an end after the loss of giant B52 bombers, and the diplomatic intrigues of Nixon's Secretary of State Henry Kissinger.

By the time the smoke cleared, the United States was retreating in defeat from Vietnam, and liberal reforms were off the agenda. Cadences such as those of Lyndon Johnson in his 15 March 1965 speech to Congress would not be heard again by Americans for many decades.

Václav Havel

'People, Your Government Has Returned To You!'

New Year Address to the Nation, Prague, 1 January 1990.

Václav Havel addresses the Joint Session of US Congress in 1990.

Václav Havel (1936–) became renowned outside of his native Czechoslovakia as one of the most candid and articulate leaders of the post-Soviet era. The acclaimed poet, dramatist and political activist took over the reins of power in late 1989 in the 'Velvet Revolution'. This followed the collapse of the Soviet Union, of which Czechoslovakia had been a satellite state.

Havel was born in Prague. In his 20s, he began writing stage plays which were well received at home and abroad. They were suppressed, however, after the collapse of the 1968 'Prague Spring' liberalizations of Czechoslovakian leader Alexander Dubcek (1921–1992). Dubcek's 'socialism with a human face' included economic reforms and ending media censorship, but the Soviet leadership responded by sending in the tanks, Dubcek was forced from power, and Havel and many other intellectuals and artists were jailed.

Havel served further prison terms during the 1970s for his stand on human rights. As the Soviet Union crumbled in 1989 and the former Eastern Bloc satellite states asserted their independence, Havel became president, and among his first acts was the political rehabilitation of Dubcek.

In this frank address to the Czechoslovak nation upon taking power, Havel confronts the problems both economic and moral facing the nation.

'My dear fellow citizens, for 40 years you heard from my predecessors on this day different variations on the same theme: how our country was flourishing, how many million tons of steel we produced, how happy we all were, how we trusted our government, and what bright perspectives were unfolding in front of us.

I assume you did not propose me for this office so that I, too, would lie to you.

Our country is not flourishing. The enormous creative and spiritual potential of our nation is not being used sensibly. Entire branches of industry are producing goods that are of no interest to anyone, while we are lacking the things we need. A state which calls itself a workers' state humiliates and exploits workers. Our obsolete economy is wasting the little energy we have available. A country that once could be proud of the educational level of its citizens spends so little on education that it ranks today as seventy-second in the world. We have polluted the soil, rivers and forests bequeathed to us by our ancestors, and we have today the most contaminated environment in Europe. Adults in our country die earlier than in most other European countries.

Allow me a small personal observation. When I flew recently to Bratislava, I found some time during discussions to look out of the plane window. I saw the industrial complex of Slovnaft chem-

'I assume you did not propose me for this office so that I, too, would lie to you. Our country is not flourishing. The enormous creative and spiritual potential of our nation is not being used sensibly. Entire branches of industry are producing goods that are of no interest to anyone, while we are lacking the things we need.'

'The previous regime—armed with its arrogant and intolerant ideology—reduced man to a force of production, and nature to a tool of production. In this it attacked both their very substance and their mutual relationship.'

ical factory and the giant Petr'alka housing estate right behind it. The view was enough for me to understand that for decades our statesmen and political leaders did not look or did not want to look out of the windows of their planes. No study of statistics available to me would enable me to understand faster and better the situation in which we find ourselves.

But all this is still not the main problem. The worst thing is that we live in a contaminated moral environment. We fell morally ill because we became used to saying something different from what we thought. We learned not to believe in anything, to ignore one another, to care only about ourselves. Concepts such as love, friendship, compassion, humility or forgiveness lost their depth and dimension, and for many of us they represented only psychological peculiarities, or they resembled gone-astray greetings from ancient times, a little ridiculous in the era of computers and spaceships. Only a few of us were able to cry out loudly that the powers that be should not be all-powerful and that the special farms, which produced ecologically pure and top-quality food just for them, should send their produce to schools, children's homes and hospitals if our agriculture was unable to offer them to all.

The previous regime—armed with its arrogant and intolerant ideology—reduced man to a force of production, and nature to a tool of production. In this it attacked both their very substance and their mutual relationship. It reduced gifted and autonomous people, skilfully working in their own country, to the nuts and bolts of some monstrously huge, noisy and stinking machine, whose real meaning was not clear to anyone. It could not do more than slowly but inexorably wear out itself and all its nuts and bolts.

When I talk about the contaminated moral atmosphere, I am not talking just about the gentlemen who eat organic vegetables and do not look out of the plane windows. I am talking about all of us. We had all become used to the totalitarian system and accepted it as an unchangeable fact and thus helped to perpetuate it. In other words, we are all—though naturally to differing extents—responsible for the operation of the totalitarian machinery. None of us is just its victim. We are all also its co-creators.

Why do I say this? It would be very unreasonable to understand the sad legacy of the last 40 years as something alien, which some distant relative bequeathed to us. On the contrary, we have to accept this legacy as a sin we committed against ourselves. If we accept it as such, we will understand that it is up to us all, and up to us alone to do something about it. We cannot blame the previous rulers for everything, not only because it would be untrue, but also because it would blunt the duty that each of us faces today: namely, the obligation to act independently, freely, reasonably and quickly. Let us not be mistaken: the best government in the world, the best parliament and the best president, cannot achieve much on their own. And it would be wrong to expect a general remedy from them alone. Freedom and democracy include participation and therefore responsibility from us all.

If we realize this, then all the horrors that the new Czechoslovak democracy inherited will cease to appear so terrible. If we realize this, hope will return to our hearts. In the effort to rectify matters of common concern, we have something to lean on. The recent period—and in particular the last six weeks of our peaceful revolution—has shown the enormous human, moral and spiritual potential, and the civic culture that slumbered in our society under the enforced mask of apathy. Whenever someone categorically claimed that we were this or that, I always objected that society is a very mysterious creature and that it is unwise to trust only the face it presents to you. I am happy that I was not mistaken...

You may ask what kind of republic I dream of. Let me reply: I dream of a republic independent, free, and democratic, of a republic economically prosperous and yet socially just; in short, of a humane republic that serves the individual and that therefore holds the hope that the individual will serve it in turn. Of a republic of well-rounded people, because without such people it is impossible to solve any of our problems—human, economic, ecological, social, or political...

People, your government has returned to you! ’

In 1992 Czechoslovakia divided into two, becoming the Czech and Slovak republics, and in 1993 Václav Havel became the first president of the Czech Republic. He left office in 2003, and in 2007 premiered *Leaving*, his first new play in two decades.

Aung San Suu Kyi

'The Quest for Democracy in Burma'

Acceptance speech for winning the 1991 Nobel Peace Prize. Delivered by Aung San Suu Kyi's son, Alexander Aris, after the Burmese military junta prevented her from attending, Oslo, 10 December 1991.

Democracy leader Aung San Suu Kyi following her release from 19 months' house arrest on 6 May 2002.

Aung San Suu Kyi (1945–) is the daughter of Burmese national leader General Aung San (1915–47), who was assassinated when she was an infant. She is recognized worldwide for her selfless and unremitting struggle over more than two decades in Myanmar (Burma) for freedom from military dictatorship.

Educated at Oxford University, England, Suu Kyi worked for the UN in New York, before marrying academic Michael Aris (1946–99). She returned to Burma (now Myanmar) in 1988 to visit her mother and became involved in the struggle to rid her country of the military dictatorship. Suu Kyi became leader of the democracy movement and was put under house arrest in 1989 and was threatened with assassination before the 1990 elections, in which her National League for Democracy (NLD) party won more than 80 per cent of seats.

The military junta refused to honour the result, and she was again placed under house arrest. In the two decades since then she has gained enormous international support, and become one of the world's best-known advocates for peaceful change. Among the many honours awarded to Suu Kyi was the 1991 Nobel Peace Prize. Her son made the following speech on her behalf.

‘The Burmese people can today hold their heads a little higher in the knowledge that in this far distant land their suffering has been heard and heeded. We must also remember that the lonely struggle taking place in a heavily guarded compound in Rangoon is part of the much larger struggle, worldwide, for the emancipation of the human spirit from political tyranny and psychological subjection. The Prize, I feel sure, is also intended to honour all those engaged in this struggle wherever they may be. It is not without reason that today's events in Oslo fall on the International Human Rights Day, celebrated throughout the world.

Mr Chairman, the whole international community has applauded the choice of your committee. Just a few days ago, the United Nations passed a unanimous and historic resolution welcoming Secretary-General Javier Pérez de Cuéllar's statement on the significance of this award and endorsing his repeated appeals for my mother's early release from detention. Universal concern at the grave human rights situation in Burma was clearly expressed. Alone and isolated among the entire nations of the world a single dissenting voice was heard, from the military junta in Rangoon, too late and too weak.

This regime has through almost 30 years of misrule reduced the once prosperous "Golden Land" of Burma to one of the world's most economically destitute nations. In their heart of hearts even those in power now in Rangoon must know that their eventual fate will be that of all totalitarian regimes who seek to impose their authority through fear, repression and hatred.

When the present Burmese struggle for democracy erupted onto the streets in 1988, it was the first of what became an international tidal wave of such movements throughout Eastern Europe, Asia and Africa. Today, in 1991, Burma stands conspicuous in its continued suffering at the hands of a repressive, intransigent junta, the State Law and Order Restoration Council.

'The quest for democracy in Burma is the struggle of a people to live whole, meaningful lives as free and equal members of the world community. It is part of the unceasing human endeavour to prove that the spirit of man can transcend the flaws of his nature.'

However, the example of those nations which have successfully achieved democracy holds out an important message to the Burmese people; that, in the last resort, through the sheer economic unworkability of totalitarianism this present regime will be swept away. And today in the face of rising inflation, a mismanaged economy and near worthless Kyat, the Burmese government is undoubtedly reaping as it has sown.

However, it is my deepest hope that it will not be in the face of complete economic collapse that the regime will fall, but that the ruling junta may yet heed such appeals to basic humanity as that which the Nobel Committee has expressed in its award of this year's prize...

Although my mother is often described as a political dissident who strives by peaceful means for democratic change, we should remember that her quest is basically spiritual. As she has said, "The quintessential revolution is that of the spirit", and she has written of the "essential spiritual aims" of the struggle. The realization of this depends solely on human responsibility.

At the root of that responsibility lies, and I quote, "the concept of perfection, the urge to achieve it, the intelligence to find a path towards it, and the will to follow that path if not to the end, at least the distance needed to rise above individual limitation..." And she links this firmly to her faith when she writes, "...Buddhism, the foundation of traditional Burmese culture, places the greatest value on man, who alone of all beings can achieve the supreme state of Buddhahood. Each man has in him the potential to realize the truth through his own will and endeavour and to help others to realize it."

Finally she says, "The quest for democracy in Burma is the struggle of a people to live whole, meaningful lives as free and equal members of the world community. It is part of the unceasing human endeavour to prove that the spirit of man can transcend the flaws of his nature."'

The campaign Aung San Suu Kyi leads for democracy in Myanmar remains one of the world's ongoing struggles for freedom and democracy. The military junta's ruthless suppression of dissent led by Buddhist monks in late 2007 refocused world attention upon the terrible plight of the Burmese people under the junta.

Paul Keating

'We Brought the Disasters'

The 'Redfern Speech' on indigenous issues, Redfern Park, Sydney, 10 December 1992.

Paul Keating during his visit to Washington in September 1993.

The character 'Sir Les Patterson', one of the memorable comic creations of the great Australian satirist Barry Humphries (1934–) once declared to his audiences: 'I am not an orator—I'm an Australian politician.' Bearing the title of Minister for Inland Drainage and Rodent Control, 'Sir Les' was perhaps a lower-flying minister, until his transfer to London to spearhead Australia's 'fine arts task-force' in Europe.

Though spoken through a comic identity, the words of Humphries, like many such uttered by comedians, ring with truth. Australian politicians may be renowned for pork-barrelling, fixing their expenses and toadying up to foreign leaders—but few are known for oratory.

While former prime minister Gough Whitlam (1916–) had the bearing of an orator, and current incumbent Kevin Rudd (1957–) has made important statements to the nation—none more so than his Apology to Australia's indigenous people for the 'Stolen Generations', the speech best remembered as a landmark is the 'Redfern Speech' of Paul Keating (1944–).

Though formidable with barbs and witticisms in Parliament, Paul Keating was not widely thought of as an orator until the day he stood up in a park in inner-city Redfern, a suburb many urban indigenous people have long made their home in Sydney, to launch the 1993 International Year of the World's Indigenous People. The speech he gave was characterized by rare vision, honesty and candour.

Keating grew up in the working-class Sydney suburb of Bankstown, worked as a council clerk and tried his hand at managing a rock band before gaining Australian Labor Party preselection for Federal Parliament at the 1969 Federal election, when he was only 25.

After Bob Hawke defeated Malcolm Fraser's conservative Coalition in 1983, Keating became Federal Treasurer, and then Prime Minister in 1991.

'Redfern is a good place to contemplate these things. Just a mile or two from the place where the first European settlers landed, in too many ways it tells us that their failure to bring much more than devastation and demoralization to Aboriginal Australia continues to be our failure.'

His speech touches in part on the Royal Commission into the deaths of indigenous prisoners in prison and police holding cells, and on the Mabo Judgement of 3 June 1992, when the High Court dismissed the notion of terra nullius, that is that Australia had belonged to no-one before the arrival of Europeans. The case brought by indigenous man Eddie Mabo—who sadly did not live to see it succeed—was a watershed in Australian law, opening the way for claims for Native Title to Crown land.

'Ladies and gentlemen,

I am very pleased to be here today at the launch of Australia's celebration of the 1993 International Year of the World's Indigenous People. It will be a year of great significance for Australia. It comes at a time when we have committed ourselves to succeeding in the test which so far we have always failed.

'We simply cannot sweep injustice aside. Even if our own conscience allowed us to, I am sure, that in due course, the world and the people of our region would not. There should be no mistake about this—our success in resolving these issues will have a significant bearing on our standing in the world.'

Because, in truth, we cannot confidently say that we have succeeded as we would like to have succeeded if we have not managed to extend opportunity and care, dignity and hope to the indigenous people of Australia—the Aboriginal and Torres Strait Island people.

This is a fundamental test of our social goals and our national will: our ability to say to ourselves and the rest of the world that Australia is a first rate social democracy, that we are what we should be—truly the land of the fair go and the better chance.

There is no more basic test of how seriously we mean these things. It is a test of our self-knowledge. Of how well we know the land we live in. How well we know our history. How well we recognize the fact that, complex as our contemporary identity is, it cannot be separated from Aboriginal Australia. How well we know what Aboriginal Australians know about Australia.

Redfern is a good place to contemplate these things. Just a mile or two from the place where the first European settlers landed, in too many ways it tells us that their failure to bring much more than devastation and demoralization to Aboriginal Australia continues to be our failure.

More I think than most Australians recognize, the plight of Aboriginal Australians affects us all. In Redfern it might be tempting to think that the reality Aboriginal Australians face is somehow contained here, and that the rest of us are insulated from it. But of course, while all the dilemmas may exist here, they are far from contained. We know the same dilemmas and more are faced all over Australia.

This is perhaps the point of this Year of the World's Indigenous People: to bring the dispossessed out of the shadows, to recognize that they are part of us, and that we cannot give indigenous Australians up without giving up many of our own most deeply held values, much of our own identity—and our own humanity. Nowhere in the world, I would venture, is the message more stark than in Australia.

We simply cannot sweep injustice aside. Even if our own conscience allowed us to, I am sure, that in due course, the world and the people of our region would not. There should be no mistake about this—our success in resolving these issues will have a significant bearing on our standing in the world.

However intractable the problems may seem, we cannot resign ourselves to failure—any more than we can hide behind the contemporary version of Social Darwinism which says that to reach back for the poor and dispossessed is to risk being dragged down.

That seems to me not only morally indefensible, but bad history. We non-Aboriginal Australians should perhaps remind ourselves that Australia once reached out for us. Didn't Australia provide opportunity and care for the dispossessed Irish? The poor of Britain? The refugees from war and famine and persecution in the countries of Europe and Asia? Isn't it reasonable to say that if we can build a prosperous and remarkably harmonious multicultural society in Australia, surely we can find just solutions to the problems which beset the first Australians—the people to whom the most injustice has been done.

And, as I say, the starting point might be to recognize that the problem starts with us non-Aboriginal Australians.

It begins, I think, with the act of recognition. Recognition that it was we who did the dispossessing. We took the traditional lands and smashed the traditional way of life. We brought the disasters. The alcohol. We committed the murders. We took the children from their mothers. We practised discrimination and exclusion.

It was our ignorance and our prejudice. And our failure to imagine these things being done to us. With some noble exceptions, we failed to make the most basic human response and enter into their hearts and minds. We failed to ask—how would I feel if this were done to me?

'We took the traditional lands and smashed the traditional way of life. We brought the disasters. The alcohol. We committed the murders. We took the children from their mothers. We practised discrimination and exclusion. It was our ignorance and our prejudice. And our failure to imagine these things being done to us.'

As a consequence, we failed to see that what we were doing degraded all of us. If we needed a reminder of this, we received it this year. The Report of the Royal Commission into Aboriginal Deaths in Custody showed with devastating clarity that the past lives on in inequality, racism and injustice in the prejudice and ignorance of non-Aboriginal Australians, and in the demoralization and desperation, the fractured identity, of so many Aborigines and Torres Strait Islanders.

For all this, I do not believe that the Report should fill us with guilt. Down the years, there has been no shortage of guilt, but it has not produced the responses we need. Guilt is not a very constructive emotion.

I think what we need to do is open our hearts a bit.

All of us.

Perhaps when we recognize what we have in common we will see the things which must be done—the practical things.

There is something of this in the creation of the Council for Aboriginal Reconciliation. The council's mission is to forge a new partnership built on justice and equity and an appreciation of the heritage of Australia's indigenous people. In the abstract those terms are meaningless. We have to give meaning to "justice" and "equity"—and, as I have said several times this year, we will only give them meaning when we commit ourselves to achieving concrete results.

If we improve the living conditions in one town, they will improve in another. And another. If we raise the standard of health by 20 per cent one year, it will be raised more the next. if we open one door others will follow.

When we see improvement, when we see more dignity, more confidence, more happiness—we will know we are going to win. We need these practical building blocks of change.

The Mabo judgement should be seen as one of these. By doing away with the bizarre conceit that this continent had no owners prior to the settlement of Europeans, Mabo establishes a fundamental truth and lays the basis for justice. It will be much easier to work from that basis than has ever been the case in the past.

For this reason alone we should ignore the isolated outbreaks of hysteria and hostility of the past few months. Mabo is an historic decision—we can make it an historic turning point, the basis of a new relationship between indigenous and non-Aboriginal Australians.

The message should be that there is nothing to fear or to lose in the recognition of historical truth, or the extension of social justice, or the deepening of Australian social democracy to include indigenous Australians.

There is everything to gain.

Even the unhappy past speaks for this. Where Aboriginal Australians have been included in the life of Australia they have made remarkable contributions. Economic contributions, particularly in the pastoral and agricultural industry. They are there in the frontier and exploration history of Australia. They are there in the ways. In sport to an extraordinary degree. In literature and art and music.

In all these things they have shaped our knowledge of this continent and of ourselves. They have shaped our identity. They are there in the Australian legend. We should never forget—they helped build this nation. And if we have a sense of justice, as well as common sense, we will forge a new partnership.

As I said, it might help us if we non-Aboriginal Australians imagined ourselves dispossessed of land we have lived on for 50,000 years—and then imagined ourselves told that it had never been ours. Imagine if ours was the oldest culture in the world and we were told that it was worthless. Imagine if we had resisted this settlement, suffered and died in the defence of our land, and then were told in history books that we had given up without a fight. Imagine if non-Aboriginal Australians had served their country in peace and war and were then ignored in history books. Imagine if our feats on sporting fields had inspired admiration and patriotism and yet did nothing to diminish prejudice. Imagine if our spiritual life was denied and ridiculed.

'It might help us if we non-Aboriginal Australians imagined ourselves dispossessed of land we have lived on for 50,000 years—and then imagined ourselves told that it had never been ours. Imagine if ours was the oldest culture in the world and we were told that it was worthless.'

Imagine if we had suffered the injustice and then were blamed for it.

It seems to me that if we can imagine the injustice then we can imagine its opposite. And we can have justice.

I say that for two reasons: I say it because I believe that the great things about Australian social democracy reflect a fundamental belief in justice. And I say it because in so many other areas we have proved our capacity over the years to go on extending the realism of participating, opportunity and care. Just as Australians living in the relatively narrow and insular Australia of the 1960s imagined a culturally diverse, worldly and open Australia, and in a generation turned the idea into reality, so we can turn the goals of reconciliation into reality...

Ever so gradually we are learning how to see Australia through Aboriginal eyes, beginning to

'Ever so gradually we are learning how to see Australia through Aboriginal eyes, beginning to recognize the wisdom contained in their epic story. I think we are beginning to see how much we owe the indigenous Australians and how much we have lost by living so apart.'

recognize the wisdom contained in their epic story. I think we are beginning to see how much we owe the indigenous Australians and how much we have lost by living so apart.

I said we non-indigenous Australians should try to imagine the Aboriginal view. It can't be too hard. Someone imagined this event today, and it is now a marvellous reality and a great reason for hope.

There is one thing today we cannot imagine. We cannot imagine that the descendants of people whose genius and resilience maintained a culture here through 50,000 years or more, through cataclysmic changes to the climate and environment, and who then survived two centuries of dispossession and abuse, will be denied their place in the modern Australian nation.

We cannot imagine that.

We cannot imagine that we will fail.

And with the spirit that is here today I am confident that we won't. I am confident that we will succeed in this decade. Thank you.'

The tide turned against Keating in the mid-1990s, and he was swept from office in the 1996 election, which handed power to conservative John Howard's Coalition. Howard had consistently refused to give an Apology to the Stolen Generations, which his Labor successor Kevin Rudd ensured occurred in the first weeks of his government, on 13 February 2008 at a special sitting of Federal Parliament in Canberra. Australians indigenous and non-indigenous were moved, many to tears, as he stated to Parliament and the nation via the media:

'For the pain, suffering and hurt of these Stolen Generations, their descendants and for the families left behind, we are sorry. To the mothers and the fathers, the brothers and the sisters, for the breaking up of families and communities, we say sorry. And for the indignity and degradation thus inflicted on a proud people and a proud culture, we say sorry.'

Yitzhak Rabin

'A Chance for Peace, a Great Chance'

Speech at a peace rally Tel Aviv, 4 November 1995, just before he was assassinated.

Yitzhak Rabin, right, and Shimon Peres at the rally for peace 4 November 1995 in Tel Aviv. Rabin was shot dead after stepping off the podium.

The former Israeli warrior turned into a messenger of peace, and it brought about his murder. Yitzhak Rabin (1922–1995) was born in Jerusalem and became a career soldier, rising to become Israel's military chief of staff in 1964. He was commander of Israeli armed forces in their resounding victory over Arab forces in the Six Day War of 1967.

He served as Ambassador to the US from 1968–1973, and on his return from Washington became leader of the Labour Party. He served as Israel's Prime Minister from 1974–1977, during which he ordered the daring hostage rescue at Entebbe Airport in Uganda in July 1976.

He served a second term as premier from 1992–1995, the highlight being the historic Oslo peace agreement which he signed with Palestine Liberation Organisation (PLO) leader Yasir Arafat (1924–2004). That gave the Palestinians limited self-government. Following the landmark Israeli–Palestinian peace accord of 1993, Rabin shared the 1994 Nobel Peace Prize with Arafat and Israel's foreign minister Shimon Peres (1923–).

Rabin's policies had remained controversial with a number of Israelis and concerns increased for his safety. Nonetheless on 4 November 1995 he spoke at a peace rally attended by thousands in the Israeli capital Tel Aviv.

'Permit me to say that I am deeply moved. I wish to thank each and every one of you, who have come here today to take a stand against violence and for peace. This government, which I am privileged to head, together with my friend Shimon Peres, decided to give peace a chance—a peace that will solve most of Israel's problems.

I was a military man for 27 years. I fought so long as there was no chance for peace. I believe that there is now a chance for peace, a great chance. We must take advantage of it for the sake of those standing here, and for those who are not here—and they are many.

'I have always believed that the majority of the people want peace and are ready to take risks for peace. In coming here today, you demonstrate, together with many others who did not come, that the people truly desire peace and oppose violence. Violence erodes the basis of Israeli democracy. It must be condemned and isolated.'

I have always believed that the majority of the people want peace and are ready to take risks for peace. In coming here today, you demonstrate, together with many others who did not come, that the people truly desire peace and oppose violence. Violence erodes the basis of Israeli democracy. It must be condemned and isolated. This is not the way of the State of Israel… the Israeli people has proven that it is possible to make peace, that peace opens the door to a better economy and society; that peace is not just a prayer. Peace is first of all in our prayers, but it is also the aspiration of the Jewish people, a genuine aspiration for peace.

There are enemies of peace who are trying to hurt us, in order to torpedo the peace process. I want to say bluntly, that we have found a partner for peace among the Palestinians as well: the

PLO, which was an enemy, and has ceased to engage in terrorism. Without partners for peace, there can be no peace. We will demand that they do their part for peace, just as we will do our part for peace, in order to solve the most complicated, prolonged, and emotionally charged aspect of the Israeli–Arab conflict: the Palestinian-Israeli conflict.

This is a course which is fraught with difficulties and pain. For Israel, there is no path that is without pain. But the path of peace is preferable to the path of war. I say this to you as one who was a military man, someone who is today Minister of Defense and sees the pain of the families of the IDF [Israeli Defense Force] soldiers. For them, for our children, in my case for our grandchildren, I want this Government to exhaust every opening, every possibility, to promote and achieve a comprehensive peace. Even with Syria, it will be possible to make peace.

This rally must send a message to the Israeli people, to the Jewish people around the world, to the many people in the Arab world, and indeed to the entire world, that the Israeli people want peace, support peace. For this, I thank you.'

He was shot soon after leaving the stage. His killer was a fanatical right-wing religious settler called Yigal Amir, intent upon derailing the peace process. Rabin was mourned around the world by people who yearned for peace in the Middle East, a peace which still remains elusive.

Bob Brown

'This Finite, Fragile Living Planet'

Maiden speech by the leader of the Australian Greens to to the Australian Parliament, Canberra, 10 September 1996.

Greens Leader Senator Bob Brown.

The leader of the Australian Greens Party, Bob Brown (1944–) is Australia's best-known environmental campaigner. He was born in country New South Wales, and educated at Blacktown Boys High School, before studying medicine at the University of Sydney.

After graduating he moved to Tasmania to practise, and soon became involved in the public campaigns of the 1970s to save the rivers, lakes and forests of the island state's unique wilderness. He became director of the Tasmanian Wilderness Society, and a key figure in the successful campaign to stop the damming of the Franklin River in 1983.

He was elected to the Tasmanian Parliament in 1989 and then the Australian Senate in 1996. Whatever their position regarding his views, few Australians would doubt he speaks from belief, integrity and honesty.

'Here we are, some 6 billion people, on this finite, fragile living planet. We do not understand as a generally accepted wisdom why. We do not know where we have come from and, indeed, we cannot clearly chart the future ahead, but this much we do know: we are an amazing organism which is able to think and reflect on the universe and its awesome and infinite wonder.

We are, indeed, the universe; a means by which the universe is able to reflect upon itself and to alter itself. We do not know whether this has ever happened before or will ever happen again but, if we stand back and look objectively at what we are, it is a precious and awesome thing which deserves to be cradled very carefully.

And yet, by that experimentation and that ability to change this planet, we have moved now into an awesomely challenging time when it is in our hands either to proceed towards the millennium which our forebears have only dreamed about, or to proceed down the road of materialism which currently has this world by the throat, pressing on the accelerator as we go towards what any person who is thinking clearly can see is an inevitable unsustainability with the planet, with our fellow species and with ourselves.

Some millions of years ago Lucy, the small-brained Australopithecus, was one of about 125,000 of the congregation of what are generally accepted as our earliest humanoid ancestors on this planet. By some 2,000 years ago the population had grown to 125 million. By the 1880s that population—including Rome becoming the first city aggregate of 1 million people on this planet—had moved through to number 1 billion people. Within the space of little more than a century that number has grown to six billion and, if we take the most hopeful indications, the projections are that it will proceed to somewhere between 8 and 14 billion people crushed together on a planet which is undergoing—as far as this human community is concerned—immense and accelerating change.

'It is in our hands either to proceed towards the millennium which our forebears have only dreamed about, or to proceed down the road of materialism which currently has this world by the throat, pressing on the accelerator.'

If looked at objectively again, it is a frightening prospect because we have to agree—before we come to grips with the moves that are necessary for us to collectively rein in our excesses and get ourselves back to sustainability—that we are not in control. We only have to look at that population pressure and what it means to this planet to know that. We only have to look at the growing gap between the haves and the have-nots within the human community to recognize that we are failing to achieve the moves to sustainability which we owe the future generations.

It is a matter of concern to me that on this planet there are now some hundreds of billionaires at the same time as there are 1.3 billion people living at a level of less than $1 income per day. These people are marginalized and living in marginalized areas on the planet with increasing frustration as they recognize through modern communications that those billionaires exist and that we in the rich, wealthy and lucky northern countries of the world have, compared with them, gross consumption and profligacy in the way in which we use this planet's finite resources.

We only have to recognize that there are already on this planet some 25 million environmental refugees compared with 22 million refugees through other causes to know that it is the environment that is, if you like, in control, rather than we human beings. Anybody who reads natural history will know that, if you flout the environment's carrying capacity, you ultimately are headed yourself towards extinction as a species.

That number of 25 million environmental refugees, by the way, is predicted to double by the year 2010, and if you look at the 1.3 billion people living in marginalized circumstances on this planet, their fortunes seem very bleak indeed. If, for example, the temperature rises, as predicted, by half a degree centigrade by the year 2025 when India will have 1.3 billion people, we can expect that the wheat crop, for one, will have been reduced by 10 per cent on current levels. There is no hope of accommodating the 300 million extra marginalized people that will be on the Indian subcontinent at that time.

We have to face this reality: either we, as a nation, are going to be outgoing and giving to the rest of the planet; either we are going to find the means for sustainable relationships for people living in much harder conditions than ours, and export it; or we are going to be the recipients of at least part of the enormous mass migrations which are going to occur for many reasons, but not least the environmental catastrophes which will overtake humanity in the coming century.

One has only to look again at the reality that if we do not rein in the Greenhouse Gas phenomenon 1 billion people on this planet will be displaced if the oceans rise by a metre at the end of the next century. This for a planet on which the wealthy ones who fly between here and London put, on average per passenger, five tonnes of carbon dioxide into the atmosphere.

'Anybody who reads natural history will know that, if you flout the environment's carrying capacity, you ultimately are headed yourself towards extinction as a species.'

Only today we heard in this parliament… British thinker Doctor Norman Myers informing us that, in terms of the value of the carbon sink in this age of enormous inherent problems, if we do not bring our warming gases under control, each hectare of forest being logged on this planet is of a value between $1,000 and $4,500 for its ability to contain carbon alone—something never written into the equation, so far as I am aware, in the debate over the value of Australia's forests, one which has been raging in this country.

To summarise what I have just been saying, maybe we ought to have taken more notice, we ought to have heard more in our press about the 1992 petition to the people of this planet from some 1,575 scientists, including 100 Nobel Prize laureates. They warned that if we do not change this material charge, this consumption of the planet, within 40 years life for many species, perhaps including our own, is likely to be unsustainable, that we are on a collision course with the planetary environment itself.

Had that warning that the planet is going to collapse under the weight of human activities been a warning of a stock exchange collapse in this day and age of economic fundamentalism, it would have grabbed the front pages of the media around the planet. As it was, it missed most Australian newspapers. It made page nine of the Hobart *Mercury*, as I remember, and one of the mainland metropolitan dailies. Less space was given to that extraordinarily telling warning from a global scientific think–tank than to the *Peanuts* cartoon of the same day around this country. It is very sobering indeed to think that, after some millions of years of divergence from our feathered friends in the bird world as far as evolution is concerned, we are studying so hard to emulate the ostrich.’

‘Had that warning that the planet is going to collapse under the weight of human activities been a warning of a stock exchange collapse in this day and age of economic fundamentalism, it would have grabbed the front pages of the media around the planet. As it was, it missed most Australian newspapers.’

Corazón Aquino

'Waiting For the Dictator To Blink'

Acceptance speech for the Fulbright Prize, Washington, DC, 11 October 1996.

Corazón Aquino announcing the abolition of the Philippine constitution and parliament and institution of a revolutionary government in 1986.

During the 1980s unrest increased in the Philippines against the dictatorial rule of Ferdinand E. Marcos (1917-89). The World War II hero had gained the presidency in 1965, but moved to extend his rule indefinitely, and imposed martial law.

He had long been opposed by Benigno ('Ninoy') Aquino (1932–83), who endured imprisonment and exile. When Aquino returned from exile in the United States in 1983 he was assassinated as he stepped from his aircraft in Manila.

His widow Corazón Aquino (1933-) ran against Marcos in a national election in 1986 but there was widespread electoral fraud, and despite Mrs Aquino's victory, Marcos claimed to be the winner. During the peaceful 'people power' uprising that followed, the US withdrew its support for its former ally. The Army eventually turned against Marcos and he fled into exile.

When the people gained access to the presidential palace in Manila they were amazed at the opulence in which Marcos and his wife, former beauty queen Imelda, had lived. They discovered Mrs Marcos possessed an astounding number of shoes, and the name Imelda has become synonymous with over-indulgence in footwear.

Ferdinand Marcos died in exile in 1989, and Corazón Aquino served as president until 1992.

'I am not a hero like Mandela. The best description for me might, after all, be that of my critics who said: "She is just a plain housewife." Indeed, as a housewife, I stood by my husband and never questioned his decision to stand alone in defence of a dead democracy against an arrogant dictatorship enjoying the support of the United States.

As a housewife, I never missed a chance to be with my husband when his jailers permitted it. Nor gave up looking for him one day when he was taken away, no one could tell me where.

As a housewife, I never chided him for the troubles he brought on my family and their businesses; nor, I must add, did my family complain. For they saw that his wife loved him very much and indeed, they loved him, too.

And when he challenged Imelda Marcos from his prison cell for the same seat in parliament, I took his place in the campaign. I, who hadn't the experience on a political stage, nor entertained much hope that he would make it. Yet, how could I doubt his wisdom at the end, when, on the eve of a surely rigged election, the country's capital city exploded in a deafening noise barrage in his name.

As a housewife, I held his hand as the life drained out of him in a self-imposed fast of 40 days, to protest a fine legal point about

'I am not a hero like Mandela. The best description for me might, after all, be that of my critics who said: "She is just a plain housewife." Indeed, as a housewife, I stood by my husband and never questioned his decision to stand alone in defence of a dead democracy against an arrogant dictatorship.'

'It was the greatest funeral since Gandhi. An estimated 2 million people lined the streets of the capital from the church to the graveyard. The coffin, on a flatbed truck, was followed by thousands of the most militant self-recruited supporters of his cause.'

the civilian jurisdiction of a military court. For seven-and-a-half years, I sat outside the gate of his maximum security prison, with his food and his books—when they allowed it—and with forced smiles from our children and myself.

Thanks to the intervention of the US State Department under President [Jimmy] Carter, the death sentence passed on him by the military court was suspended and my husband went into exile in the United States. I joined him, of course. They were the three happiest years of our lives together.

But just when I was getting used to having him to myself, indeed, just when our youngest, who was a year-old when he was detained, was basking in the special affection he lavished on her to make up for the time he had lost, I lost him again. He returned to our country, against the advice of his friends and the warning of his worst enemy.

I followed a few days later, no longer as a housewife but as a widow to lay his body in the grave. A military escort had shot him in the back of the head, in the midst of more than 1,000 soldiers sent out to arrest him.

It was the greatest funeral since Gandhi. An estimated 2 million people lined the streets of the capital from the church to the graveyard. The coffin, on a flatbed truck, was followed by thousands of the most militant self-recruited supporters of his cause. All had answered his call when his mouth could no longer speak.

The government shut down public transportation to discourage people from going out, but the people came out. The government sent out buses when rain started to pour, to show its concern, but the people would not ride. Everyone wore a strip of yellow fabric, instead of the customary black. They came from the yellow ribbons tied around trees and lamp posts for his return. Ninoy Aquino had made yellow the colour of courage.

That night, the dictator lost the country's capital and never got it back again. Demonstrations would continue, and grow in size and boldness, over the next three years, coming to a head in the snap election campaign.

By then there was another description of me. Perhaps because he grew uneasy calling me the widow he had made, President Marcos turned to calling me "just a woman" instead, whose place was in the bedroom.

Fine, I said; the next time I appeared before a mammoth crowd of supporters, I would do my nails first. But he, I countered, was just a coward and a lonely one at that. A coward for threatening to take me out with a single bullet; and a loser, because I promised him no more than a single ballot in return.

On the night of a bloody election, while he prepared his victory statement, I read mine on the air.

His rubber-stamp parliament immediately convened to declare him the winner. The people staged a mammoth rally to proclaim me instead. European Community ambassadors came to me to congratulate… I mention this fact to show how crucial to the morale of a freedom movement is international support of its cause. A point we should bear in mind as the freedom struggle of Burma comes to a head.

There were other foreign friends of freedom at the rebirth of Philippine democracy. Congressman Stephen Solarz never wavered in his devotion to the democratic cause in the Philippines, even when it looked most forlorn. Senator Kerry stood guard by the women tabulators who had staged a walkout on the cheating being done at the computer centre of the Commission on Elections. Secretary of State George Shultz convinced the US President that this time a policy that was morally right coincided with the geopolitics of realism. Senator Richard Lugar convinced him that it was time to cut a dictatorship loose and take a chance with democracy in fighting communism. The support shown by others like them, too many to name here, needs to be mentioned now because of events in Burma. Such concern and concerted action by the friends of democracy do count in the final political equation.

President Reagan sent a special envoy to broker a truce and offer a compromise. I could have any position in the Marcos government or spend the rest of my days trying to topple it in vain. Basically, I wanted what I won in the presidential election or else, no matter how long it would take, I would not stop until the government fell. I called for a civil disobedience movement and the boycott of all businesses linked to the cronies of the dictator.

Within two weeks, the government fell, between a massive gathering of people power and the military mutiny it went out to protect…

My parents, especially my mother, taught me the value of hard work and to persevere in whatever it is that I set out to do. And from my father, I learned what kindness, patience and humility are all about.

When I married Ninoy, my conscious world went beyond that of the family and the family business. I married a dedicated politician in the best sense of the word, a worker in politics. He, too, taught me to persevere in a good cause. I was lucky, for although he died before his persistence paid off, I lived to see it happen.

When I look back now on all those years—waiting outside the prison to see my husband, waiting in the house in Boston for the confirmation of his death, waiting for the dictator to blink in our face-off because I certainly wouldn't, facing down the military rebels—I realize how really hard it is to come by freedom and democracy. And that it is mainly by perseverance that one is won and the other is kept.

Some leaders, like Mr Mandela, had to fight much longer for them. He had to suffer personally much more, too. Twenty-seven years as a prisoner in pitch-black confinement or in the bright blinding wastes of the South African pit mines. But the sweet taste of winning back freedom and gaining democracy for his South Africa must have been multiplied a hundred fold for every minute spent in prison. There are still a number of leaders who have not lost their will to fight, who still display the proud perseverance to win their country's freedom. We cannot

'President Reagan sent a special envoy to broker a truce and offer a compromise. I could have any position in the Marcos government or spend the rest of my days trying to topple it in vain. Basically, I wanted what I won in the presidential election.'

help but think of Burma and Aung Sang Suu Kyi. Each national experience of winning freedom is unique... The message is that the struggle never ends, the work is never finished, nor does the task devolve mainly on the great. It belongs rather to ordinary people, the improvement of whose lives is this Prize's main concern.

Today is my wedding anniversary, which brings to mind the other half who may well be here and the words of a moving poem for J. William Fulbright: "Then think that every time, alone in darkness, someone finds the courage to take a stand against the arrogance of power or lifts one hesitant hand against the tyranny of mad momentum, there is a monument. And there. And there."

Two statues stand in different squares, one in Arkansas, the other in my country; the distance and the years between them gone. One is of a man who worked to make the human spirit nobler and the other of one who showed it could be done. ’

Julius Nyerere

'Poverty Is An Enemy of Good Governance'

Speech opening 'Governance in Africa' Conference, Addis Ababa, 2 March 1998.

Tanzanian statesman Julius Nyerere in 1979.

Julius Nyerere (1921–99) gained fame as the gifted African leader who through persuasion and diplomacy convinced Britain to grant independence to his East African country of Tanganyika (now Tanzania). His intellect, integrity and power of oratory helped ensure a peaceful transition for the British colony, something which sadly did not occur in neighbouring Kenya.

The son of a tribal chief, Nyerere showed promise at school, trained as a teacher, and went on to study at Edinburgh University. He gained an interest in politics, and on his return in 1954 founded the Tanganyikan African National Union to push for independence from Britain. He became prime minister at Independence in 1961, and three years later, after union with the island of Zanzibar, the new republic took the name Tanzania.

Nyerere propounded his own African style of socialism of 'Ujamaa' ('living together'), which blended socialism with traditional communal living. He initiated advances in education and health, though widespread poverty remained a major hurdle. Nyerere retired from the presidency in 1985 and when he died in 1999, he was considered among the most respected statesmen of Africa.

In this, one of his last major speeches, Nyerere considers the pressures from the developed world ('The North'), upon the developing world ('The South') to tie the provision of aid to a developed world definition of 'good governance'. In this considered and insightful address, he candidly confronts the problems Africa has experienced in the post-colonial era and looks at the dangers of African states acceding to demands for 'smaller government', which he sees as weakening government in Africa as a whole.

'Government is an instrument of state. Today there is a call, emanating from the North, for the weakening of the state. In my view, Africa should ignore this call. Our states are so weak and anaemic already that it would almost amount to a crime to weaken them further. We have a duty to strengthen the African states almost in every respect you can think of; one of the objectives of improving the governance of our countries is to strengthen the African state and thus enable it to serve the people of Africa better.

One result of weakening the state can be observed in Somalia. There are many potential Somalias in Africa if we heed the Northern call to weaken the state. In any case dieting and other slimming exercises are appropriate for the opulent who over-eat, but very inappropriate for the emaciated and starving! Incidentally, the world has changed indeed! The withering of the State used to be the ultimate objective of good Marxists. Today the weakening of the state is the immediate objective of the Free-Marketers!

In advocating a strong state I am not advocating an overburdened state, nor a state with bloated bureaucracy. To advocate for a strong state is to advocate for a state, which, among other things has power to act on behalf of the people in accordance with their wishes. And in a market economy, with its laws of the jungle, we need a state that has the capacity to intervene on behalf of the weak. No state is really strong unless its government has the full consent of at least the majority of the people; and it is difficult to envisage how that consent of at least the majority can be obtained outside democracy. So a call for a strong state is not a call for dictatorship either. Indeed all dictatorships are basically weak, because the means they apply in governance make them inherently unstable...

All the institutions and processes of democracy and democratic administration cost a great deal of money to establish, to maintain, and to operate... Yet Africa is at present poverty-stricken. I am the first to admit that a country does not have to be rich in order to be democratic. But a minimum amount of resources is needed in order to meet some minimum requirements of good governance... Poverty is an enemy of good governance; for persistent poverty is a destabiliser, especially, if such poverty is shared in a grossly unequal manner, or is widely regarded as being unfairly distributed as the few who are relatively rich indulge in conspicuous consumption. Known or suspected corruption among the political leaders often makes the problem worse—and corruption through the society more difficult to overcome. Good wages or salaries will not stop bad people from being corrupt; but miserable wages and salaries are not conducive to rectitude. Political instability, real or imagined, can be a source, and is often used as an excuse for bad governance.

But to say this is very different from saying that because Africa is poor, Africans do not deserve good governance. This continent is not distinguished for its good governance of the peoples of Africa and their affairs. Poverty may be a problem, and I believe that it is a problem as we try to establish the conditions for good governance throughout Africa. But without good governance we cannot eradicate poverty; for no corrupt government is interested in the eradication of poverty; on the contrary, and as we have seen in many parts of Africa and elsewhere, widespread corruption in high places breeds poverty.

'Poverty is an enemy of good governance; for persistent poverty is a destabiliser, especially, if such poverty is shared in a grossly unequal manner, or is widely regarded as being unfairly distributed as the few who are relatively rich indulge in conspicuous consumption.'

Nor in saying this am I asking this conference to accept the widespread belief that Africa has more corrupt, more tyrannical and more power-hungry elites, than have other continents either now or historically.

While avoiding the living and naming only a few of the dead, it is surely easy to see that in the past 75 years alone, our Mobutus, our Idi Amins, our Bokassas and our military coup leaders, can be paralleled by the Francos, the Mussolinis, the Hitlers, and the military Juntas of Europe and elsewhere. In all European countries where the term of office is not limited by the constitution, my fellow politicians there pride themselves on how long not on how short they remain in power. The trouble is that our Amins and Bokassas and Mobutus are Africans; but the Francos, and Hitlers and Mussolinis are Spanish or German or Italians and Africa played no role in putting them in power...

'Most of our countries are now living in a state of internal peace, and a peace which is deepening; we do not hear such peace unless it is broken. Despite the artificial and often unclear national borders of Africa, our states have very largely avoided violent conflict among themselves.'

Let me mention some of the encouraging factors. Most countries of Africa are now once again 'coping' with the worst of their economic problems, and some are making well-based progress towards better living conditions for their people. We hear little about such difficult triumphs over adversity in the context of such things as international recessions and violent changes in primary commodity prices.

Most of our countries are now living in a state of internal peace, and a peace which is deepening; we do not hear such peace unless it is broken. Despite the artificial and often unclear national borders of Africa, our states have very largely avoided violent conflict among themselves. Despite the histories of other continents, that accomplishment is ignored—even within Africa. And although this important success has been achieved largely through the work of the Organisation of African Unity (which African states themselves established) the media and the international community generally refers to the OAU with derision—if at all.

Our children's expectation of life, and all that those statistics imply, has greatly improved—except where countries became the direct or indirect surrogates in Cold War conflicts, or were for other special reasons among the countries involved in prolonged civil strife.

Africa does now have a core of highly educated and internationally recognized experts in different fields. Your presence here and the quality of the papers you have produced are proof of that. Given the number of technically and professionally educated Africans in our countries at independence, and the paucity of secondary or tertiary educational institutions at that time, the number of high calibre experts in Africa is now much larger than could reasonably have been expected after this lapse of time. Perhaps we are misusing them, but they are there now. At independence some of our countries had no trained people at all.

Finally, good or bad, the first generation of our leaders is fast being replaced by the second or even the third; most of these are better educated, relatively free from the mental hangovers of colonialism, and have had the opportunity to learn from the mistakes and the successes of their predecessors.

With the help of work done at this conference, I am confident that African states, individually and in co-operation with one another, can step by step and in an ordered fashion move towards good governance.'

Desmond Tutu

'Let the Waters of Healing Flow'

Speech made as Tutu handed the report of the South African Truth and Reconciliation Commission to President Nelson Mandela, Pretoria, 29 October 1998.

Archbishop Desmond Tutu outside the Civic Centre in Cape Town on 20 May 1998, prior to receiving the Freedom of the City.

The Anglican Archbishop of Cape Town Desmond Tutu became one of the world's most recognizable faces during the long years of the anti-apartheid struggle in South Africa. All throughout it he argued for mutual understanding and an end to state-sponsored violence, with his trademark calm and intelligence, and manifest persistence.

Desmond Tutu (1931–) was born in Kierksdorp in Transvaal, and after being educated in Johannesburg trained as a teacher in Pretoria. He undertook theological studies in Britain during the 1960s, and taught theology in South Africa upon his return. In 1975, he became the first black African to hold the post of Dean at Saint Mary's Cathedral in Johannesburg, and three years later was the first black Secretary-General of the South African Council of Churches.

His commitment to a peaceful end to South Africa's apartheid policy led to his Nobel Peace Prize in 1984, and two years later he became the Archbishop of Cape Town. His outspokenness and resoluteness during the nation's wrenching decades of troubles made him an obvious choice to head the Truth and Reconciliation Commission which sat during the 1990s following the abolition of apartheid and the election of Nelson Mandela as president of the South African republic.

'Your Excellency Mr President, I ask that we stand to observe a minute's silence in honour and memory of all those who were victims of gross violations of their rights at, for instance, Sharpeville, Boipatong, Sebokeng, Soweto, Table Mountain, Pietermaritzburg, King William's Town Golf Course, Church Street and St James Church, Bisho, Heidelberg Tavern, who were tortured or executed in prisons and camps inside and outside South Africa and those who died on the border needlessly in unnecessary wars...

The world has looked in amazement and indeed awe at the remarkable example that you have set of magnanimity and generosity in your willingness to forgive and to work for reconciliation. They have thrilled as they heard the stories of Mrs Savage, of Mr Smit, of the mothers of the Gugulethu Seven, of Mrs Roux, the Biehl family, of Neville Clarence and many, many others. They have seen the miracle of April 1994 continuing in people who suffered grievously, ready to forgive.

'The world has looked in amazement and indeed awe at the remarkable example that you have set of magnanimity and generosity in your willingness to forgive and to work for reconciliation.'

And the world sees South Africa as a beacon of hope for those places like Northern Ireland, Bosnia, Rwanda—so different from Sierra Leone where just last week they executed 24 people by firing squad. They see a new way, a better way to deal with a post-conflict, a post-repression period. This report speaks about that. It contains more than just accounts of findings against perpetrators. It seeks to give as complete a picture as possible of the gross human rights violations that occurred as a result of the conflict of the past. It provides a setting against which to understand our past; it gives insight into the perspectives of those who supported apartheid and those who opposed it.

It makes comprehensive recommendations about rehabilitation and reparation proposals. It makes specific proposals about how we can cultivate a culture of human rights and of structures to ensure that the atrocities of the past do not recur and strong suggestions about how to advance the process of hearing and reconciliation of our traumatized and wounded nation.

The Commission can make but a contribution to this, perhaps a significant one but only a contribution. It is up to all of us South Africans to say "this is our land"; we are committed to it. We are concerned about the welfare of all South Africans, not just of my particular section or group.

'We will have looked the beast in the eye. We will have come to terms with our horrendous past and it will no longer keep us hostage. We will cast off its shackles and, holding hands together, black and white will stride into the future.'

We have not been facile or superficial, heeding the cry of the prophet against those who healed the sickness of their people, superficially crying "peace, peace" where there was no peace. We care about our land, about her people, black, white, coloured, Indian, young and old.

Many will be upset by this report. Some have sought to discredit it pre-emptively. Even if they were to succeed, what is that to the point? It won't change the fact that they killed Stanza Bopape, that they bombed Khotso House, that they tortured their own people in their camps in Tanzania, in Angola, that they necklaced people. That is what the perpetrators told us—not an invention by the Commission.

No, dear fellow South Africans, accept this report as a way, an indispensable way to healing. Let the waters of healing flow from Pretoria today as they flowed from the altar in Ezekiel's vision to cleanse our land, its people, and to bring unity and reconciliation.

We will have looked the beast in the eye. We will have come to terms with our horrendous past and it will no longer keep us hostage. We will cast off its shackles and, holding hands together, black and white will stride into the future, the glorious future God holds out before us—we who are the Rainbow people of God—and looking at our past we will commit ourselves: Never again! ’

Michelle Bachelet

'I Personify a Whole History'

Inaugural address, Santiago, Chile, 11 March 2006.

Michelle Bachelet waves to people from the balcony of La Moneda palace in Santiago, 11 March 2006, after being sworn in as Chile's first female president.

Michelle Bachelet (1951–) is Chile's first female president. Her father, Alberto Bachelet, was a general in the Chilean Air Force and a key figure in President Salvadore Allende's government. He was imprisoned and tortured following the September 1973 military coup of Augusto Pinochet (1915–2006) and died of a heart attack shortly after his release.

A medical student in the capital Santiago, Michelle Bachelet witnessed the bombing of the presidential palace from the rooftop of a university building. The death of her father was not to be the only trauma she would suffer, however.

In January 1975 Bachelet and her mother were taken from their home by Pinochet's secret police agents and subjected to torture for several weeks. After their release they went into exile, firstly in Australia, and then in East Germany, where she continued her studies. She married a fellow Chilean in exile and in 1979 returned to Chile.

In 1982 Bachelet graduated as a surgeon from the national university. Following the restoration of democracy in 1990, she entered politics in 1996. In 2000, when economist Richard Lagos (1938–) was elected prime minister, Bachelet became health minister. She was elected president on 15 January 2006. The following is Bachelet's inaugural address.

'There have been times in our history when we were divided amongst ourselves. We looked at each other with distrust, suspicion and disdain. Over the past 16 years of democracy, we have worked hard together to smoothe over the sharp edges of a divided society, a society that separated "us" from "them". Now is the time that we all feel part of a larger "us".

Today, there is something different in the air. We have been able to build a new society, where the noble desire for a better future for all Chileans unites us. Everyone has a place in that future, with an inclusive homeland, where no diversity is left out and no one feels like their destiny is left dangling in the breeze.

We have prepared ourselves for this great challenge. The 21st century will bring new tasks for us, some of which are unknown to us at this moment. Aside from the technological revolution unfolding before our eyes, I think that there is another revolution afoot in the way we relate to each other, the way we interact within our communities, and our manner of combating individualism, indifference and hopelessness. The time has come for us to look one another in the eye, without resentments or suspicion.

The past is what it is: the past. We will never forget it. As [former president] President Lagos said, "there is no tomorrow without yesterday", and we do not want to repeat the errors of the past. We want a more prosperous, just, egalitarian and participative future.

We know that we are not going to solve all our problems in four years—that was never part of the discourse of my campaign. But we are going to take a great step forward.

This will be a government of citizens, from the most neglected to the most entrepreneurial,

'Difficulties will arise, without a doubt; every government experiences them. "Campaigns," a great thinker once said, "happen in poetry, but governments happen in prose".'

an infinite range of colours, perceptions and faces that imbue our society with so much richness. These citizens, you, have in me a President that will also speak the language of the truth.

Difficulties will arise, without a doubt; every government experiences them. "Campaigns," a great thinker once said, "happen in poetry, but governments happen in prose." However, the relationship between you and us, and I, will not be affected by any such difficulties, because I want to establish a dialogue based on frankness and participation. It will be a great pact between the citizens and those who govern.

You know that I follow through with my commitments. I will say what I think, and I will do what I say. I give you my word! In our quest to move towards a Chile that is better every day for every one of our citizens, I want to gather the efforts of citizens and the Congress, which is the expression of the legitimacy of our laws. With all of them, we will work towards a shared ideal: the good of Chileans, and justice throughout our country. And to do this, I am asking for the support of all women and men in Congress...

My friends: this is a very solemn moment for the country. I ask you to turn your heads and look at the statues of the illustrious citizens adorning this plaza. This is the Republic, my friends. There in the front is Diego Portales, the symbol of a small, growing Republic, modest at the time, but thriving, orderly and able to resolve disputes with the law rather than by taking up arms. Jorge Alessandri, Salvador Allende and Eduardo Frei Montalva also stand in this plaza. I pay tribute to them, as they symbolize our modern homeland, the country of the 20th century, vocations for democracy and eras of development and social progress.

I personify a whole history, which had dark and bitter moments, but I knew how to recover. Today, we Chileans live better and more free than before. We have had three successful administrations. I feel proud to continue along a path that has borne so many fruits...

My friends: We will continue working to make our country more developed, with more justice and better opportunities.

The world is watching us. The world is closely observing what is happening in this small country in the south of the world that was able to restore freedom and rights—with effort and pain, yes—but it built a solid democracy. It brought about reconciliation and it is progressing. It has been able to pull millions out of poverty, in the name of freedom and dignity. '

Barack Obama

'A More Perfect Union'

Speech during the 2008 presidential election campaign, Philadelphia, 18 March 2008.

Barack Obama, as a presidential candidate, gives a speech at the National Constitution Center in Philadelphia, Pennsylvania, in March 2008.

Barack Obama made history when he was elected as the first African American president of the United States on 4 November 2008.

Obama was born in Hawaii in 1961, the son of the interracial union between Kenyan-born Barack Obama Sr and Ann Dunham. The couple had met as students at the University of Hawaii but separated when the young Barack was two. His father returned to Kenya, while his mother, an anthropologist, remarried, taking him to live for several years in his new stepfather's native land, Indonesia. When Barack was 10, he returned with his mother and half-sister, Maya, to Hawaii. They lived in Honolulu, although Ann Dunham later returned to Indonesia to further her academic research. Barack and his sister lived with his maternal grandparents during that time.

As a young man Obama went to college in Los Angeles, before transferring to Columbia University in New York, where he graduated with a political science degree. He moved to Chicago, where he worked in community activism in the city's poorer districts. He later studied law at Harvard University, meeting his future wife Michelle (née Robinson, 1964–) while interning at a Chicago law firm. He graduated from Harvard in 1991. While working as a civil rights advocate in Chicago, he became involved in the Democratic Party. He later served in the Illinois legislature before his election to the US Senate in 2004.

His meteoric political rise did not stop at the Senate. In 2007 he joined the field of contenders to become the Democratic Party's candidate in the 2008 US presidential election, and by June of 2008 had secured the delegates required.

Obama faced and defeated Republican John McCain (1936–) in November 2008, and was inaugurated as president in Washington, DC, on 20 January 2009.

Already a renowned orator, Obama's speech 'a more perfect Union' is considered to be perhaps his finest of the campaign, and is said to have swung to his side many of the Democrats who supported his rival for the nomination, Hillary Rodham Clinton (1947–), who became secretary of state under his administration. In the following speech, Obama directly confronts his connection with a controversially outspoken black pastor—and the race issue itself in the campaign.

❛ 'We the people, in order to form a more perfect union.'

Two hundred and twenty-one years ago, in a hall that still stands across the street, a group of men gathered and, with these simple words, launched America's improbable experiment in democracy. Farmers and scholars, statesmen and patriots who had travelled across an ocean to escape tyranny and persecution finally made real their declaration of independence at a Philadelphia convention that lasted through the spring of 1787.

The document they produced was eventually signed but ultimately unfinished. It was stained by this nation's original sin of slavery, a question that divided the colonies and brought the convention to a stalemate until the founders chose to allow the slave trade to continue for at least 20 more years, and to leave any final resolution to future generations.

Of course, the answer to the slavery question was already embedded within our Constitution—a Constitution that had at its very core the ideal of equal citizenship under the law; a Constitution that promised its people liberty, and justice, and a union that could be and should be perfected over time.

And yet words on a parchment would not be enough to deliver slaves from bondage, or provide men and women of every colour and creed their full rights and obligations as citizens of the United States. What would be needed were Americans in successive generations who were willing to do their part—through protests and struggle, on the streets and in the courts, through a civil war and civil disobedience and always at great risk—to narrow that gap between the promise of our ideals and the reality of their time.

This was one of the tasks we set forth at the beginning of this campaign—to continue the long march of those who came before us, a march for a more just, more equal, more free, more caring and more prosperous America.

I chose to run for the presidency at this moment in history because I believe deeply that we cannot solve the challenges of our time unless we solve them together—unless we perfect our union by understanding that we may have different stories, but we hold common hopes; that we may not look the same and we may not have come from the same place, but we all want to move in the same direction—towards a better future for our children and our grandchildren.

'I have brothers, sisters, nieces, nephews, uncles and cousins, of every race and every hue, scattered across three continents, and for as long as I live, I will never forget that in no other country on earth is my story even possible.'

This belief comes from my unyielding faith in the decency and generosity of the American people. But it also comes from my own American story.

I am the son of a black man from Kenya and a white woman from Kansas. I was raised with the help of a white grandfather who survived a Depression to serve in Patton's Army during World War II and a white grandmother who worked on a bomber assembly line at Fort Leavenworth while he was overseas. I've gone to some of the best schools in America and lived in one of the world's poorest nations. I am married to a black American who carries within her the blood of slaves and slave owners—an inheritance we pass on to our two precious daughters. I have brothers, sisters, nieces, nephews, uncles and cousins, of every race and every hue, scattered across three continents, and for as long as I live, I will never forget that in no other country on earth is my story even possible.

It's a story that hasn't made me the most conventional candidate. But it is a story that has seared into my genetic make-up the idea that this nation is more than the sum of its parts—that out of many, we are truly one.

Throughout the first year of this campaign, against all predictions to the contrary, we saw

'This is not to say that race has not been an issue in the campaign. At various stages in the campaign, some commentators have deemed me either "too black", or "not black enough". We saw racial tensions bubble to the surface during the week before the South Carolina primary.'

how hungry the American people were for this message of unity. Despite the temptation to view my candidacy through a purely racial lens, we won commanding victories in states with some of the whitest populations in the country. In South Carolina, where the Confederate Flag still flies, we built a powerful coalition of African Americans and white Americans.

This is not to say that race has not been an issue in the campaign. At various stages in the campaign, some commentators have deemed me either "too black", or "not black enough". We saw racial tensions bubble to the surface during the week before the South Carolina primary. The press has scoured every exit poll for the latest evidence of racial polarization, not just in terms of white and black, but black and brown as well. And yet, it has only been in the last couple of weeks that the discussion of race in this campaign has taken a particularly divisive turn.

On one end of the spectrum, we've heard the implication that my candidacy is somehow an exercise in affirmative action; that it's based solely on the desire of wide-eyed liberals to purchase racial reconciliation on the cheap. On the other end, we've heard my former pastor, Reverend Jeremiah Wright, use incendiary language to express views that have the potential not only to widen the racial divide, but views that denigrate both the greatness and the goodness of our nation; that rightly offend white and black alike.

I have already condemned, in unequivocal terms, the statements of Reverend Wright that have caused such controversy. For some, nagging questions remain. Did I know him to be an occasionally fierce critic of American domestic and foreign policy? Of course. Did I ever hear him make remarks that could be considered controversial while I sat in church? Yes. Did I strongly disagree with many of his political views? Absolutely—just as I'm sure many of you have heard remarks from your pastors, priests, or rabbis with which you strongly disagreed.

But the remarks that have caused this recent firestorm weren't simply controversial. They weren't simply a religious leader's effort to speak out against perceived injustice. Instead, they expressed a profoundly distorted view of this country—a view that sees white racism as endemic, and that elevates what is wrong with America above all that we know is right with America; a view that sees the conflicts in the Middle East as rooted primarily in the actions of stalwart allies like Israel, instead of emanating from the perverse and hateful ideologies of radical Islam.

As such, Reverend Wright's comments were not only wrong but divisive, divisive at a time when we need unity; racially charged at a time when we need to come together to solve a set of monumental problems—two wars, a terrorist threat, a falling economy, a chronic health care crisis and potentially devastating climate change; problems that are neither black or white or Latino or Asian, but rather problems that confront us all.

Given my background, my politics, and my professed values and ideals, there will no doubt be those for whom my statements of condemnation are not enough. Why associate myself with

Reverend Wright in the first place, they may ask? Why not join another church? And I confess that if all that I knew of Reverend Wright were the snippets of those sermons that have run in an endless loop on the television and YouTube, or if Trinity United Church of Christ conformed to the caricatures being peddled by some commentators, there is no doubt that I would react in much the same way.

But the truth is, that isn't all that I know of the man. The man I met more than 20 years ago is a man who helped introduce me to my Christian faith, a man who spoke to me about our obligations to love one another; to care for the sick and lift up the poor. He is a man who served his country as a US Marine, who has studied and lectured at some of the finest universities and seminaries in the country, and who for over 30 years led a church that serves the community by doing God's work here on Earth—by housing the homeless, ministering to the needy, providing day care services and scholarships and prison ministries, and reaching out to those suffering from HIV/AIDS.

In my first book, *Dreams From My Father*, I described the experience of my first service at Trinity: "People began to shout, to rise from their seats and clap and cry out, a forceful wind carrying the reverend's voice up into the rafters... And in that single note—hope!—I heard something else; at the foot of that cross, inside the thousands of churches across the city, I imagined the stories of ordinary black people merging with the stories of David and Goliath, Moses and Pharaoh, the Christians in the lion's den, Ezekiel's field of dry bones. Those stories—of survival, and freedom, and hope—became our story, my story; the blood that had spilled was our blood, the tears our tears; until this black church, on this bright day, seemed once more a vessel carrying the story of a people into future generations and into a larger world. Our trials and triumphs became at once unique and universal, black and more than black; in chronicling our journey, the stories and songs gave us a means to reclaim memories that we didn't need to feel shame about... memories that all people might study and cherish—and with which we could start to rebuild."

That has been my experience at Trinity. Like other predominantly black churches across the country, Trinity embodies the black community in its entirety—the doctor and the welfare mom, the model student and the former gang-banger. Like other black churches, Trinity's services are full of raucous laughter and sometimes bawdy humour. They are full of dancing, clapping, screaming and shouting that may seem jarring to the untrained ear. The church contains in full the kindness and cruelty, the fierce intelligence and the shocking ignorance, the struggles and successes, the love and yes, the bitterness and bias that make up the black experience in America.

'Like other predominantly black churches across the country, Trinity embodies the black community in its entirety—the doctor and the welfare mom, the model student and the former gang-banger. Like other black churches, Trinity's services are full of raucous laughter and sometimes bawdy humour.'

And this helps explain, perhaps, my relationship with Reverend Wright. As imperfect as he may be, he has been like family to me. He strengthened my faith, officiated my wedding, and baptised my children. Not once in my conversations with him have I heard him talk about any ethnic group in derogatory terms, or treat whites with whom he interacted with anything but courtesy and respect. He contains within him the contradictions—the good and the bad—of the community that he has served diligently for so many years.

I can no more disown him than I can disown the black community. I can no more disown him than I can my white grandmother—a woman who helped raise me, a woman who sacrificed again and again for me, a woman who loves me as much as she loves anything in this world, but a woman who once confessed her fear of black men who passed by her on the street, and who on more than one occasion has uttered racial or ethnic stereotypes that made me cringe.

These people are a part of me. And they are a part of America, this country that I love.

Some will see this as an attempt to justify or excuse comments that are simply inexcusable. I can assure you it is not. I suppose the politically safe thing would be to move on from this episode and just hope that it fades into the woodwork. We can dismiss Reverend Wright as a crank or a demagogue, just as some have dismissed Geraldine Ferraro, in the aftermath of her recent statements, as harbouring some deep-seated racial bias. But race is an issue that I believe this nation cannot afford to ignore right now. We would be making the same mistake that Reverend Wright made in his offending sermons about America—to simplify and stereotype and amplify the negative to the point that it distorts reality.

'The fact is that the comments that have been made and the issues that have surfaced over the last few weeks reflect the complexities of race in this country that we've never really worked through—a part of our union that we have yet to perfect.'

The fact is that the comments that have been made and the issues that have surfaced over the last few weeks reflect the complexities of race in this country that we've never really worked through—a part of our union that we have yet to perfect. And if we walk away now, if we simply retreat into our respective corners, we will never be able to come together and solve challenges like health care, or education, or the need to find good jobs for every American.

Understanding this reality requires a reminder of how we arrived at this point. As William Faulkner once wrote, "The past isn't dead and buried. In fact, it isn't even past." We do not need to recite here the history of racial injustice in this country. But we do need to remind ourselves that so many of the disparities that exist in the African-American community today can be directly traced to inequalities passed on from an earlier generation that suffered under the brutal legacy of slavery and Jim Crow.

Segregated schools were, and are, inferior schools; we still haven't fixed them, 50 years after Brown v. Board of Education, and the inferior education they provided, then and now, helps explain the pervasive achievement gap between today's black and white students.

Legalized discrimination—where blacks were prevented, often through violence, from owning property, or loans were not granted to African-American business owners, or black homeowners could not access FHA mortgages, or blacks were excluded from unions, or the police force, or fire departments—meant that black families could not amass any meaningful wealth to bequeath to future generations. That history helps explain the wealth and income gap between black and white, and the concentrated pockets of poverty that persist in so many of today's urban and rural communities.

A lack of economic opportunity among black men, and the shame and frustration that came from not being able to provide for one's family, contributed to the erosion of black families—a problem that welfare policies for many years may have worsened. And the lack of basic services in so many urban black neighbourhoods—parks for kids to play in, police walking the beat, regular garbage pick-up and building code enforcement—all helped create a cycle of violence, blight and neglect that continues to haunt us.

This is the reality in which Reverend Wright and other African Americans of his generation grew up. They came of age in the late 50s and early 60s, a time when segregation was still the law of the land and opportunity was systematically constricted. What's remarkable is not how many failed in the face of discrimination, but rather how many men and women overcame the odds; how many were able to make a way out of no way for those like me who would come after them.

'A lack of economic opportunity among black men, and the shame and frustration that came from not being able to provide for one's family, contributed to the erosion of black families—a problem that welfare policies for many years may have worsened.'

But for all those who scratched and clawed their way to get a piece of the American Dream, there were many who didn't make it—those who were ultimately defeated, in one way or another, by discrimination. That legacy of defeat was passed on to future generations—those young men and increasingly young women who we see standing on street corners or languishing in our prisons, without hope or prospects for the future. Even for those blacks who did make it, questions of race, and racism, continue to define their worldview in fundamental ways. For the men and women of Reverend Wright's generation, the memories of humiliation and doubt and fear have not gone away; nor has the anger and the bitterness of those years. That anger may not get expressed in public, in front of white co-workers or white friends. But it does find voice in the barbershop or around the kitchen table. At times, that anger is exploited by politicians, to gin up votes along racial lines, or to make up for a politician's own failings.

And occasionally it finds voice in the church on Sunday morning, in the pulpit and in the pews. The fact that so many people are surprised to hear that anger in some of Reverend Wright's sermons simply reminds us of the old truism that the most segregated hour in American life occurs on Sunday morning.

That anger is not always productive; indeed, all too often it distracts attention from solving real problems; it keeps us from squarely facing our own complicity in our condition, and prevents the African-American community from forging the alliances it needs to bring about real change. But the anger is real; it is powerful; and to simply wish it away, to condemn it without understanding its roots, only serves to widen the chasm of misunderstanding that exists between the races.

In fact, a similar anger exists within segments of the white community. Most working- and middle-class white Americans don't feel that they have been particularly privileged by their race. Their experience is the immigrant experience—as far as they're concerned, no-one's handed them anything, they've built it from scratch. They've worked hard all their lives, many times only to see their jobs shipped overseas or their pension dumped after a lifetime of labor. They are anxious about their futures, and feel their dreams slipping away; in an era of stagnant wages and global competition, opportunity comes to be seen as a zero sum game, in which your dreams come at my expense. So when they are told to bus their children to a school across town; when they hear that an African American is getting an advantage in landing a good job or a spot in a good college because of an injustice that they themselves never committed; when they're told that their fears about crime in urban neighbourhoods are somehow prejudiced, resentment builds over time.

Like the anger within the black community, these resentments aren't always expressed in polite company. But they have helped shape the political landscape for at least a generation. Anger over welfare and affirmative action helped forge the Reagan Coalition. Politicians routinely exploited fears of crime for their own electoral ends. Talk show hosts and conservative commentators built entire careers unmasking bogus claims of racism while dismissing legitimate discussions of racial injustice and inequality as mere political correctness or reverse racism.

Just as black anger often proved counterproductive, so have these white resentments distracted attention from the real culprits of the middle-class squeeze—a corporate culture rife with inside dealing, questionable accounting practices, and short-term greed; a Washington dominated by lobbyists and special interests; economic policies that favour the few over the many. And yet, to wish away the resentments of white Americans, to label them as misguided or even racist, without recognizing they are grounded in legitimate concerns—this too widens the racial divide, and blocks the path to understanding.

'Just as black anger often proved counterproductive, so have these white resentments distracted attention from the real culprits of the middle-class squeeze—a corporate culture rife with inside dealing, questionable accounting practices, and short-term greed; a Washington dominated by lobbyists and special interests.'

This is where we are right now. It's a racial stalemate we've been stuck in for years. Contrary to the claims of some of my critics, black and white, I have never been so naive as to believe that we can get beyond our racial divisions in a single election cycle, or with a single candidacy—particularly a candidacy as imperfect as my own.

But I have asserted a firm conviction—a conviction rooted in my faith in God and my faith in the American people—that working together we can move beyond some of our old racial wounds, and that in fact we have no choice if we are to continue on the path of a more perfect union.

For the African-American community, that path means embracing the burdens of our past without becoming victims of our past. It means continuing to insist on a full measure of justice in every aspect of American life. But it also means binding our particular grievances—for better health care, and better schools, and better jobs—to the larger aspirations of all Americans—the white woman struggling to break the glass ceiling, the white man who's been laid off, the immigrant trying to feed his family. And it means taking full responsibility for our own lives—by demanding more from our fathers, and spending more time with our children, and reading to them, and teaching them that while they may face challenges and discrimination in their own lives, they must never succumb to despair or cynicism; they must always believe that they can write their own destiny.

'And it means taking full responsibility for our own lives—by demanding more from our fathers, and spending more time with our children, and reading to them, and teaching them that while they may face challenges and discrimination in their own lives, they must never succumb to despair or cynicism.'

Ironically, this quintessentially American—and yes, conservative—notion of self-help found frequent expression in Reverend Wright's sermons. But what my former pastor too often failed to understand is that embarking on a program of self-help also requires a belief that society can change. The profound mistake of Reverend Wright's sermons is not that he spoke about racism in our society. It's that he spoke as if our society was static; as if no progress has been made; as if this country—a country that has made it possible for one of his own members to run for the highest office in the land and build a coalition of white and black, Latino and Asian, rich and poor, young and old—is still irrevocably bound to a tragic past.

But what we know—what we have seen—is that America can change. That is true genius of this nation. What we have already achieved gives us hope—the audacity to hope—for what we can and must achieve tomorrow.

In the white community, the path to a more perfect union means acknowledging that what ails the African American community does not just exist in the minds of black people; that the legacy of discrimination—and current incidents of discrimination, while less overt than in the past—are real and must be addressed. Not just with words, but with deeds—by investing in our schools and our communities; by enforcing our civil rights laws and ensuring fairness in our criminal justice system; by providing this generation with ladders of opportunity that were unavailable for previous generations. It requires all Americans to realize that your dreams do not have to come at the expense of my dreams; that investing in the health, welfare, and education of black and brown and white children will ultimately help all of America prosper.

In the end, then, what is called for is nothing more, and nothing less, than what all the world's great religions demand—that we do unto others as we would have them do unto us. Let us be our brother's keeper, Scripture tells us. Let us be our sister's keeper. Let us find that common stake we all have in one another, and let our politics reflect that spirit as well.

For we have a choice in this country. We can accept a politics that breeds division, and conflict, and cynicism. We can tackle race only as spectacle—as we did in the OJ trial—or in the wake of tragedy, as we did in the aftermath of Katrina—or as fodder for the nightly news. We can play Reverend Wright's sermons on every channel, every day and talk about them from now until the election, and make the only question in this campaign whether or not the American people think that I somehow believe or sympathize with his most offensive words. We can pounce on some gaffe by a Hillary supporter as evidence that she's playing the race card, or we can speculate on whether white men will all flock to John McCain in the general election regardless of his policies.

We can do that.

But if we do, I can tell you that in the next election, we'll be talking about some other distraction. And then another one. And then another one. And nothing will change.

That is one option. Or, at this moment, in this election, we can come together and say, "Not this time". This time we want to talk about the crumbling schools that are stealing the future of black children and white children and Asian children and Hispanic children and Native American children. This time we want to reject the cynicism that tells us that these kids can't learn; that those kids who don't look like us are somebody else's problem. The children of America are not those kids, they are our kids, and we will not let them fall behind in a 21st century economy. Not this time.

'This time we want to reject the cynicism that tells us that these kids can't learn; that those kids who don't look like us are somebody else's problem. The children of America are not those kids, they are our kids, and we will not let them fall behind in a 21st century economy. Not this time.'

This time we want to talk about how the lines in the Emergency Room are filled with whites and blacks and Hispanics who do not have health care; who don't have the power on their own to overcome the special interests in Washington, but who can take them on if we do it together.

This time we want to talk about the shuttered mills that once provided a decent life for men and women of every race, and the homes for sale that once belonged to Americans from every religion, every region, every walk of life. This time we want to talk about the fact that the real problem is not that someone who doesn't look like you might take your job; it's that the corporation you work for will ship it overseas for nothing more than a profit.

This time we want to talk about the men and women of every colour and creed who serve together, and fight together, and bleed together under the same proud flag. We want to talk about how to bring them home from a war that never should've been authorized and never should've been waged, and we want to talk about how we'll show our patriotism by caring for them, and their families, and giving them the benefits they have earned.

I would not be running for President if I didn't believe with all my heart that this is what the vast majority of Americans want for this country. This union may never be perfect, but generation after generation has shown that it can always be perfected. And today, whenever I find myself feeling doubtful or cynical about this possibility, what gives me the most hope is the next generation—the young people whose attitudes and beliefs and openness to change have already made history in this election.

There is one story in particular that I'd like to leave you with today—a story I told when I had the great honour of speaking on Dr King's birthday at his home church, Ebenezer Baptist, in Atlanta. There is a young, 23-year-old white woman named Ashley Baia who organized for our campaign in Florence, South Carolina. She had been working to organize a mostly African American community since the beginning of this campaign, and one day she was at a roundtable discussion where everyone went around telling their story and why they were there.

And Ashley said that when she was nine years old, her mother got cancer. And because she had to miss days of work, she was let go and lost her health care. They had to file for bankruptcy, and that's when Ashley decided that she had to do something to help her mom.

She knew that food was one of their most expensive costs, and so Ashley convinced her mother that what she really liked and really wanted to eat more than anything else was mustard and relish sandwiches. Because that was the cheapest way to eat.

She did this for a year until her mom got better, and she told everyone at the roundtable that the reason she joined our campaign was so that she could help the millions of other children in the country who want and need to help their parents too.

Now Ashley might have made a different choice. Perhaps somebody told her along the way that the source of her mother's problems were blacks who were on welfare and too lazy to work, or Hispanics who were coming into the country illegally. But she didn't. She sought out allies in her fight against injustice.

Anyway, Ashley finishes her story and then goes around the room and asks everyone else why they're supporting the campaign. They all have different stories and reasons. Many bring up a specific issue. And finally they come to this elderly black man who's been sitting there quietly the entire time. And Ashley asks him why he's there. And he does not bring up a specific issue. He does not say health care or the economy. He does not say education or the war. He does not say that he was there because of Barack Obama. He simply says to everyone in the room, "I am here because of Ashley."

"I'm here because of Ashley."

By itself, that single moment of recognition between that young white girl and that old black man is not enough. It is not enough to give health care to the sick, or jobs to the jobless, or education to our children.

But it is where we start. It is where our union grows stronger. And as so many generations have come to realize over the course of the 221 years since a band of patriots signed that document in Philadelphia, that is where the perfection begins. ’

The Conservative Backlash

After nearly two decades of rapid social change and progress, by the mid to late 1970s the public mood had begun to turn in many Western nations, including the United States and Britain.

Part of the problem for the progressive movement was that it had been to an extent fed by a youth culture which had by the late 1970s run out of energy, exemplified by growing political and social apathy. Music, literature and art, all aspects of the push for change of the 60s and early 70s, had begun to lose direction, edge and focus.

Beneath these more obvious outward changes was a far more potent, hidden one: the middle classes of Britain and the United States had felt left behind by such rapid changes as those won by the civil rights movement. Encouraged by conservative elements, they came to resent paying for positive change through their taxes. The immediate result was a hard swing back to the right in Britain through the election of Margaret Thatcher (1925–) as prime minister in 1979. The following year, former B movie actor and extreme conservative Ronald W. Reagan (1911–2004) was elected president of the United States.

The new era was marked by a neo-conservative rhetoric of 'small government', low taxation and the privatization of major public assets, a reassertion of 'traditional' values such as on the family and religion, and a very dangerous new phase in the Cold War between the Soviet Union and the Western powers.

Recent research has suggested the world came perilously close to all-out nuclear war in 1983, following provocative speeches by President Reagan, as well as a Soviet early-warning computer malfunction and the Soviets' shooting down of a South Korean civilian airliner that had strayed into its airspace.

The conservative agenda was to mark Western politics for three decades, becoming ever more strident after the contested election of Republican Christian fundamentalist neo-conservative George W. Bush (1946–) in 2000 in the United States. It concluded only with the global economic crisis that began in 2008—which threw into serious question the freemarket and neo-liberal views that had long dominated debate—and the inauguration of Democrat Barack Obama as US president in January 2009.

But the right-wing backlash went far deeper than mere party political changes into the social order itself. With the election of Thatcher and Reagan, the youth culture of the 60s and 70s was replaced by a new class which had little or no interest in social change, which fetishized the free market and exalted individual over community.

Corporate suits supplanted T-shirts and jeans, and sport trumped protest. Suddenly, it was acceptable, even fashionable, to wear the T-shirt logo of a corporation, where even a few years earlier it would have been one sporting a political slogan. Revolt transmuted into style and corporate became chic. The neocon era of free-market triumphalism and social conservatism had begun. And, almost inevitably, a new round of armed conflicts began.

Margaret Thatcher

'Their Way of Life is British'

Speech to the House of Commons, London, on the 'grave situation' in the Falkland Islands, 3 April 1982.

Margaret Thatcher during the British election campaign in 1983.

Margaret Thatcher, Britain's first female prime minister, once said 'if you want anything said, ask a man... if you want something done, ask a woman'.

One of the most controversial figures of global politics in the late 20th century, the headstrong style and conservative economic policies of the lady 'not for turning' led to the coining of her personalized adjective: 'Thatcherite'.

Margaret Thatcher (née Roberts) was born in 1925 into a grocer's family in a small town in the north of England. She did well at school and went on to study chemistry at Oxford University. She married wealthy industrialist Dennis Thatcher in 1951 and practised as a barrister from 1954.

Thatcher won the North London seat of Finchley for the Conservatives in 1959; two years later she was promoted to the ministry. She served as secretary of state for education and science under Edward Heath's administration and was elected leader of the Conservative Party in 1975. She led her party to victory four years later after the 'Winter of Discontent' in Britain at the 1979 general election.

Thatcher's early years were dogged by severe economic problems in Britain. Favouring individualism over state intervention favoured by the previous Labour government, she cut public spending, selling off state-owned public industries to private business and cutting subsidies. As a result, unemployment rose sharply during her first years and she appeared destined for a short time in office. The 1982 war with Argentina over the Falklands Islands (Islas Malvenas) changed all that.

Argentina had, since the 19th century, laid claim to the remote, sparsely populated sheep-pasturing islands near its coastline, but Britain had seized them in 1833 and had since resisted all attempts to give them up. When Argentine troops invaded, Thatcher responded by setting up an exclusion zone in the adjacent waters. When a British submarine sank the Argentine battleship General Belgrano, outside of the exclusion zone, resulting in the loss of several hundred lives, the British popular press went into jingoistic overdrive, with one infamous tabloid headline gloating 'Gotcha!'

In the following speech, made at the start of the conflict, Thatcher sketches the history of Britain's claim to the remote islands, and reaffirms her intention to re-take them.

'The House meets this Saturday to respond to a situation of great gravity. We are here because, for the first time for many years, British sovereign territory has been invaded by a foreign power. After several days of rising tension in our relations with Argentina, that country's armed forces attacked the Falkland Islands yesterday and established military control of the islands.

Yesterday was a day of rumour and counter-rumour. Throughout the day we had no communication from the Government of the Falklands. Indeed, the last message that we received was at 21.55 hours on Thursday night, 1 April. Yesterday morning at 8.33am we sent a telegram which was acknowledged. At 8.45am all communications ceased. I shall refer to that again in a moment. By late afternoon yesterday it became clear that an Argentine invasion had taken place and that the lawful British Government of the islands had been usurped.

I am sure that the whole House will join me in condemning totally this unprovoked aggression by the Government of Argentina against British territory. It has not a shred of justification and not a scrap of legality.

It was not until 8.30 this morning, our time, when I was able to speak to the governor, who had arrived in Uruguay, that I learnt precisely what had happened. He told me that the Argentines had landed at approximately 6am Falklands' time, 10 am our time. One party attacked the capital from the landward side and another from the seaward side. The governor then sent a signal to us which we did not receive.

'Fortunately, as far as he is aware, there were no civilian casualties. When he left the Falklands, he said that the people were in tears. They do not want to be Argentine. He said that the islanders are still tremendously loyal. I must say that I have every confidence in the governor and the action that he took.'

Communications had ceased at 8.45am our time. It is common for atmospheric conditions to make communications with Port Stanley difficult. Indeed, we had been out of contact for a period the previous night.

The governor reported that the Marines, in the defence of Government House, were superb. He said that they acted in the best traditions of the Royal Marines. They inflicted casualties, but those defending Government House suffered none. He had kept the local people informed of what was happening through a small local transmitter which he had in Government House. He is relieved that the islanders heeded his advice to stay indoors.

Fortunately, as far as he is aware, there were no civilian casualties. When he left the Falklands, he said that the people were in tears. They do not want to be Argentine. He said that the islanders are still tremendously loyal. I must say that I have every confidence in the governor and the action that he took.

I must tell the House that the Falkland Islands and their dependencies remain British territory. No aggression and no invasion can alter that simple fact. It is the Government's objective to see that the islands are freed from occupation and are returned to British administration at the earliest possible moment.

Argentina has, of course, long disputed British sovereignty over the islands. We have absolutely no doubt about our sovereignty, which has been continuous since 1833. Nor have we any doubt about the unequivocal wishes of the Falkland Islanders, who are British in stock and tradition, and they wish to remain British in allegiance. We cannot allow the democratic rights of the islanders to be denied by the territorial ambitions of Argentina.

Over the past 15 years, successive British Governments have held a series of meetings with the Argentine Government to discuss the dispute. In many of these meetings elected representatives of the islanders have taken part. We have always made it clear that their wishes were paramount and that there would be no change in sovereignty without their consent and without the approval of the House.

The most recent meeting took place this year in New York at the end of February between my honourable friend the Member for Shoreham accompanied by two members of the islands council, and the Deputy Foreign Secretary of Argentina. The atmosphere at the meeting was cordial and positive, and a communiqué was issued about future negotiating procedures. Unfortunately, the joint communiqué which had been agreed was not published in Buenos Aires.

There was a good deal of bellicose comment in the Argentine press in late February and early March, about which my hon. Friend [Richard Luce] the Minister of State for Foreign and Commonwealth Affairs expressed his concern in the House on 3 March following the Anglo–Argentine talks in New York. However, this has not been an uncommon situation in Argentina over the years. It would have been absurd to dispatch the fleet every time there was bellicose talk in Buenos Aires. There was no good reason on 3 March to think that an invasion was being planned, especially against the background of the constructive talks on which my hon. Friend had just been engaged. The joint communiqué on behalf of the Argentine deputy Minister of Foreign Affairs and my hon. Friend read: "The meeting took place in a cordial and positive spirit. The two sides reaffirmed their resolve to find a solution to the sovereignty dispute and considered in detail an Argentine proposal for procedures to make better progress in this sense."

'It would have been absurd to dispatch the fleet every time there was bellicose talk in Buenos Aires. There was no good reason on 3 March to think that an invasion was being planned, especially against the background of the constructive talks on which my hon. Friend had just been engaged.'

There had, of course, been previous incidents affecting sovereignty before the one in South Georgia, to which I shall refer in a moment. In December 1976 the Argentines illegally set up a scientific station on one of the dependencies within the Falklands group—Southern Thule. The Labour Government attempted to solve the matter through diplomatic exchanges, but without success. The Argentines remained there and are still there.

Two weeks ago—on 19 March—the latest in this series of incidents affecting sovereignty occurred; and the deterioration in relations between the British and Argentine Governments which culminated in yesterday's Argentine invasion began. The incident appeared at the start to be relatively minor. But we now know it was the beginning of much more.

The commander of the British Antarctic Survey base at Grytviken on South Georgia—a dependency of the Falkland Islands over which the United Kingdom has exercised sovereignty since 1775 when the island was discovered by Captain Cook—reported to us that an Argentine navy cargo ship had landed about 60 Argentines at nearby Leith harbour. They had set up camp and hoisted the Argentine flag. They were there to carry out a valid commercial contract to remove scrap metal from a former whaling station.

The leader of the commercial expedition, Davidoff, had told our embassy in Buenos Aires that he would be going to South Georgia in March. He was reminded of the need to obtain permission from the immigration authorities on the island. He did not do so. The base commander told the Argentines that they had no right to land on South Georgia without the permission of the British authorities. They should go either to Grytviken to get the necessary clearances, or leave. The ship and some 50 of them left on 22 March. Although about 10 Argentines remained behind, this appeared to reduce the tension.

In the meantime, we had been in touch with the Argentine Government about the incident. They claimed to have had no prior knowledge of the landing and assured us that there were no Argentine military personnel in the party. For our part we made it clear that, while we had no wish to interfere in the operation of a normal commercial contract, we could not accept the illegal presence of these people on British territory.

We asked the Argentine Government either to arrange for the departure of the remaining men or to ensure that they obtained the necessary permission to be there. Because we recognized the potentially serious nature of the situation, HMS Endurance was ordered to the area. We told the Argentine Government that, if they failed to regularize the position of the party on South Georgia or to arrange for their departure, HMS Endurance would take them off, without using force, and return them to Argentina.

This was, however, to be a last resort. We were determined that this apparently minor problem of 10 people on South Georgia in pursuit of a commercial contract should not be allowed to escalate and we made it plain to the Argentine Government that we wanted to achieve a peaceful resolution of the problem by diplomatic means. To help in this, HMS Endurance was ordered not to approach the Argentine party at Leith but to go to Grytviken.

But it soon became clear that the Argentine Government had little interest in trying to solve the problem. On 25 March another Argentine navy ship arrived at Leith to deliver supplies to the 10 men ashore. Our ambassador in Buenos Aires sought an early response from the Argentine Government to our previous requests that they should arrange for the men's departure. This request was refused. Last Sunday, on Sunday 28 March, the Argentine Foreign Minister sent a message to my right hon. and noble friend the Foreign Secretary refusing outright to regularize the men's position. Instead, it restated Argentina's claim to sovereignty over the Falkland Islands and their dependencies...

The Government has now decided that a large task force will sail as soon as all preparations are complete. HMS Invincible will be in the lead and will leave port on Monday.

I stress that I cannot foretell what orders the task force will receive as it proceeds. That will depend on the situation at the time. Meanwhile, we hope that our continuing diplomatic efforts, helped by our many friends, will meet with success.

The Foreign Ministers of the European Community member states yesterday condemned the intervention and urged withdrawal. The NATO Council called on both sides to refrain from force and continue diplomacy.

'The Government has now decided that a large task force will sail as soon as all preparations are complete. HMS Invincible will be in the lead and will leave port on Monday. I stress that I cannot foretell what orders the task force will receive as it proceeds. That will depend on the situation at the time.'

The United Nations Security Council met again yesterday and will continue its discussions today. Opposition Members laugh. They would have been the first to urge a meeting of the Security Council if we had not called one. They would have been the first to urge restraint and to urge a solution to the problem by diplomatic means. They would have been the first to accuse us of sabre rattling and war mongering…

The people of the Falkland Islands, like the people of the United Kingdom, are an island race. They are few in number, but they have the right to live in peace, to choose their own way of life and to determine their own allegiance. Their way of life is British; their allegiance is to the Crown. It is the wish of the British people and the duty of Her Majesty's Government to do everything that we can to uphold that right. That will be our hope and our endeavour and, I believe, the resolve of every Member of the House.'

'The United Nations Security Council met again yesterday and will continue its discussions today. Opposition Members laugh. They would have been the first to urge a meeting of the Security Council if we had not called one. They would have been the first to urge restraint and to urge a solution to the problem by diplomatic means.'

During the fighting from 2 April to 14 June 1982, 655 Argentine and 255 British servicemen lost their lives, as well as three Falklands civilians. Hostilities ended with the capture by British forces of the capital, Port Stanley.

Dubbed 'the Iron Lady' by the press, Thatcher saw her popularity skyrocket as a result of this war. She was easily re-elected in 1983, and pursued a Conservative program of privatization and anti-unionism. The following year though she was lucky to survive an IRA attempt on her life, when a bomb exploded in the Brighton (Sussex) hotel, where she was staying during a Conservative Party conference. Several people were killed, and the hotel was severely damaged.

During 1984 she also made a controversial speech to Conservative Party backbenchers, in which she drew parallels between the Falklands war and the long-running British miners' strike, urging a fight not only against the enemy without, but also 'the enemy within', which she said was much more difficult to combat but just as dangerous to liberty.

Re-elected for a third term in 1987, she found herself in increasing difficulty. The introduction of the highly unpopular Poll Tax (Council Tax) helped feed the perception that she was becoming increasingly out of touch with the electorate, and the nation was unsettled by race riots in London in 1990. Her downfall came in her own party room in November of that year when she resigned from office. Her replacement was John Major (1943–).

Though considered a strong and resolute leader by some, to others she merely gave chauvinist males ammunition in the old argument about women and power. Her influence is still obvious, however, carrying on into the Major and (Labour) Blair governments, neither of which returned to the kind of welfare state she had dismantled. In the case of Tony Blair (1953–), he followed the US into two new wars that the latter started in Afghanistan and Iraq, respectively.

Ronald Reagan

'The Ash Heap of History'

Speech on Soviet Communism to Britain's House of Commons,
London, 8 June 1982.

Ronald Reagan in 1982.

Former Hollywood actor Ronald Reagan won the US presidency in the conservative Republican landslide in 1980. A veteran of more than 50 Hollywood B movies, he became active in the actors' union, the Screen Actors Guild (SAG), and became its president in the late 1940s.

Reagan fought against communist infiltration of SAG and much to his fellow unionists' disgust testified as a 'friendly witness' at the House Un-American Activities Committee (HUAC) hearings, the witchhunts carried out against alleged communists by Senator Joseph McCarthy, which led to the blacklisting of many prominent Hollywood people.

Reagan's personal politics moved from liberal to arch conservative. He officially became a member of the Republican Party in 1962. Elected governor of California in 1966, he cut taxes but also social services, a policy which gained him the support of the burgeoning Californian suburban middle class. He secured the Republican Party nomination for the 1980 presidential election, and with Democrat president Jimmy Carter entrenched in the Iran hostage crisis, won easily.

He survived an attempt on his life just a few weeks into his presidency in early 1981, and returned to the Oval Office with a policy of lower taxes and reduced spending. His enthusiasm for smaller government did not extend to military expenditure, which blew out with massive proposed projects such his anti-ballistic missile Star Wars programme.

Dubbed by friends as 'the Great Communicator', in this speech to Britain's House of Commons in 1982 he declares the Soviet Union a failed state, and Marxism–Leninism a failed ideology.

'Historians looking back at our time will note the consistent restraint and peaceful intentions of the West. They will note that it was the democracies who refused to use the threat of their nuclear monopoly in the 40s and early 50s for territorial or imperial gain. Had that nuclear monopoly been in the hands of the Communist world, the map of Europe—indeed, the world—would look very different today. And certainly they will note it was not the democracies that invaded Afghanistan or suppressed Polish Solidarity or used chemical and toxin warfare in Afghanistan and Southeast Asia.

If history teaches anything, it teaches self-delusion in the face of unpleasant facts is folly. We see around us today the marks of our terrible dilemma—predictions of doomsday, anti-nuclear demonstrations, an arms race in which the West must, for its own protection, be an unwilling participant. At the same time we see totalitarian forces in the world who seek subversion and conflict around the globe to further their barbarous assault on the human spirit. What, then, is our course? Must civilization perish in a hail of fiery atoms? Must freedom wither in a quiet, deadening accommodation with totalitarian evil?

Sir Winston Churchill refused to accept the inevitability of war or even that it was imminent. He said, "I do not believe that Soviet Russia desires war. What they desire is the fruits of war and the indefinite expansion of their power and doctrines. But what we have to consider here today while time remains is the permanent prevention of war and the establishment of conditions of freedom and democracy as rapidly as possible in all countries."

Well, this is precisely our mission today: to preserve freedom as well as peace. It may not be easy to see; but I believe we live now at a turning point.

In an ironic sense Karl Marx was right. We are witnessing today a great revolutionary crisis, a crisis where the demands of the economic order are conflicting directly with those of the political order. But the crisis is happening not in the free, non-Marxist West but in the home of Marxism–Leninism, the Soviet Union. It is the Soviet Union that runs against the tide of history by denying human freedom and human dignity to its citizens.

It also is in deep economic difficulty. The rate of growth in the national product has been steadily declining since the 50s and is less than half of what it was then. The dimensions of this failure are astounding: a country which employs one-fifth of its population in agriculture is unable to feed its own people. Were it not for the private sector, the tiny private sector tolerated in Soviet agriculture, the country might be on the brink of famine. These private plots occupy a bare 3 per cent of the arable land but account for nearly one-quarter of Soviet farm output and nearly one-third of meat products and vegetables.

'We are witnessing today a great revolutionary crisis, a crisis where the demands of the economic order are conflicting directly with those of the political order. But the crisis is happening not in the free, non-Marxist West but in the home of Marxism–Leninism, the Soviet Union.'

Overcentralized, with little or no incentives, year after year the Soviet system pours its best resources into the making of instruments of destruction. The constant shrinkage of economic growth combined with the growth of military production is putting a heavy strain on the Soviet people. What we see here is a political structure that no longer corresponds to its economic base, a society where productive forces are hampered by political ones.

The decay of the Soviet experiment should come as no surprise to us. Wherever the comparisons have been made between free and closed societies—West Germany and East Germany, Austria and Czechoslovakia, Malaysia and Vietnam—it is the democratic countries that are prosperous and responsive to the needs of their people. And one of the simple but overwhelming facts of our time is this: of all the millions of refugees we've seen in the modern world, their flight is always away from, not toward the Communist world. Today on the NATO line, our military forces face east to prevent a possible invasion. On the other side of the line, the Soviet forces also face east to prevent their people from leaving.

The hard evidence of totalitarian rule has caused in mankind an uprising of the intellect and will. Whether it is the growth of the new schools of economics in America or England or the appearance of the so-called new philosophers in France, there is one unifying thread running through the intellectual work of these groups—rejection of the arbitrary power of the state, the refusal to subordinate the rights of the individual to the superstate, the realization that collectivism stifles all the best human impulses... Chairman Brezhnev repeatedly has stressed that the competition of ideas and systems must continue and that this is entirely consistent with relaxation of tensions and peace. Well, we ask only that these systems begin by living up to their own constitutions, abiding by their own laws, and complying with the international obligations they have undertaken. We ask only for a process, a direction, a basic code of decency, not for an instant transformation.

We cannot ignore the fact that even without our encouragement there has been and will continue to be repeated explosion against repression and dictatorships. The Soviet Union itself is not immune to this reality. Any system is inherently unstable that has no peaceful means to legitimize its leaders. In such cases, the very repressiveness of the state ultimately drives people to resist it, if necessary, by force.

While we must be cautious about forcing the pace of change, we must not hesitate to declare our ultimate objectives and to take concrete actions to move toward them. We must be staunch in our conviction that freedom is not the sole prerogative of a lucky few but the inalienable and universal right of all human beings. So states the United Nations Universal Declaration of Human Rights, which, among other things, guarantees free elections.

The objective I propose is quite simple to state: to foster the infrastructure of democracy, the system of a free press, unions, political parties, universities, which allows a people to choose their own way to develop their own culture, to reconcile their own differences through peaceful means.

This is not cultural imperialism; it is providing the means for genuine self-determination and protection for diversity. Democracy already flourishes in countries with very different cultures and historical experiences...

It is time that we committed ourselves as a nation—in both the public and private sectors—to assisting democratic development... What I am describing now is a plan and a hope for the long term—the march of freedom and democracy which will leave Marxism–Leninism on the ash heap of history as it has left other tyrannies which stifle the freedom and muzzle the self-expression of the people. And that's why we must continue our efforts to strengthen NATO even as we move forward with our zero-option initiative in the negotiations on intermediate-range forces and our proposal for a one-third reduction in strategic ballistic missile warheads.

'What I am describing now is a plan and a hope for the long term—the march of freedom and democracy which will leave Marxism–Leninism on the ash heap of history as it has left other tyrannies which stifle the freedom and muzzle the self-expression of the people.'

Our military strength is a prerequisite to peace, but let it be clear we maintain this strength in the hope it will never be used, for the ultimate determinant in the struggle that's now going on in the world will not be bombs and rockets but a test of wills and ideas, a trial of spiritual resolve, the values we hold, the beliefs we cherish, the ideals to which we are dedicated.

The British people know that, given strong leadership, time, and a little bit of hope, the forces of good ultimately rally and triumph over evil. Here among you is the cradle of self-government, the Mother of Parliaments. Here is the enduring greatness of the British contribution to mankind, the great civilized ideas: individual liberty, representative government, and the rule of law under God.'

Reagan was re-elected in 1984, and during his second term allowed US military intelligence new freedoms, which led to the 'Iran–Contragate' scandal, in which the US used laundered money from arms sales to Iran (then at war with Iraq, which was also buying weapons from the US) to finance an insurgency against the left-wing government of Nicaragua in Central America.

His increased military spending, which the Soviets sought to match, seems to have been a factor in the implosion of what Reagan famously labelled the 'Evil Empire'. He also demanded the tearing down of the Berlin Wall—which in fact occurred soon after he left office. His legacy was a US as dominant world superpower, but one more divided at home between rich and poor, a gulf which only widened further after his time in power.

George H.W. Bush

'A New World Order'

Speech to the Joint Session of Congress, Washington, 11 September 1990.

George H. W. Bush delivering a speech during an Export Council luncheon in 1991.

George H.W. Bush (1924–) was born in Massachusetts and educated at Yale University. A decorated World War II airman, he served as a senator and as director of the CIA before Ronald Reagan invited him to be his running mate in the 1980 American presidential election.

After Reagan completed his second term, Bush ran for the White House in 1988, defeating the Democratic Party's Michael Dukakis (1933–). During his administration, the Berlin Wall came down in 1989, and the Soviet Union collapsed.

Then, in 1990, he faced the invasion of Kuwait by the Iraqi troops of Saddam Hussein (1937–2006). With UN approval he assembled a US-led multinational force to re-take the tiny, oil-rich nation, famously drawing his 'line in the sand'. In this landmark address, as the US responds to the invasion of oil-rich Kuwait by Iraqi forces, Bush articulates what he envisions as the opportunity for a post-Cold War 'new world order', one in which war and terrorism become relegated to history. It was not to be.

'We gather tonight, witness to events in the Persian Gulf as significant as they are tragic. In the early morning hours of August 2nd, following negotiations and promises by Iraq's dictator Saddam Hussein not to use force, a powerful Iraqi army invaded its trusting and much weaker neighbour, Kuwait. Within three days, 120,000 Iraqi troops with 850 tanks had poured into Kuwait and moved south to threaten Saudi Arabia. It was then that I decided to check that aggression...

As you know, I've just returned from a very productive meeting with Soviet President Gorbachev. And I am pleased that we are working together to build a new relationship. In Helsinki, our joint statement affirmed to the world our shared resolve to counter Iraq's threat to peace. Let me quote: "We are united in the belief that Iraq's aggression must not be tolerated. No peaceful international order is possible if larger states can devour their smaller neighbours."

Clearly, no longer can a dictator count on East–West confrontation to stymie concerted United Nations action against aggression. A new partnership of nations has begun. We stand today at a unique and extraordinary moment. The crisis in the Persian Gulf, as grave as it is, also offers a rare opportunity to move toward an historic period of co-operation. Out of these troubled times, our fifth objective—a new world order—can emerge: a new era—freer from the threat of terror, stronger in the pursuit of justice, and more secure in the quest for peace. An era in which the nations of the world, East and West, North and South, can prosper and live in harmony.

A hundred generations have searched for this elusive path to peace, while a thousand wars raged across the span of human endeavour. Today that new world is struggling to be born. A world quite different from the one we've known. A world where the rule of law supplants the rule of the jungle. A world in which nations recognize the shared responsibility for freedom and justice. A world where the strong respect the rights of the weak.

This is the vision that I shared with President Gorbachev in Helsinki. He and other leaders from Europe, the Gulf and around the world, understand that how we manage this crisis today could shape the future for generations to come. The test we face is great—and so are the stakes. This is the first assault on the new world that we seek, the first test of our mettle. Had we not responded to this first provocation with clarity of purpose, if we do not continue to demonstrate our determination, it would be a signal to actual and potential despots around the world.

America and the world must defend common vital interests. And we will. And the world must support the rule of law. And we will. America and the world must stand up to aggression. And we will. And one thing more—in the pursuit of these goals America will not be intimidated.

Vital issues of principle are at stake. Saddam Hussein is literally trying to wipe a country off the face of the earth. We do not exaggerate. Nor do we exaggerate when we say Saddam Hussein will fail.

Vital economic interests are at risk as well. Iraq itself controls some 10 per cent of the world's proven oil reserves. Iraq plus Kuwait controls twice that. An Iraq permitted to swallow Kuwait would have the economic and military power, as well as the arrogance, to intimidate and coerce its neighbours—neighbours who control the lion's share of the world's remaining oil reserves. We cannot permit a resource so vital to be dominated by one so ruthless. And we won't...

Together with our friends and allies, ships of the United States Navy are today patrolling Mideast waters. They've already intercepted more than 700 ships to enforce the sanctions. Three regional leaders I spoke with just yesterday told me that these sanctions are working. Iraq is feeling the heat.

We continue to hope that Iraq's leaders will recalculate just what their aggression has cost them. They are cut off from world trade, unable to sell their oil. And only a tiny fraction of goods gets through.

The communiqué with President Gorbachev made mention of what happens when the embargo is so effective that children of Iraq literally need milk or the sick truly need medicine. Then, under strict international supervision that guarantees the proper destination, then food will be permitted...

At home, the material cost of our leadership can be steep. That's why Secretary of State Baker and Treasury Secretary Brady have met with many world leaders to underscore that the burden of this collective effort must be shared. We are prepared to do our share and more to help carry that load; we insist that others do their share as well.

The response of most of our friends and allies has been good. To help defray costs, the leaders of Saudi Arabia, Kuwait, and the UAE [the United Arab Emirates] have pledged to provide our deployed troops with all the food and fuel they need. Generous assistance will also be provided to stalwart front-line nations, such as Turkey and Egypt. I am also heartened to report that this international response extends to the neediest victims

'Let me also make clear that the United States has no quarrel with the Iraqi people. Our quarrel is with Iraq's dictator and with his aggression. Iraq will not be permitted to annex Kuwait. That's not a threat, that's not a boast, that's just the way it's going to be.'

'Once again, Americans have stepped forward to share a tearful good-bye with their families before leaving for a strange and distant shore. At this very moment, they serve together with Arabs, Europeans, Asians and Africans in defence of principle and the dream of a new world order.'

of this conflict—those refugees. For our part, we've contributed $28 million for relief efforts. This is but a portion of what is needed. I commend, in particular, Saudi Arabia, Japan, and several European nations who have joined us in this purely humanitarian effort.

There's an energy-related cost to be borne as well. Oil-producing nations are already replacing lost Iraqi and Kuwaiti output. More than half of what was lost has been made up. And we're getting superb cooperation. If producers, including the United States, continue steps to expand oil and gas production, we can stabilize prices and guarantee against hardship.

Additionally, we and several of our allies always have the option to extract oil from our strategic petroleum reserves if conditions warrant. As I've pointed out before, conservation efforts are essential to keep our energy needs as low as possible. And we must then take advantage of our energy sources across the board: coal, natural gas, hydro, and nuclear. Our failure to do these things has made us more dependent on foreign oil than ever before. Finally, let no one even contemplate profiteering from this crisis. We will not have it.

I cannot predict just how long it will take to convince Iraq to withdraw from Kuwait. Sanctions will take time to have their full intended effect. We will continue to review all options with our allies, but let it be clear: we will not let this aggression stand.

Let me also make clear that the United States has no quarrel with the Iraqi people. Our quarrel is with Iraq's dictator and with his aggression. Iraq will not be permitted to annex Kuwait. That's not a threat, that's not a boast, that's just the way it's going to be. Our ability to function effectively as a great power abroad depends on how we conduct ourselves at home. Our economy, our armed forces, our energy dependence, and our cohesion all determine whether we can help our friends and stand up to our foes.

For America to lead, America must remain strong and vital. Our world leadership and domestic strength are mutual and reinforcing; a woven piece, strongly bound as Old Glory…

In the final analysis, our ability to meet our responsibilities abroad depends upon political will and consensus at home. This is never easy in democracies—for we govern only with the consent of the governed. And although free people in a free society are bound to have their differences, Americans traditionally come together in times of adversity and challenge.

Once again, Americans have stepped forward to share a tearful good-bye with their families before leaving for a strange and distant shore. At this very moment, they serve together with Arabs, Europeans, Asians and Africans in defence of principle and the dream of a new world order. That's why they sweat and toil in the sand and the heat and the sun. If they can come together under such adversity, if old adversaries like the Soviet Union and the United States can work in common cause, then surely we who are so fortunate to be in this great chamber—Democrats, Republicans, liberals, conservatives—can come together to fulfil our responsibilities here. ’

After weeks of air attacks on its forces in the desert, the Iraqi army was routed in days and Kuwait retaken in January 1991. The triumph did not translate into further electoral fortune for Bush, however: he was destined to be a single-term president. Facing domestic economic and social problems, he was defeated by the Democratic Party's Bill Clinton in 1992.

Eleven years to the day after George H.W. Bush's 'New World Order' speech to the US Congress, a terrible new world did arrive with the Al Qaeda terrorist attacks on New York City and Washington, DC, that left 3,000 Americans dead.

Two years later, in 2003, Bush's son, President George W. Bush, ordered US forces to lead an invasion of Iraq that toppled Saddam Hussein's regime. The reason given for the invasion was claimed intelligence that Iraq possessed 'weapons of mass destruction'—later shown to be false. Saddam Hussein was convicted of war crimes and executed in 2006.

War and Peace in the New Millennium

The fall of the Berlin Wall in 1989 and the collapse of the Soviet Union and the subsequent foundation of the Russian federation two years later, led many in the West to hope for a new era of peace and co-operation.

But hardly had George H.W. Bush pronounced his 'New World Order', when terror attacks on US interests at home and abroad signalled that the world had entered a dangerous new era, one with new kinds of challenges to peace.

The attacks continued throughout the presidency of Bill Clinton (1946–; in office 1993–2001), starting on 26 February 1993, the month after he took office, when a massive truck bomb attack on the World Trade Center towers in New York threatened to topple them. Other bombing attacks on US embassies in Kenya and Tanzania in 1998 killed more than 200 people and demonstrated that the US faced a dangerous adversary in the terrorist leader Osama bin Laden (1957–). Leader of the Islamic fundamentalist Al Qaeda network, bin Laden had also been linked to the deadly attack on the American warship the USS Cole in the Yemeni port of Aden in October 2000.

The US presidential election of November 2000 saw the Republican Party's George W. Bush, son of George H.W. Bush, take the Oval Office over the Democrat Al Gore (1948–), who had served as vice-president under Bill Clinton since 1993.

George W. Bush's early months were of little note, and despite his ideological positioning among the neocons (neo-conservatives) and the Christian evangelical Religious Right, he was already being labelled a do-little president when matters changed on 11 September 2001. In a carefully planned co-ordinated terrorist assault of epic proportions and horrifying results, two airliners, hijacked by Islamic terrorists, flew into New York's World Trade Center twin towers, causing both subsequently to collapse; another plane hit the Pentagon in Washington. Thousands died in these attacks and the US and the world community entered a new battle against international terrorism, a 'War on Terror'.

Bin Laden was born in 1957 into one of the wealthiest families in Saudi Arabia, one of some 50 alleged children of a construction magnate. At university he came into contact with radical Islamic teachings. During the Soviet occupation of Afghanistan of 1979–89, with CIA backing he set up training camps for the US-backed resistance fighters, and reputedly saw action. He returned home only to become increasingly upset with what he viewed as the corruption of Saudi authorities.

He became vehemently anti-American in the wake of Iraq's 1990 invasion of Kuwait, which saw the stationing of US troops in Saudi Arabia. He saw this as an affront to Islam, and also blamed the Saudi regime for allowing it to happen.

Sent into exile in 1991, he based himself in Sudan for several years, until international pressure prompted the Sudanese to expel him. Relocating to Afghanistan, bin Laden set up the first of a number of training camps for his Al Qaeda ('the Base') terrorist network.

He oversaw a series of attacks on American interests in Kenya, Tanzania and Yemen. The terror attacks of 9/11 made bin Laden infamous. They galvanized the United States, and flung the world into the age of terror.

President Bush declared a 'War on Terror', and a month after 9/11, the US and its allies launched a controversial military campaign against Afghanistan's Taliban regime, believed to be harbouring bin Laden. Despite the speedy fall of that regime, and the 'cornering' of bin Laden in mountains on the Pakistan border, he eluded capture, his tape and video messages to the world via Arabic television channels mocking efforts to find him.

An unready world found itself in an age where terrorists felt no compunction about murdering innocent people, and the citizens of major cities braced themselves for further outrages without warning at any moment. The list of attacks grew with bombings by Islamic extremists in Bali in 2002 and 2005, and in Madrid and London in 2004 and 2005 ('7/7'), respectively.

The situation worsened when George W. Bush ordered American troops to lead an invasion of Iraq in 2003 on the grounds that it held weapons of mass destruction, a claim later found to be false. The conflict divided the international community.

The first decade of the new millennium has also been one of profound change technologically. The internet, a 'new technology' in the 1990s, has become an essential part of everyday life in much of the world, spawning a host of new sites that have become household names almost overnight, such as Google, YouTube, Facebook and Twitter.

At the same time, the world has had to face up to a technological challenge of a different kind: how to curb carbon emissions in an evermore populated and busy world, when those harmful emissions are causing global warming through the Greenhouse Effect. While a small minority of scientists and a rump of media commentators still remain sceptical about the science, most world governments do not, and capping and reducing carbon emissions will be a major challenge to the entire human race in this new century and millennium of change.

George W. Bush

'We Mourn the Loss of Thousands of Our Citizens'

'Bullhorn Speech' to rescue workers at Ground Zero, World Trade Center site, New York City, 14 September 2001.

followed by

'You Are With Us, Or You Are With The Terrorists'

Address to a Joint Session of Congress and the American People, Washington, DC, 20 September 2001.

George W. Bush addresses a joint session of Congress on 20 September 2001.

George W. Bush (1946–) survived problems with alcohol and years of obscurity to snatch the US presidency in 2000.

Educated at Yale University, where he was a member of the notorious Skull & Bones Club, he served in the domestic National Guard during the Vietnam War, prompting some to suspect that strings had been pulled to keep him away from combat. He managed a Texan baseball team, and rose to become the state governor in 1994. Re-elected in 1998, Bush ran for president in 2000 and defeated Democratic contender Al Gore by the slimmest of margins. His victory was not confirmed for several weeks, and then only enforced by a decision of the US Supreme Court.

It was the destiny of both the former baseball team manager, and of the people of the United States, that America's most perilous period since World War II should occur during the watch of the man widely considered to be the most hapless US president in living memory.

On the morning of 11 September 2001, terrorists hijacked four civilian airliners and flew them towards planned targets. Two flew into the skyscraper towers of the World Trade Center in New York City, levelling them, while another seriously damaged the Pentagon in Washington. A fourth crashed into a field in Pennsylvania after passengers apparently battled with the hijackers. In all, more than 3,000 lives were lost.

Despite initially seeming incapable of dealing with the news of the attacks as he sat reading to children in a Florida classroom, three days later Bush was at 'Ground Zero', the former site of the World Trade Center, on a bullhorn, speaking to rescue teams, America and the rest of the world.

The message from the Christian fundamentalist president was as predictable as it was simple: America would get even.

❛ Thank you all. I want you all to know—it can't go any louder [loud hailer]—I want you all to know that America today, America today is on bended knee, in prayer for the people whose lives were lost here, for the workers who work here, for the families who mourn. The nation stands with the good people of New York City and New Jersey and Connecticut as we mourn the loss of thousands of our citizens.

Voices from crowd: "I can't hear you!"

Bush: I can hear you! I can hear you! The rest of the world hears you! And the people—and the people who knocked these buildings down will hear all of us soon!

Chanting from crowd: "USA! USA! USA!"

President Bush: The nation...the nation sends its love and compassion to everybody who is here. Thank you for your hard work. Thank you for makin' the nation proud, and may God bless America.

Chanting from crowd: "USA! USA! USA! USA!"

'I can hear you! I can hear you! The rest of the world hears you! And the people—and the people who knocked these buildings down—will hear all of us soon!'

Six days later, President Bush addressed the US Congress on the attacks.

'On September the 11th, enemies of freedom committed an act of war against our country. Americans have known wars—but for the past 136 years they have been wars on foreign soil, except for one Sunday in 1941. Americans have known the casualties of war—but not at the centre of a great city on a peaceful morning. Americans have known surprise attacks—but never before on thousands of civilians. All of this was brought upon us in a single day—and night fell on a different world, a world where freedom itself is under attack.

Americans have many questions tonight. Americans are asking: Who attacked our country? The evidence we have gathered all points to a collection of loosely affiliated terrorist organizations known as Al Qaeda. They are the same murderers indicted for bombing American embassies in Tanzania and Kenya, and responsible for bombing the USS Cole.

Al Qaeda is to terror what the mafia is to crime. But its goal is not making money; its goal is remaking the world—and imposing its radical beliefs on people everywhere. The terrorists practise a fringe form of Islamic extremism that has been rejected by Muslim scholars and the vast majority of Muslim clerics—a fringe movement that perverts the peaceful teachings of Islam. The terrorists' directive commands them to kill Christians and Jews, to kill all Americans, and make no distinction among military and civilians, including women and children.

This group and its leader—a person named Osama bin Laden—are linked to many other organizations in different countries, including the Egyptian Islamic Jihad and the Islamic Movement of Uzbekistan. There are thousands of these terrorists in more than 60 countries. They are recruited from their own nations and neighbourhoods and brought to camps in places like Afghanistan, where they are trained in the tactics of terror. They are sent back to their homes or sent to hide in countries around the world to plot evil and destruction.

The leadership of Al Qaeda has great influence in Afghanistan and supports the Taliban regime in controlling most of that country. In Afghanistan, we see Al Qaeda's vision for the world. Afghanistan's people have been brutalized—many are starving and many have fled. Women are not allowed to attend school. You can be jailed for owning a television. Religion can be practised only as their leaders dictate. A man can be jailed in Afghanistan if his beard is not long enough.

'In Afghanistan, we see Al Qaeda's vision for the world. Afghanistan's people have been brutalized—many are starving and many have fled. Women are not allowed to attend school. You can be jailed for owning a television. Religion can be practised only as their leaders dictate.'

The United States respects the people of Afghanistan—after all, we are currently its largest source of humanitarian aid—but we condemn the Taliban regime. It is not only repressing its own people, it is threatening people everywhere by sponsoring and sheltering and supplying terrorists.

By aiding and abetting murder, the Taliban regime is committing murder. And tonight, the United States of America makes the following demands on the Taliban: Deliver to United States authorities all the leaders of Al Qaeda who hide in your land. Release all foreign nationals, including American citizens, you have unjustly imprisoned. Protect foreign journalists, diplomats and aid workers in your country. Close immediately and permanently every terrorist training camp in Afghanistan, and hand over every terrorist, and every person in their support structure, to appropriate authorities. Give the United States full access to terrorist training camps, so we can make sure they are no longer operating. These demands are not open to negotiation or discussion. The Taliban must act, and act immediately. They will hand over the terrorists, or they will share in their fate.

'We are not deceived by their pretences to piety. We have seen their kind before. They are the heirs of all the murderous ideologies of the 20th century. By sacrificing human life to serve their radical visions—by abandoning every value except the will to power—they follow in the path of Fascism, and Nazism and totalitarianism.'

I also want to speak tonight directly to Muslims throughout the world. We respect your faith. It's practised freely by many millions of Americans, and by millions more in countries that America counts as friends. Its teachings are good and peaceful, and those who commit evil in the name of Allah blaspheme the name of Allah. The terrorists are traitors to their own faith, trying, in effect, to hijack Islam itself. The enemy of America is not our many Muslim friends; it is not our many Arab friends. Our enemy is a radical network of terrorists, and every government that supports them. Our war on terror begins with Al Qaeda, but it does not end there. It will not end until every terrorist group of global reach has been found, stopped and defeated.

Americans are asking, why do they hate us? They hate what we see right here in this chamber—a democratically elected government. Their leaders are self-appointed. They hate our freedoms—our freedom of religion, our freedom of speech, our freedom to vote and assemble and disagree with each other.

They want to overthrow existing governments in many Muslim countries, such as Egypt, Saudi Arabia, and Jordan. They want to drive Israel out of the Middle East. They want to drive Christians and Jews out of vast regions of Asia and Africa. These terrorists kill not merely to end lives, but to disrupt and end a way of life. With every atrocity, they hope that America grows fearful, retreating from the world and forsaking our friends. They stand against us, because we stand in their way.

We are not deceived by their pretences to piety. We have seen their kind before. They are the heirs of all the murderous ideologies of the 20th century. By sacrificing human life to serve their radical visions—by abandoning every value except the will to power—they follow in the path of Fascism, and Nazism, and totalitarianism. And they will follow that path all the way, to where it ends: in history's unmarked grave of discarded lies.

Americans are asking: How will we fight and win this war? We will direct every resource at our command—every means of diplomacy, every tool of intelligence, every instrument of law enforcement, every financial influence, and every necessary weapon of war—to the disruption and to the defeat of the global terror network.

This war will not be like the war against Iraq a decade ago, with a decisive liberation of territory and a swift conclusion. It will not look like the air war above Kosovo two years ago, where no ground troops were used and not a single American was lost in combat. Our response involves far more than instant retaliation and isolated strikes. Americans should not expect one battle, but a lengthy campaign, unlike any other we have ever seen. It may include dramatic strikes, visible on TV, and covert operations, secret even in success.

We will starve terrorists of funding, turn them one against another, drive them from place to place, until there is no refuge or no rest. And we will pursue nations that provide aid or safe haven to terrorism. Every nation, in every region, now has a decision to make. Either you are with us, or you are with the terrorists. From this day forward, any nation that continues to harbour or support terrorism will be regarded by the United States as a hostile regime.’

Despite the deployment of massive resources and claims to some success, the ‘War on Terror’ failed to apprehend the man responsible for the 9/11 attacks, Osama bin Laden, who remained at large and seemingly still outspoken when Bush left office in January 2009.

Queen Elizabeth II

'We Struggled To Find Ways of Expressing Our Horror'

Queen Elizabeth II's 2001 Christmas message broadcast, 25 December 2001.

Queen Elizabeth II in November 2001.

Elizabeth II, Queen of England (Elizabeth Alexandra Mary Windsor, 1926–) has reigned since 1953, during which time Britain emerged from post-war austerity and the loss of empire into a new era of prosperity. The severe downturn that began in 2008 notwithstanding, the reassertion of British influence and a new flowering of creativity in the arts and letters have constituted a kind of second Elizabethan era.

The elder daughter of George VI and Queen Elizabeth, Elizabeth was educated privately. In 1947 she married Philip Mountbatten, her fourth cousin, and they had four children.

While on a visit to Africa, she was informed of the death of her father, and was subsequently crowned in Westminster Abbey, London, in June 1953. She celebrated her Silver Jubilee in 1977, while 1992, a year of scandals within the family, she nominated as her *annus horribilis*.

In her annual Christmas message of 2001, Elizabeth II reflected on the terror attacks just three months earlier, stressing the importance of community as a means for dealing with the frightening new era the world faced.

‘The terrorist outrages in the United States last September brought home to us the pain and grief of ordinary people the world over who find themselves innocently caught up in such evil. During the following days we struggled to find ways of expressing our horror at what had happened.

As so often in our lives at times of tragedy—just as on occasions of celebration and thanksgiving—we look to the Church to bring us together as a nation or as a community in commemoration and tribute. It is to the Church that we turn to give meaning to these moments of intense human experience through prayer, symbol and ceremony.

In these circumstances so many of us, whatever our religion, need our faith more than ever to sustain and guide us. Every one of us needs to believe in the value of all that is good and honest; we need to let this belief drive and influence our actions.

All the major faiths tell us to give support and hope to others in distress. We in this country have tried to bring comfort to all those who were bereaved, or who suffered loss or injury in September's tragic events through those moving services at St Paul's and more recently at Westminster Abbey.

On these occasions and during the countless other acts of worship during this past year, we came together as a community—of relations, friends and neighbours—to draw strength in troubled times from those around us.

I believe that strong and open communities matter both in good times as well as bad. Certainly they provide a way of helping one another. I would like to pay tribute to so many of you

‘I believe that strong and open communities matter both in good times as well as bad. Certainly they provide a way of helping one another. I would like to pay tribute to so many of you who work selflessly for others in your neighbourhood needing care and support.’

who work selflessly for others in your neighbourhood needing care and support.

Communities also give us an important sense of belonging, which is a compelling need in all of us. We all enjoy moments of great happiness and suffer times of profound sadness; the happiness is heightened, the sadness softened when it is shared.

But there is more than that. A sense of belonging to a group, which has in common the same desire for a fair and ordered society, helps to overcome differences and misunderstanding by reducing prejudice, ignorance and fear. We all have something to learn from one another, whatever our faith—be it Christian or Jewish, Muslim, Buddhist, Hindu or Sikh—whatever our background, whether we be young or old, from town or countryside.

'A sense of belonging to a group, which has in common the same desire for a fair and ordered society, helps to overcome differences and misunderstanding by reducing prejudice, ignorance and fear.'

This is an important lesson for us all during this festive season. For Christmas marks a moment to pause, to reflect and believe in the possibilities of rebirth and renewal. Christ's birth in Bethlehem so long ago remains a powerful symbol of hope for a better future. After all the tribulations of this year, this is surely more relevant than ever.

As we come together amongst family and friends and look forward to the coming year, I hope that in the months to come we shall be able to find ways of strengthening our own communities as a sure support and comfort to us all—whatever may lie ahead.’

When her reign comes to an end she will be remembered as a steadfast monarch, measured, and known for the occasional wry witticism. Her eldest son Prince Charles remains her heir-apparent.

Kofi Annan

'Peace Has No Parade, No Pantheon of Victory'

**Accepting the Nobel Peace Prize,
Oslo, Norway, 10 December 2001.**

Kofi Annan at the headquarters of the United Nations in New York in December 2001.

Kofi Annan (1938–) served as secretary-general of the United Nations (UN) during some of the most testing times for the global institution.

Born in Ghana, he graduated in economics from Macalester College in the United States in 1961, and later gained a master's degree. He joined the UN in 1962, working for the World Health Organization (WHO) in Geneva, before moving to the UN Headquarters in New York, where he held a number of key posts.

He was secretary-general from 1996 to 2006, dealing with a plethora of weighty issues, including the breakaway Yugoslav republic of Kosovo, UN sanctions in Iraq and weapons inspections, and the ongoing Arab–Israeli crisis in the Middle East.

After the terrorist attacks of 9/11 against the United States, he worked through the UN General Assembly and the Security Council to combat terrorism. In the following speech, he reflects upon the nature of peace and tolerance, and on the UN's role to preserve peace in the new millennium.

'Ladies and Gentlemen, we have entered the third millennium through a gate of fire. If today, after the horror of 11 September, we see better, and we see further—we will realize that humanity is indivisible. New threats make no distinction between races, nations or regions. A new insecurity has entered every mind, regardless of wealth or status. A deeper awareness of the bonds that bind us all—in pain as in prosperity—has gripped young and old.

In the early beginnings of the 21st century—a century already violently disabused of any hopes that progress towards global peace and prosperity is inevitable—this new reality can no longer be ignored. It must be confronted.

The 20th century was perhaps the deadliest in human history, devastated by innumerable conflicts, untold suffering, and unimaginable crimes. Time after time, a group or a nation inflicted extreme violence on another, often driven by irrational hatred and suspicion, or unbounded arrogance and thirst for power and resources. In response to these cataclysms, the leaders of the world came together at mid-century to unite the nations as never before.

A forum was created—the United Nations—where all nations could join forces to affirm the dignity and worth of every person, and to secure peace and development for all peoples. Here states could unite to strengthen the rule of law, recognize and address the needs of the poor, restrain man's brutality and greed, conserve the resources and beauty of nature, sustain the equal rights of men and women, and provide for the safety of future generations.

We thus inherit from the 20th century the political, as well as the scientific and technological power, which—if only we have the will to use them—give us the chance to vanquish poverty, ignorance and disease.

In the 21st century I believe the mission of the United Nations will be defined by a new, more profound, awareness of the sanctity and dignity of every human life, regardless of race or religion. This will require us to look beyond the framework of states, and beneath the surface

'A genocide begins with the killing of one man—not for what he has done, but because of who he is. A campaign of "ethnic cleansing" begins with one neighbour turning on another. Poverty begins when even one child is denied his or her fundamental right to education.'

of nations or communities. We must focus, as never before, on improving the conditions of the individual men and women who give the state or nation its richness and character. We must begin with the young Afghan girl, recognizing that saving that one life is to save humanity itself.

Over the past five years, I have often recalled that the United Nations' Charter begins with the words: "We the peoples." What is not always recognized is that "we the peoples" are made up of individuals whose claims to the most fundamental rights have too often been sacrificed in the supposed interests of the state or the nation.

A genocide begins with the killing of one man—not for what he has done, but because of who he is. A campaign of "ethnic cleansing" begins with one neighbour turning on another. Poverty begins when even one child is denied his or her fundamental right to education. What begins with the failure to uphold the dignity of one life, all too often ends with a calamity for entire nations.

In this new century, we must start from the understanding that peace belongs not only to states or peoples, but to each and every member of those communities. The sovereignty of states must no longer be used as a shield for gross violations of human rights. Peace must be made real and tangible in the daily existence of every individual in need. Peace must be sought, above all, because it is the condition for every member of the human family to live a life of dignity and security.

The rights of the individual are of no less importance to immigrants and minorities in Europe and the Americas than to women in Afghanistan or children in Africa. They are as fundamental to the poor as to the rich; they are as necessary to the security of the developed world as to that of the developing world.

From this vision of the role of the United Nations in the next century flow three key priorities for the future: eradicating poverty, preventing conflict, and promoting democracy. Only in a world that is rid of poverty can all men and women make the most of their abilities. Only where individual rights are respected can differences be channelled politically and resolved peacefully. Only in a democratic environment, based on respect for diversity and dialogue, can individual self-expression and self-government be secured, and freedom of association be upheld.

Throughout my term as secretary-general, I have sought to place human beings at the centre of everything we do—from conflict prevention to development to human rights. Securing real and lasting improvement in the lives of individual men and women is the measure of all we do at the United Nations.

It is in this spirit that I humbly accept the Centennial Nobel Peace Prize. Forty years ago today, the Prize for 1961 was awarded for the first time to a secretary-general of the United Nations—posthumously, because Dag Hammarskjöld had already given his life for peace in Central Africa. And on the same day, the Prize for 1960 was awarded for the first time to an

African—Albert Luthuli, one of the earliest leaders of the struggle against apartheid in South Africa. For me, as a young African beginning his career in the United Nations a few months later, those two men set a standard that I have sought to follow throughout my working life.

This award belongs not just to me. I do not stand here alone. On behalf of all my colleagues in every part of the United Nations, in every corner of the globe, who have devoted their lives—and in many instances risked or given their lives in the cause of peace—I thank the Members of the Nobel Committee for this high honour. My own path to service at the United Nations was made possible by the sacrifice and commitment of my family and many friends from all continents—some of whom have passed away—who taught me and guided me. To them, I offer my most profound gratitude.

In a world filled with weapons of war and all too often words of war, the Nobel Committee has become a vital agent for peace. Sadly, a prize for peace is a rarity in this world. Most nations have monuments or memorials to war, bronze salutations to heroic battles, archways of triumph. But peace has no parade, no pantheon of victory.

What it does have is the Nobel Prize—a statement of hope and courage with unique resonance and authority. Only by understanding and addressing the needs of individuals for peace, for dignity, and for security can we at the United Nations hope to live up to the honour conferred today, and fulfil the vision of our founders. This is the broad mission of peace that United Nations staff members carry out every day in every part of the world...

In every great faith and tradition one can find the values of tolerance and mutual understanding. The Qur'an, for example, tells us that "We created you from a single pair of male and female and made you into nations and tribes, that you may know each other." Confucius urged his followers: "when the good way prevails in the state, speak boldly and act boldly. When the state has lost the way, act boldly and speak softly." In the Jewish tradition, the injunction to "love thy neighbour as thyself," is considered to be the very essence of the Torah.

This thought is reflected in the Christian Gospel, which also teaches us to love our enemies and pray for those who wish to persecute us. Hindus are taught that "truth is one, the sages give it various names." And in the Buddhist tradition, individuals are urged to act with compassion in every facet of life.

Each of us has the right to take pride in our particular faith or heritage. But the notion that what is ours is necessarily in conflict with what is theirs is both false and dangerous. It has resulted in endless enmity and conflict, leading men to commit the greatest of crimes in the name of a higher power.

It need not be so. People of different religions and cultures live side by side in almost every part of the world, and most of us have overlapping identities which unite us with very different groups. We can love what we are, without hating what—and

'In a world filled with weapons of war and all too often words of war, the Nobel Committee has become a vital agent for peace. Sadly, a prize for peace is a rarity in this world. Most nations have monuments or memorials to war, bronze salutations to heroic battles, archways of triumph. But peace has no parade, no pantheon of victory.'

who—we are not. We can thrive in our own tradition, even as we learn from others, and come to respect their teachings. This will not be possible, however, without freedom of religion, of expression, of assembly, and basic equality under the law. Indeed, the lesson of the past century has been that where the dignity of the individual has been trampled or threatened—where citizens have not enjoyed the basic right to choose their government, or the right to change it regularly—conflict has too often followed, with innocent civilians paying the price, in lives cut short and communities destroyed.

The obstacles to democracy have little to do with culture or religion, and much more to do with the desire of those in power to maintain their position at any cost. This is neither a new phenomenon nor one confined to any particular part of the world. People of all cultures value their freedom of choice, and feel the need to have a say in decisions affecting their lives.

The United Nations, whose membership comprises almost all the states in the world, is founded on the principle of the equal worth of every human being. It is the nearest thing we have to a representative institution that can address the interests of all states, and all peoples. Through this universal, indispensable instrument of human progress, states can serve the interests of their citizens by recognizing common interests and pursuing them in unity. No doubt, that is why the Nobel Committee says that it "wishes, in its centenary year, to proclaim that the only negotiable route to global peace and co-operation goes by way of the United Nations". ’

Yoko Ono

'Don't Fight for Peace, Stand for Peace'

**Speech at Oxford University,
16 October 2002.**

Yoko Ono before a charity concert to commemorate
her late husband, John Lennon, in Saitama, suburban Tokyo, in December 2002.

Yoko Ono (1933–) was born into an aristocratic Tokyo family. They moved to the United States when she was in her teens, and she studied at Sarah Lawrence College before moving to downtown Manhattan, where she exhibited her conceptual art works.

She met musician John Lennon, one of the Beatles, in 1967, and their affair ended both their marriages. Their week-long honeymoon 'Bed-In for Peace' at the Amsterdam Hilton in 1969 attracted global media attention.

After the break-up of the Beatles—which she was widely accused of precipitating—the couple devoted themselves to the cause of world peace, writing message songs like 'Give Peace a Chance'. The couple moved to the United States, where Lennon died in 1980, gunned down outside their New York apartment building by a troubled misfit. Yoko Ono later returned to the recording studio, making a series of albums in the 1980s and 1990s, and to creating art.

The following is a speech she made at Oxford University as the drums of war had begun to beat for a conflict with Iraq, and around the world movements for peace sprang up to try to prevent the coming conflict.

'Only a few weeks ago, on October 5th, there was a large Peace Rally in Central Park, and over 10,000 people came together to protest the US policy and to say "Not In My Name". This was the first Peace Rally in NY against the impending war. A surprisingly large number of people gathered that day for the rally, despite the intense political climate in the States at this time.

It delights me, and concerns me, at the same time. It is delightful that so many Americans are thinking Peace. It concerns me that this may bring another destruction on some remote island, to make a sacrificial lamb out of innocent people in an effort to urge us to go to war. That was done in the beginning of the Second World War. There's no reason to think that history will not repeat itself.

You may know that Al Gore came out with strong anti-Iraq War statements, and Ted Kennedy immediately expressed his support. The press, however, tried to discredit their statements as being made by professional politicians. Nevertheless, the effect of their statements is creating strong ripples. I hope you will pick up Al Gore's recent interviews and Op-Ed statement on the internet. He is going beyond the call of duty, possibly jeopardizing his chances for the next election, if anything.

The latest polls in the States show that although 57 per cent of the Americans support invasion of Iraq, if the UN and the Congress do not authorize the action, the number of Americans who would support the invasion on that basis drops to 37 per cent. This shows that the United Nations still carries weight in the American Mind, and you, through writing to the United Nations to support their position, can too.

Write to your statesmen, write to any institution which exerts power in the decision-making of war or peace. Send letters to the editors of magazines and newspapers. Write to fashion designers, for instance, and ask them to stamp Peace on his/her advertisements. Don't fight for

Peace, stand for Peace. Write, voice and appeal. With your appeal, instil the word Peace in the minds of every being in our society.

A week ago, on John Lennon's birthday, October 9th, I inaugurated A LennonOno Grant For Peace at the United Nations. The idea of the grant came to me in 1999 when I did two art shows, one in Jerusalem, and the other in Um El Fachem, at the same time. The grant focuses on the issues where healing is needed. The first recipients were one Israeli artist and one Palestinian artist selected by curators of each region. The two artists were chosen to celebrate the fact that they have continued to be inspirational and creative in spite of the intense political climate we all live in. The artists shook hands in front of UN ambassadors, government officials, and fellow artists. The Secretary-General, Kofi Annan, congratulated me and the artists and said that the prize showed the fact that "peace is everybody's business not just an issue for governments".

The two artists, Zvi Goldstein and Khalil Rabah, the curators and the organizers of the grant, me and my friends in NY, went to a SoHo restaurant later for drinks and meal, and hugged and celebrated each other. It was an evening of meeting of the minds, of friends, so much so, that for a moment I forgot the fact that the friends from the Middle East will be going back to the war zone the next morning. But once I thought of it, then I wasn't entirely sure whether they were returning to the war zone, or leaving us in one. Hey, stay well. Let's all stay well and survive. Promise to meet again soon. Okay?

You may say my attempt was naive that it would not even move a mouse, let alone a mountain. Well, this was my humble attempt to plant a seed. A tree can be cut down. But a seed is not so easy to destroy. It is a psychotic act to go around digging for seeds, though the most recent suggestion of 'a pre-emptive strike' sounds very much like one. Let's all of us plant seeds, give water, and Imagine all the people living life in Peace. Remember, our hearts are one. Even when we are at war with each other, our hearts are always beating in unison.

'Well, this was my humble attempt to plant a seed. A tree can be cut down. But a seed is not so easy to destroy. It is a psychotic act to go around digging for seeds, though the most recent suggestion of 'a pre-emptive strike' sounds very much like one. Let's all of us plant seeds, give water, and Imagine all the people living life in Peace.'

During World War II, Saint Petersburg was surrounded by the German Army and cut off from the other part of Russia for months. Finally, there was no food. No heat. Just the sound of the German bombings. But the people of Saint Petersburg did not surrender. They were determined not to give up their city. The radio DJ tried to cheer people up by playing music, talking and cracking jokes. Finally, he became lethargic as well. Nevertheless, he felt he could still do something to help people survive. He let a metronome tick live on the radio. People lay down and just listened and held on to that sound of the metronome ticking through day and night. That's how Saint Petersburg managed not to fall.

During the same war but in Japan, my brother and I were stranded at a farm in the country we had been evacuated to. We were starving. One day, I saw my brother looking extremely tired and sad. It pained me to see him like that. Usually, he was an active, jolly little boy who laughed at the drop of a hat. But now, he looked as helpless and confused as the rest of us. Suddenly, a good idea came to me. I explained to my brother that we were going to think of a dream menu. "Think of the dinner you want to eat." He started slowly. "I want ice cream." "But that's a dessert. We should start with soup, of course." We created an elaborate meal in the air. My brother's face started to light up. Finally, he gave me the sweet chuckle I loved so much.

John was a war child and so was I. He was born during the bombing of Liverpool. While I was in a bomb shelter in Tokyo. In a war, which is another name for organized killing, civilians are the ones who suffer the most.

Don't be misled by euphemistic expressions such as "the attack was made with surgical precision." In the wars of the 20th century approximately 62 million civilians have perished, while nearly 43 million military personnel were killed. Soldiers came second on the death list. But then one must remember the soldiers' families. How they cope with the change in their lives as a result of the loss, emotionally, physically, and financially.

We must reclaim what we are. Once we were told that we were created in the image of God. But now, we discovered that we can clone ourselves, in OUR image, by the millions, from one cell in our hair. With that kind of power, we can do almost anything. The war profiteers are strong because we allow them to confuse us and cause suspicion of each other. Divide and conquer. Their policy of deception, manipulation and intimidation is working. Find peace in your heart and it will spread over the world. The effect of it is strong and immediate. Keep your quiet centre, and stand for peace, instead of fighting for peace. We can do it.

Let's visualize the boat all of us are on. If this sinks like the Titanic, or if we would get to the shore safely all depends on what we will do. Are we to fight the people who stand for war? Fight them and the boat will sink. Our sanity and peace is what is needed to keep the boat afloat.

In early 1981, the coroner's office gave me back John's belongings in a plain brown paper bag. Aside of being a man of peace, John was "The King of the World"... John, who had everything any man could ever want... came back to me in a brown paper bag in the end. I want you to know that. AND we were not alone. The number of people who have died by gunshot alone since John's death is10 times larger than the total number of American soldiers lost in the Vietnam War. We are indeed living in a war zone called the world. I want all of us to realize that, and so, hopefully, the healing process can begin. John would have wanted to say this to you, too. ’

Benazir Bhutto

'The Wheel of History Turns'

Hindustan Times Peace Seminar, New Delhi,
India, 13 December 2003.

Benazir Bhutto in December 2003.

The tragic murder of former Pakistan prime minister Benazir Bhutto (1953–2007) in December 2007 ended the life of one of the most courageous politicians of recent history. Mrs Bhutto had returned to Pakistan two months before from self-imposed exile in Britain, and was campaigning for the national elections which ultimately broke the grip on power of General Perves Musharraf (1953–), who had seized power in a coup d'état in 1999.

Benazir Bhutto became the first female prime minister of an Islamic country, and wrestled with corruption and authoritarianism in Pakistan, only to see her country slide back into dictatorship. Born into Pakistan's elite, she experienced more than her share of troubles during her lifetime, with arrest, detention and dismissal from office twice. Her father, Zulfikar Ali Bhutto (1928–79), who served as both president and prime minister of Pakistan in the 1970s, was executed by military dictator Mohammad Zia ul-Haq (1924–88) in 1979.

Educated abroad at Harvard University and Oxford University, Bhutto returned to her homeland in the 1980s, and led her father's Pakistan People's Party (PPP) back to power in 1988. She pursued a social welfare agenda, before being dismissed by the president in 1990. Elected to power again in 1993, she was again dismissed in 1996.

After the coup that brought General Musharraf to power in 1997, Bhutto's husband was imprisoned and she was forced to take her two children into exile in the United Kingdom, from where she worked for the restoration of democracy in Pakistan. After her return to Pakistan in October 2007, there were two attempts on her life in the space of just weeks, the second one sadly successful.

In this important and candid speech, delivered in late 2003, Bhutto comments on the war in Iraq, the continuing flashpoint of Kashmir, and how South Asia has become 'the most dangerous place on earth'.

'I thought long and hard about whether to accept the gracious invitation to speak at this forum today. The politics of a former Prime Minister of Pakistan—and the leader of Pakistan's most popular party—travelling to India to discuss bilateral relations between our two nations were truly complex.

In the end I decided to attend. I did this because the threat of a conflict in South Asia ending up in the first nuclear war since Hiroshima is real. Such a conflict could annihilate hundreds of millions without distinguishing whether they were Pakistanis or Indians or Kashmiris. The determination to make a contribution to avoid this nuclear nightmare far outweighed other arguments that could have crossed my mind.

We meet today with the world a different and more dangerous place than we expected when the Berlin Wall fell. The end of the Cold War promised to herald an era of global peace. The principles of Freedom and Free Markets promised to shake up sluggish economies. The prospect of a Peace Dividend was before us.

It was not to be. The world is at war, not peace. The US-led coalition occupies a major Islamic nation, suffering daily attacks and many casualties. No one knows whether Iraq will survive the present phase. Both India and Pakistan are under pressure to send troops to Iraq. And both are considering that option separately. How much better it would be if countries in this South Asian region could consult each other on such important measures before taking a final decision.

And as I talk to you, the resurgent Taliban are mounting fresh attacks against the Karzai government in Afghanistan. They are mounting attacks against the Coalition forces and the NGOs working there. In Jammu and Kashmir, despite the present welcome ceasefire at the Line of Control, the intensity of violence has yet to decrease.

We must ask ourselves: are we to condemn our future generations to a world of violence, of conflict, of bloodshed, of war, blood and destruction.

This conference, organized to explore peace initiatives, is an important step in building a different kind of world. A world of peace and harmony that protects the life, liberty and livelihood of every individual irrespective of their race, religion, gender or political affiliation.

This is an important responsibility on the shoulders of the leadership of South Asia. This responsibility is all the more grave as the world is involved in the war against terrorism.

Few nations or regions have been spared. Christian churches and Muslim masjids were targets of suicide bombers in Pakistan. Your own Parliament became a bloody target. Great Britain is a target. Saudi Arabia is a target. Turkey is a target. Indonesia is a target. Australia is a target. There are seemingly constant acts of terrorism in the Middle East, every day, every week. The world is threatened with carnage in many corners.

'The threat of a conflict in South Asia ending up in the first nuclear war since Hiroshima is real. Such a conflict could annihilate hundreds of millions without distinguishing whether they were Pakistanis or Indians or Kashmiris. The determination to make a contribution to avoid this nuclear nightmare far outweighed other arguments.'

We owe it to ourselves and to our people, to all of South Asia, to make every effort, to strive, to seek, to pursue peaceful means for the resolution of outstanding disputes, for confidence building and for reduction of tension in our region…

It is tragic that this subcontinent, so full of history, has remained for so long the most likely site for a nuclear exchange on our planet. South Asia must begin its search for a peace dividend. We can think of the peace dividend as the sum of resources no longer devoted to the military and available for the social sector. The peace dividend can be the traditional guns for butter trade-off. In the longer term, a peace dividend is defined by investment. We must invest in technology. We must invest in infrastructure. Above all we must invest in human capital—specifically on education and health.

The 1990s began with falling defence budgets in the United States. But the United States quickly assumed its role as the world's only superpower. Now the US spends more on defence than during the Cold War.

Another test of the peace dividend soon emerged following the Declaration signed by Israeli Prime Minister Rabin and Palestinian President Arafat on the White House lawn in September 1993. Foreign investment into Israel and Palestine soared. A Palestinian Development Bank was established funded by the IMF [International Monetary Fund], the United States and the EU [European Union]. All this finished with the Intifida.

We know that a South Asian peace dividend could dramatically increase the quality of life of our huge populations. Scholars expect peace to break down poverty. A Harvard Professor, David Landes, writing in *The Wealth and Poverty of Nations* said, "poverty is inextricably linked to armed conflict." Poverty creates an atmosphere that encourages war for the purpose of national identification, national mobilization, and as a distraction from social inequality and hopelessness...

For now, I am an exile. I am banned from my country. I am banned from contesting for premiership of my country, banned from contesting even as a backbencher, banned from seeing my husband who is in the eighth year of his imprisonment, banned from entering my ancestral homes, banned from praying at the graves of my Martyred Father and brothers.

I do not despair. In life, an individual makes choices.

I made mine on the last day of my father's life in a prison that our colonial masters built in the city of Rawalpindi. That was the choice to fight for peace and democracy, to fight for human dignity that must come when people can combat hunger, poverty and illiteracy.

I know that realities change. That a person can go from Prime Minister to prisoner and from prisoner to Prime Minister. I have seen power from the time that I was a child. I must tell you that the sense of satisfaction and joy that I felt never came from the chandeliered halls or the turbaned staff, or the pomp and power of governing a state.

It came from small acts. It came from giving a child polio drops knowing those small drops would change its life forever. It came from inaugurating a school, providing electricity and water to places that had none. It came from seeing the smile on the face of a boy or girl who got a job.

The wheel of history turns. There was a time when Prime Minister Gujral could not visit Jhelum, the city he was born in because our two countries were at cross purposes. Now he, though an Indian, can visit Jhelum and I, though a Pakistani, cannot visit my Larkana.

The wheel of history turns. For individuals and nations.

And as the wheel of history turns for the children of Partition, I hope we bequeath them a better future than our bitter past.

Ladies and Gentlemen, I conclude with a quote from Alexander Pope, which I used during my last visit to New Delhi two years back. He said: "What war could ravish, Commerce could bestow, And he returned a friend, Who was a foe". Thank you. ’

It is a final bitter irony of the Bhutto family that Benazir Bhutto was assassinated in the same city, Rawalpindi, where her father was hanged by his political foes 28 years before.

General Musharraf was forced from power after the assassination of Mrs Bhutto, and her widower Asif Ali Zardari (1955–) became the new president of Pakistan in 2008.

Nelson Mandela

'Make Poverty History'

Speech at a rally in Trafalgar Square,
London, 3 February 2005, before a G7 leaders' meeting.

Nelson Mandela speaks in Mpumalanga, South Africa, in November 1993.

A man of unquestionable integrity, courage and vision, Nelson Mandela (1918–) has long been the international community's leading elder statesman.

Born into one of South Africa's ruling tribal families, he studied law and practised in Johannesburg, where he founded one of the first black law firms with Oliver Tambo (1917–93); president of the African National Congress (ANC) from 1969). He joined the black rights organization the ANC in 1944, and began actively opposing the discriminatory apartheid policy of the ruling National Party. Under this system, the right to vote was confined to whites and the races were kept separate. He was accused of treason, standing trial between 1956 and 1961, charges of which he was subsequently acquitted.

Following the Sharpeville massacre in 1960 and the banning of the ANC, Mandela was jailed in 1962 and sent to Robben Island Prison, off Cape Town (where he remained until 1982 before moving to Pollsmoor Prison). In 1964, he was given a life sentence on a charge of plotting the overthrow of the government. During the long years of his incarceration, however, his commitment to ending apartheid never wavered and his fame spread throughout the world as he became an inspirational figure of resistance to tyranny.

State-sponsored violence saw South Africa increasingly isolated by the international community that imposed a series of economic, cultural and sporting sanctions on the country. After F.W. de Klerk's administration, Mandela's eventual release became an international cause célèbre. When he walked to freedom from prison on 11 February 1990, the peaceful end of apartheid was imminent. Mandela replaced Tambo as president of the ANC, after the latter became ill, and de Klerk and Mandela worked together to bring about the peaceful transition of their country from apartheid to democracy, something for which they were both awarded the Nobel Prize. Mandela was subsequently elected president of South Africa in 1994, serving in that office until his retirement in 1999. A celebrated orator, he toured the world on speaking engagements, a sought-after mentor in troubled times.

Despite having retired from public life, in early 2005 Mandela spoke at a rally of thousands against world poverty in London's Trafalgar Square.

'I am privileged to be here today at the invitation of the campaign to Make Poverty History. As you know, I recently formally announced my retirement from public life and should really not be here. However, as long as poverty, injustice and gross inequality persist in our world, none of us can truly rest. Moreover, the Global Campaign for Action Against Poverty represents such a noble cause that we could not decline the invitation.

Massive poverty and obscene inequality are such terrible scourges of our times—times in which the world boasts breathtaking advances in science, technology, industry and wealth accumulation—that they have to rank alongside slavery and apartheid as social evils. The Global Campaign for Action Against Poverty can take its place as a public movement alongside the movement to abolish slavery and the international solidarity against apartheid.

And I can never thank the people of Britain enough for their support through those days of the struggle against apartheid. Many stood in solidarity with us, just a few yards from this spot. Through your will and passion, you assisted in consigning that evil system forever to history.

But in this new century, millions of people in the world's poorest countries remain imprisoned, enslaved, and in chains. They are trapped in the prison of poverty. It is time to set them free. Like slavery and apartheid, poverty is not natural. It is man-made and it can be overcome and eradicated by the actions of human beings.

And overcoming poverty is not a gesture of charity. It is an act of justice. It is the protection of a fundamental human right, the right to dignity and a decent life. While poverty persists, there is no true freedom. The steps that are needed from the developed nations are clear.

The first is ensuring trade justice. I have said before that trade justice is a truly meaningful way for the developed countries to show commitment to bringing about an end to global poverty. The second is an end to the debt crisis for the poorest countries. The third is to deliver much more aid and make sure it is of the highest quality.

In 2005, there is a unique opportunity for making an impact. In September, world leaders will gather in New York to measure progress since they made the Millennium Declaration in the year 2000. That declaration promised to halve extreme poverty. But at the moment, the promise is falling tragically behind. Those leaders must now honour their promises to the world's poorest citizens.

Tomorrow, here in London, the G7 finance ministers can make a significant beginning. I am happy to have been invited to meet with them. The G8 leaders, when they meet in Scotland in July, have already promised to focus on the issue of poverty, especially in Africa.

'Millions of people in the world's poorest countries remain imprisoned, enslaved, and in chains. They are trapped in the prison of poverty. It is time to set them free. Like slavery and apartheid, poverty is not natural. It is man-made and it can be overcome and eradicated by the actions of human beings.'

I say to all those leaders: do not look the other way; do not hesitate. Recognize that the world is hungry for action, not words. Act with courage and vision.

I am proud to wear the symbol of this global call to action in 2005. This white band is from my country. In a moment, I want to give this band to you—young people of Britain—and ask you to take it forward along with millions of others to the G8 summit in July. I entrust it to you. I will be watching with anticipation.

We thank you for coming here today. Sometimes it falls upon a generation to be great. You can be that great generation. Let your greatness blossom. Of course the task will not be easy. But not to do this would be a crime against humanity, against which I ask all humanity now to rise up.

Make Poverty History in 2005. Make History in 2005. Then we can all stand with our heads held high.'

Muhammad Yunus

'Unleash Their Energy and Creativity'

Receiving the Nobel Peace Prize
Oslo, Norway, 10 December 2006.

2006 Peace Nobel Prize winner, Bangladeshi Muhammad Yunus in May 2007.

The Bangladeshi university professor and economist known as the 'Banker to the Poor' Muhammad Yunus (1940–) was born in Chittagong and studied economics at Dhaka University. He gained a Fulbright scholarship to study at Vanderbilt University in the United States, from where he gained his PhD before returning to Bangladesh to head the Economics department at Chittagong University.

Inspired by the belief that credit is a fundamental human right, he established the Grameen Bank in Bangladesh in 1983, to help the poor escape from poverty by providing loans on terms suitable to them. He also taught them about finance and economics. The Grameen Bank's 'micro-lending' practices have spread around the world to more than 100 countries, and it is lauded as having made a major contribution to combating poverty worldwide.

In Yunus's 2006 Nobel lecture, he recounts how he came to set up the Grameen Bank, and how he sees ending poverty as a crucial step towards achieving global peace. Yunus notes repayments to Grameen from some of the poorest people on earth run at 99 per cent.

The speech also makes interesting reading in the light of the US sub-prime crisis and the unethical lending practices of US banks, which helped precipitate the global economic crisis that began in 2008.

'Since the Nobel Peace Prize was announced, I have received endless messages from around the world, but what moves me most are the calls I get almost daily, from the borrowers of Grameen Bank in remote Bangladeshi villages, who just want to say how proud they are to have received this recognition.

Nine elected representatives of the 7 million borrowers-cum-owners of Grameen Bank have accompanied me all the way to Oslo to receive the prize. I express thanks on their behalf to the Norwegian Nobel Committee for choosing Grameen Bank for this year's Nobel Peace Prize. By giving their institution the most prestigious prize in the world, you give them unparalleled honour. Thanks to your prize, nine proud women from the villages of Bangladesh are at the ceremony today as Nobel laureates, giving an altogether new meaning to the Nobel Peace Prize...

This year's prize gives highest honour and dignity to the hundreds of millions of women all around the world who struggle every day to make a living and bring hope for a better life for their children. This is a historic moment for them. By giving us this prize, the Norwegian Nobel Committee has given important support to the proposition that peace is inextricably linked to poverty. Poverty is a threat to peace.

The world's income distribution gives a very telling story. Ninety-four per cent of the world income goes to 40 per cent of the population while 60 per cent of people live on only 6 per cent of world income. Half of the world population lives on two dollars a day. Over 1 billion people live on less than a dollar a day. This is no formula for peace.

The new millennium began with a great global dream. World leaders gathered at the United Nations in 2000 and adopted, among others, a historic goal to reduce poverty by half by 2015. Never in human history had such a bold goal been adopted by the entire world in one voice, one that specified time and size.

But then came September 11 and the Iraq war, and suddenly the world became derailed from the pursuit of this dream, with the attention of world leaders shifting from the war on poverty to the war on terrorism. Till now over $530 billion has been spent on the war in Iraq by the USA alone.

I believe terrorism cannot be won over by military action. Terrorism must be condemned in the strongest language. We must stand solidly against it, and find all the means to end it. We must address the root causes of terrorism to end it for all time to come...

Poverty is the absence of all human rights. The frustrations, hostility and anger generated by abject poverty cannot sustain peace in any society. For building stable peace we must find ways to provide opportunities for people to live decent lives. The creation of opportunities for the majority of people, the poor, is at the heart of the work that we have dedicated ourselves to during the past 30 years.

I became involved in the poverty issue not as a policymaker or a researcher. I became involved because poverty was all around me, and I could not turn away from it. In 1974, I found it difficult to teach elegant theories of economics in the university classroom, in the backdrop of a terrible famine in Bangladesh. Suddenly, I felt the emptiness of those theories in the face of crushing hunger and poverty. I wanted to do something immediate to help people around me, even if it was just one human being, to get through another day with a little more ease.

'The world's income distribution gives a very telling story. Ninety-four per cent of the world income goes to 40 per cent of the population while 60 per cent of people live on only 6 per cent of world income. Half of the world population lives on two dollars a day. Over 1 billion people live on less than a dollar a day. This is no formula for peace.'

That brought me face to face with poor people's struggle to find the tiniest amounts of money to support their efforts to eke out a living. I was shocked to discover a woman in the village, borrowing less than a dollar from the money-lender, on the condition that he would have the exclusive right to buy all she produces at the price he decides. This, to me, was a way of recruiting slave labor.

I decided to make a list of the victims of this money-lending "business" in the village next door to our campus.

When my list was done, it had the names of 42 victims who borrowed a total amount of US $27. I offered US $27 from my own pocket to get these victims out of the clutches of those money-lenders. The excitement that was created among the people by this small action got me further involved in it. If I could make so many people so happy with such a tiny amount of money, why not do more of it?

That is what I have been trying to do ever since. The first thing I did was to try to persuade the bank located in the campus to lend money to the poor. But that did not work. The bank said that the poor were not creditworthy. After all my efforts, over several months, failed I offered to become a guarantor for the loans to the poor. I was stunned by the result. The poor paid back their loans, on time, every time!

But still I kept confronting difficulties in expanding the program through the existing banks. That was when I decided to create a separate bank for the poor, and in 1983, I finally succeeded in doing that. I named it Grameen Bank or Village bank.

Today, Grameen Bank gives loans to nearly 7 million poor people, 97 per cent of whom are women, in 73,000 villages in Bangladesh. Grameen Bank gives collateral-free income generating housing, student and micro-enterprise loans to the poor families and offers a host of attractive savings, pension funds and insurance products for its members.

'Since it introduced them in 1984, housing loans have been used to construct 640,000 houses. The legal ownership of these houses belongs to the women themselves. We focused on women because we found giving loans to women always brought more benefits to the family.'

Since it introduced them in 1984, housing loans have been used to construct 640,000 houses. The legal ownership of these houses belongs to the women themselves. We focused on women because we found giving loans to women always brought more benefits to the family.

In a cumulative way the bank has given out loans totalling about US $6 billion. The repayment rate is 99 per cent. Grameen Bank routinely makes profit. Financially, it is self-reliant and has not taken donor money since 1995. Deposits and own resources of Grameen Bank today amount to 143 per cent of all outstanding loans. According to Grameen Bank's internal survey, 58 per cent of our borrowers have crossed the poverty line.

Grameen Bank was born as a tiny home-grown project run with the help of several of my students, all local girls and boys. Three of these students are still with me in Grameen Bank, after all these years, as its topmost executives. They are here today to receive this honour you give us. This idea, which began in Jobra, a small village in Bangladesh, has spread around the world and there are now Grameen type programs in almost every country...

Information and communication technology (ICT) is quickly changing the world, creating distanceless, borderless world of instantaneous communications. Increasingly, it is becoming less and less costly. I saw an opportunity for the poor people to change their lives if this technology could be brought to them to meet their needs.

As a first step to bring ICT to the poor we created a mobile phone company, Grameen Phone. We gave loans from Grameen Bank to the poor women to buy mobile phones to sell phone services in the villages. We saw the synergy between microcredit and ICT.

The phone business was a success and became a coveted enterprise for Grameen borrowers. Telephone-ladies quickly learned and innovated the ropes of the telephone business, and it has become the quickest way to get out of poverty and to earn social respectability. Today there are nearly 300,000 telephone ladies providing telephone service in all the villages of Bangladesh. Grameen Phone has more than 10 million subscribers, and is the largest mobile phone company in the country....

I support globalization and believe it can bring more benefits to the poor than its alternative. But it must be the right kind of globalization. To me, globalization is like a hundred-lane highway criss-crossing the world. If it is a free-for-all highway, its lanes will be taken over by the giant trucks from powerful economies. Bangladeshi rickshaws will be thrown off the highway. In order to have a win-win globalization we must have traffic rules, traffic police, and traffic authority for this global highway. Rule of "strongest takes it all" must be replaced by rules that ensure that the poorest have a place and piece of the action, without being elbowed out by the strong. Globalization must not become financial imperialism.

Powerful multinational social businesses can be created to retain the benefit of globalization for the poor people and poor countries. Social businesses will either bring ownership to the poor people, or keep the profit within the poor countries, since taking dividends will not be their objective. Direct foreign investment by foreign social businesses will be exciting news for recipient countries. Building strong economies in the poor countries by protecting their national interest from plundering companies will be a major area of interest for the social businesses.

Grameen has given me an unshakeable faith in the creativity of human beings. This has led me to believe that human beings are not born to suffer the misery of hunger and poverty.

To me poor people are like bonsai trees. When you plant the best seed of the tallest tree in a flowerpot, you get a replica of the tallest tree, only inches tall. There is nothing wrong with the seed you planted, only the soil-base that is too inadequate. Poor people are bonsai people. There is nothing wrong in their seeds. Simply, society never gave them the base to grow on. All it needs to get the poor people out of poverty is for us to create an enabling environment for them. Once the poor can unleash their energy and creativity, poverty will disappear very quickly. Let us join hands to give every human being a fair chance to unleash their energy and creativity. ’

The Dalai Lama

'I Am Seeking a Meaningful Autonomy'

**Receiving the US Congressional Gold Medal,
Washington, DC, 18 October 2007.**

Tibetan spiritual leader and Nobel laureate the Dalai Lama in New Delhi, November 2007.

Tibetan spiritual and temporal leader, the 14th Dalai Lama, Tenzin Gyatso, was born in 1935. The child known as Lhamo Dhondup was part of a peasant family living in a small village in northeastern Tibet (today Tsinghai province, China). Recognized as a young boy as the reincarnation of the 13th Dalai Lama, he was taken to Lhasa, where he was invested in 1940 and educated, eventually gaining a doctorate in Buddhist Philosophy.

He assumed full political power over Tibet while still in his teens, in 1950, following China's invasion of his country. He engaged in negotiations with the latter power, but to no avail. The brutal Chinese suppression of a Tibetan uprising in 1959 forced him to seek refuge in northern India, where he set up his capital in exile at Dharamsala in the Himalayan foothills.

Despite repeated UN resolutions mandating that the Chinese withdraw from Tibet, and approaches from the Dalai Lama to negotiate and reach an accommodation, the Chinese continue to occupy Tibet. In an era often marked by conflict, terror and misunderstanding, the Dalai Lama has become increasingly valued as an articulate advocate for peaceful change.

Renowned across the world for his compassion, intelligence, candour and wit and his unwavering commitment to his cause, he continues to gather popular support for the Tibetan cause.

Among many other honours he has been awarded, he received the Nobel Peace Prize in 1989 and the US Congressional Gold Medal in 2007, at which ceremony he made the following speech.

‘Today we watch China as it rapidly moves forward. Economic liberalization has led to wealth, modernization and great power. I believe that today's economic success of both India and China, the two most populated nations with long history of rich culture, is most deserving. With their newfound status, both of these two countries are poised to play an important leading role on the world stage. In order to fulfil this role, I believe it is vital for China to have transparency, rule of law and freedom of information.

Much of the world is waiting to see how China's concepts of harmonious society and peaceful rise would unfold. Today's China, being a state of many nationalities, a key factor here would be how it ensures the harmony and unity of these various peoples. For this, the equality and the rights of its nationalities to maintain their distinct identities are crucial.

With respect to my own homeland Tibet, today many people, both from inside and outside, feel deeply concerned about the consequences of the rapid change taking place. Every year, the Chinese population inside Tibet is increasing at an alarming rate. And, if we are to judge by the example of the population of Lhasa, there is a real danger that the Tibetans will be reduced to an insignificant minority in their own homeland. This rapid increase in population combined also posing serious threat to Tibet's fragile environment. Being the source of many of Asia's great rivers, any substantial disturbance in Tibet's ecology will impact the lives of hundreds of millions. Furthermore, being situated between India and China, the peaceful resolution of the Tibet problem also has important implications for lasting peace and friendly relations between these two great neighbours.

On the future of Tibet, let me take this opportunity to restate categorically that I am not seeking independence. I am seeking a meaningful autonomy for the Tibetan people within the People's Republic of China. If the real concern of the Chinese leadership is the unity and stability of PRC, I have fully addressed their concerns. I have chosen to adopt this position because I believe, given the obvious benefits especially in economic development, this would be in the best interest of the Tibetan people. Furthermore, I have no intention of using any agreement on autonomy as a stepping stone for Tibet's independence.

I have conveyed these thoughts to successive Chinese leaders. In particular, following the renewal of direct contact with the Chinese government in 2002, I have explained these in detail through my envoys. Despite all this, Beijing continues to allege that my hidden agenda is separation and restoration of Tibet's old socio-political system. Such a notion is unfounded and untrue. Even in my youth, when I was compelled to take on the full responsibility of governance, I began to initiate fundamental changes in Tibet. Unfortunately, these were interrupted because of the political upheavals that took place. Nevertheless, following our arrival in India as refugees, we have democratized our political system and adopted a democratic charter that sets guidelines for our exiled administration.

Even our political leadership is now directly chosen by the people on a five-year term basis. Moreover, we have been able to preserve and practise most of the important aspects of our culture and spirituality in exile. This is due largely to the kindness of India and its people.

Another major concern of the Chinese government is its lack of legitimacy in Tibet. While I cannot rewrite the past, a mutually agreeable solution could bring legitimacy, and I am certainly prepared to use my position and influence among the Tibetan people to bring consensus on this question. So I would also like to restate here that I have no hidden agenda. My decision not to accept any political office in a future Tibet is final.

The Chinese authorities assert that I harbour hostility towards China and that I actively seek to undermine China's welfare. This is totally untrue. I have always encouraged world leaders to engage with China; I have supported China's entry into WTO [World Trade Organization] and the awarding of summer Olympics to Beijing. I chose to do so with the hope that China would become a more open, tolerant and responsible country.

A major obstacle in our ongoing dialogue has been the conflicting perspectives on the current situation inside Tibet. So in order to have a common understanding of the real situation, my envoys in their sixth meeting with their Chinese counterparts suggested that we be given an opportunity to send study groups to look at the actual reality on the ground, in the spirit of seeking

'On the future of Tibet, let me take this opportunity to restate categorically that I am not seeking independence. I am seeking a meaningful autonomy for the Tibetan people within the Peoples Republic of China. If the real concern of the Chinese leadership is the unity and stability of PRC, I have fully addressed their concerns.'

'Let me take this opportunity to once again appeal to the Chinese leadership to recognize the grave problems in Tibet, the genuine grievances and deep resentments of the Tibetan people inside Tibet, and to have the courage and wisdom to address these problems realistically in the spirit of reconciliation.'

truth from facts. This could help both sides to move beyond each others' contentions.

The time has now come for our dialogue with the Chinese leadership to progress towards the successful implementation of a meaningful autonomy for Tibet, as guaranteed in the Chinese constitution and detailed in the Chinese State Council White Paper on Regional Ethnic Autonomy of Tibet.

Let me take this opportunity to once again appeal to the Chinese leadership to recognize the grave problems in Tibet, the genuine grievances and deep resentments of the Tibetan people inside Tibet, and to have the courage and wisdom to address these problems realistically in the spirit of reconciliation. To you, my American friends, I appeal to you to make every effort to seek ways to help convince the Chinese leadership of my sincerity and help make our dialogue process move forward.

Since you have recognized my efforts to promote peace, understanding and nonviolence, I would like to respectfully share a few related thoughts. I believe this is precisely the time that the United States must increase its support to those efforts that help bring greater peace, understanding and harmony between peoples and cultures. As a champion of democracy and freedom, you must continue to ensure the success of those endeavours aimed at safeguarding basic human rights in the world. Another area where we need US leadership is the environment. As we all know, today our earth is definitely warming up and many scientists tell us that our own action is to a large part responsible. So each one of us must, in whatever way we can, use our talents and resources to make a difference so that we can pass on to our future generations a planet that is at least safe to live on.

Many of the world's problems are ultimately rooted in inequality and injustice, whether economic, political or social. Ultimately, this is a question of the well-being of all of us. Whether it is the suffering of poverty in one part of the world, or whether it is the denial of freedom and basic human rights in another part, we should never perceive these events in total isolation. Eventually their repercussions will be felt everywhere. I would like to appeal to you to take a leadership role in an effective international action in addressing this huge economic imbalance. I believe the time has now come to address all these global issues from the perspective of the oneness of humanity, and from a profound understanding of the deeply interconnected nature of our today's world.

In conclusion, on behalf of 6 million Tibetan people, I wish to take this opportunity to recognize from the depth of my heart the support extended to us by the American people and their government. Your continued support is critical. I thank you once again for the high honour that you have bestowed on me today. Thank you.'

Al Gore

'The Earth Has a Fever'

Receiving the Nobel Peace Prize
Oslo, Norway, 10 December 2007.

Al Gore gives an environment speech at Palazzo Mezzanotte in Milan, December 2008.

Al Gore (1948–) was the son of a Democrat congressman. Educated at Harvard University, he worked as a journalist before serving as a Democratic Party congressman and a senator from Tennessee in the 1970s and 80s. He became vice-president under Bill Clinton from 1993 to 2001.

Controversially defeated for the presidency by the Republican Party's George W. Bush in the 2000 election, Gore subsequently threw himself into the intensifying international campaign against global warming, touring the world, where he gave speeches and recruited climate activists to his cause. In 2006, he wrote and appeared in the Oscar-winning climate change documentary *An Inconvenient Truth.*

The following year, jointly with the Intergovernmental Panel on Climate Change (IPCC), he was honoured with the Nobel Peace Prize. Accepting the prize, in the speech that follows, he urged the world to urgent action to reduce carbon emissions, or face disastrous consequences.

'Sometimes, without warning, the future knocks on our door with a precious and painful vision of what might be. One-hundred-and-nineteen years ago, a wealthy inventor read his own obituary, mistakenly published years before his death. Wrongly believing the inventor had just died, a newspaper printed a harsh judgement of his life's work, unfairly labelling him "The Merchant of Death" because of his invention—dynamite. Shaken by this condemnation, the inventor made a fateful choice to serve the cause of peace.

Seven years later, Alfred Nobel created this prize and the others that bear his name. Seven years ago tomorrow, I read my own political obituary in a judgement that seemed to me harsh and mistaken—if not premature. But that unwelcome verdict also brought a precious if painful gift: an opportunity to search for fresh new ways to serve my purpose.

Unexpectedly, that quest has brought me here. Even though I fear my words cannot match this moment, I pray what I am feeling in my heart will be communicated clearly enough that those who hear me will say, "We must act."

The distinguished scientists with whom it is the greatest honour of my life to share this award have laid before us a choice between two different futures—a choice that to my ears echoes the words of an ancient prophet: "Life or death, blessings or curses. Therefore, choose life, that both thou and thy seed may live."

We, the human species, are confronting a planetary emergency—a threat to the survival of our civilization that is gathering ominous and destructive potential even as we gather here. But there is hopeful news as well: we have the ability to solve this

'We, the human species, are confronting a planetary emergency—a threat to the survival of our civilization that is gathering ominous and destructive potential even as we gather here. But there is hopeful news as well: we have the ability to solve this crisis and avoid the worst—though not all—of its consequences, if we act boldly, decisively and quickly.'

crisis and avoid the worst—though not all—of its consequences, if we act boldly, decisively and quickly.

However, despite a growing number of honourable exceptions, too many of the world's leaders are still best described in the words Winston Churchill applied to those who ignored Adolf Hitler's threat: "They go on in strange paradox, decided only to be undecided, resolved to be irresolute, adamant for drift, solid for fluidity, all powerful to be impotent."

So today, we dumped another 70 million tons of global-warming pollution into the thin shell of atmosphere surrounding our planet, as if it were an open sewer. And tomorrow, we will dump a slightly larger amount, with the cumulative concentrations now trapping more and more heat from the sun.

As a result, the Earth has a fever. And the fever is rising. The experts have told us it is not a passing affliction that will heal by itself. We asked for a second opinion. And a third. And a fourth. And the consistent conclusion, restated with increasing alarm, is that something basic is wrong.

We are what is wrong, and we must make it right.

'As a result, the Earth has a fever. And the fever is rising. The experts have told us it is not a passing affliction that will heal by itself. We asked for a second opinion. And a third. And a fourth. And the consistent conclusion, restated with increasing alarm, is that something basic is wrong. We are what is wrong, and we must make it right.'

Last September 21, as the Northern Hemisphere tilted away from the sun, scientists reported with unprecedented distress that the North Polar ice cap is "falling off a cliff". One study estimated that it could be completely gone during summer in less than 22 years. Another new study, to be presented by US Navy researchers later this week, warns it could happen in as little as seven years.

Seven years from now.

In the last few months, it has been harder and harder to misinterpret the signs that our world is spinning out of kilter. Major cities in North and South America, Asia and Australia are nearly out of water due to massive droughts and melting glaciers. Desperate farmers are losing their livelihoods. Peoples in the frozen Arctic and on low-lying Pacific islands are planning evacuations of places they have long called home. Unprecedented wildfires have forced a half million people from their homes in one country and caused a national emergency that almost brought down the government in another. Climate refugees have migrated into areas already inhabited by people with different cultures, religions, and traditions, increasing the potential for conflict. Stronger storms in the Pacific and Atlantic have threatened whole cities. Millions have been displaced by massive flooding in South Asia, Mexico, and 18 countries in Africa. As temperature extremes have increased, tens of thousands have lost their lives. We are recklessly burning and clearing our forests and driving more and more species into extinction. The very web of life on which we depend is being ripped and frayed.

We never intended to cause all this destruction, just as Alfred Nobel never intended that dynamite be used for waging war. He had hoped his invention would promote human progress. We shared that same worthy goal when we began burning massive quantities of coal, then oil and methane. Even in Nobel's time, there were a few warnings of the likely consequences. One of the very first winners of the Prize in chemistry worried that, "We are evaporating our coal mines into the air." After performing 10,000 equations by hand, Svante Arrhenius calculated that the earth's average temperature would increase by many degrees if we doubled the amount of CO_2 in the atmosphere.

Seventy years later, my teacher, Roger Revelle, and his colleague, Dave Keeling, began to precisely document the increasing CO_2 levels day by day.

But unlike most other forms of pollution, CO_2 is invisible, tasteless, and odourless—which has helped keep the truth about what it is doing to our climate out of sight and out of mind. Moreover, the catastrophe now threatening us is unprecedented—and we often confuse the unprecedented with the improbable.

We also find it hard to imagine making the massive changes that are now necessary to solve the crisis. And when large truths are genuinely inconvenient, whole societies can, at least for a time, ignore them. Yet, as George Orwell reminds us: "Sooner or later a false belief bumps up against solid reality, usually on a battlefield."

In the years since this prize was first awarded, the entire relationship between humankind and the earth has been radically transformed. And still, we have remained largely oblivious to the impact of our cumulative actions. Indeed, without realizing it, we have begun to wage war on the earth itself. Now, we and the earth's climate are locked in a relationship familiar to war planners: "Mutually assured destruction."

More than two decades ago, scientists calculated that nuclear war could throw so much debris and smoke into the air that it would block life-giving sunlight from our atmosphere, causing a "nuclear winter". Their eloquent warnings here in Oslo helped galvanise the world's resolve to halt the nuclear arms race.

Now science is warning us that if we do not quickly reduce the global warming pollution that is trapping so much of the heat our planet normally radiates back out of the atmosphere, we are in danger of creating a permanent "carbon summer".

As the American poet Robert Frost wrote, "Some say the world will end in fire; some say in ice". Either, he notes, "would suffice".

But neither need be our fate. It is time to make peace with the planet.

'As the American poet Robert Frost wrote, 'Some say the world will end in fire; some say in ice'. Either, he notes, 'would suffice'. But neither need be our fate. It is time to make peace with the planet.'

We must quickly mobilize our civilization with the urgency and resolve that has previously been seen only when nations mobilized for war. These prior struggles for survival were won when leaders found words at the 11th hour that released a mighty surge of courage, hope and readiness to sacrifice for a protracted and mortal challenge.

These were not comforting and misleading assurances that the threat was not real or imminent; that it would affect others but not ourselves; that ordinary life might be lived even in the presence of extraordinary threat; that Providence could be trusted to do for us what we would not do for ourselves.

No, these were calls to come to the defence of the common future. They were calls upon the courage, generosity and strength of entire peoples, citizens of every class and condition who were ready to stand against the threat once asked to do so. Our enemies in those times calculated that free people would not rise to the challenge; they were, of course, catastrophically wrong.

Now comes the threat of climate crisis—a threat that is real, rising, imminent, and universal. Once again, it is the 11th hour. The penalties for ignoring this challenge are immense and growing, and at some near point would be unsustainable and unrecoverable...

The future is knocking at our door right now. Make no mistake, the next generation will ask us one of two questions. Either they will ask: "What were you thinking; why didn't you act?" Or they will ask instead: "How did you find the moral courage to rise and successfully resolve a crisis that so many said was impossible to solve?"

We have everything we need to get started, save perhaps political will, but political will is a renewable resource.

So let us renew it, and say together: "We have a purpose. We are many. For this purpose we will rise, and we will act." ❜

Doris Lessing

'It Is Our Stories That Will Recreate Us'

Nobel Lecture, receiving the 2007 Nobel Prize for Literature, Oslo, 7 December 2007.

Doris Lessing at a literary party in 1957.

The eminent Southern African author Doris Lessing (1919–) attained prominence with a series of works from the 1950s onwards. Her many awards and honours were capped by the Nobel Prize for Literature in 2007. Lessing was born into an expatriate British family in Persia (now Iran); she was five when the family moved to Southern Rhodesia (now Zimbabwe). She was educated in Rhodesia, and was twice married before she moved to London in 1949.

'I felt as if my real life was beginning when I at last arrived in war-torn, grubby, cold England,' she has said of her coming to Britain. 'And of course, it was. Since then, I have written, that has been my life. Very hard work, life is—that's my summing up as I reach the end of life.'

Her first novel, *The Grass Is Singing*, a critique of colonial attitudes in Africa, was published in 1950. She followed it with the semi-autobiographical *Martha Quest* (1952), *A Proper Marriage* (1954) and *A Ripple In The Storm* (1958), chronicling a woman growing up in Africa, her marriage and rejection of it, and her involvement in Leftist politics. Lessing, herself, was a Communist, though later she became disillusioned with it.

Later books included *The Good Terrorist* (1985), for which she received the W.H. Smith Literary Award, while *The Fifth Child* won the Grinzane Cavour Prize. During the 1990s she wrote her much-lauded autobiography. The following is from her speech accepting the Nobel Prize.

'I would like you to imagine yourselves somewhere in Southern Africa, standing in an Indian store, in a poor area, in a time of bad drought. There is a line of people, mostly women, with every kind of container for water. This store gets a bowser of precious water every afternoon from the town, and here the people wait.

The Indian is standing with the heels of his hands pressed down on the counter, and he is watching a black woman, who is bending over a wadge of paper that looks as if it has been torn from a book. She is reading *Anna Karenina*.

She is reading slowly, mouthing the words. It looks a difficult book. This is a young woman with two little children clutching at her legs. She is pregnant. The Indian is distressed, because the young woman's headscarf, which should be white, is yellow with dust. Dust lies between her breasts and on her arms. This man is distressed because of the lines of people, all thirsty. He doesn't have enough water for them. He is angry because he knows there are people dying out there, beyond the dust clouds. His older brother had been here holding the fort, but he had said he needed a break, had gone into town, really rather ill, because of the drought.

This man is curious. He says to the young woman, "What are you reading?"

"It is about Russia," says the girl.

"Do you know where Russia is?" He hardly knows himself.

The young woman looks straight at him, full of dignity, though her eyes are red from dust, "I was best in the class. My teacher said I was best."

'The Indian knows he shouldn't do this but he reaches down to a great plastic container beside him, behind the counter, and pours out two mugs of water, which he hands to the children. He watches while the girl looks at her children drinking, her mouth moving.'

The young woman resumes her reading. She wants to get to the end of the paragraph.

The Indian looks at the two little children and reaches for some Fanta, but the mother says, "Fanta makes them thirstier."

The Indian knows he shouldn't do this but he reaches down to a great plastic container beside him, behind the counter, and pours out two mugs of water, which he hands to the children. He watches while the girl looks at her children drinking, her mouth moving. He gives her a mug of water. It hurts him to see her drinking it, so painfully thirsty is she.

Now she hands him her own plastic water container, which he fills. The young woman and the children watch him closely so that he doesn't spill any.

She is bending again over the book. She reads slowly. The paragraph fascinates her and she reads it again.

"Varenka, with her white kerchief over her black hair, surrounded by the children and gaily and good-humouredly busy with them, and at the same visibly excited at the possibility of an offer of marriage from a man she cared for, looked very attractive. Koznyshev walked by her side and kept casting admiring glances at her. Looking at her, he recalled all the delightful things he had heard from her lips, all the good he knew about her, and became more and more conscious that the feeling he had for her was something rare, something he had felt but once before, long, long ago, in his early youth. The joy of being near her increased step by step, and at last reached such a point that, as he put a huge birch mushroom with a slender stalk and up-curling top into her basket, he looked into her eyes and, noting the flush of glad and frightened agitation that suffused her face, he was confused himself, and in silence gave her a smile that said too much."

This lump of print is lying on the counter, together with some old copies of magazines, some pages of newspapers with pictures of girls in bikinis.

It is time for the woman to leave the haven of the Indian store, and set off back along the four miles to her village. Outside, the lines of waiting women clamour and complain. But still the Indian lingers. He knows what it will cost this girl—going back home, with the two clinging children. He would give her the piece of prose that so fascinates her, but he cannot really believe this splinter of a girl with her great belly can really understand it.

Why is perhaps a third of *Anna Karenina* here on this counter in a remote Indian store? It is like this.

A certain high official, from the United Nations as it happens, bought a copy of this novel in a bookshop before he set out on his journey to cross several oceans and seas. On the plane, settled in his business class seat, he tore the book into three parts. He looked around his fellow passengers as he did this, knowing he would see looks of shock, curiosity, but some of amusement. When he was settled, his seat belt tight, he said aloud to whomever could hear, "I always do this when I've a long trip. You don't want to have to hold up some heavy great book."

The novel was a paperback, but, true, it is a long book. This man is well used to people listening when he spoke. "I always do this, travelling," he confided. "Travelling at all these days, is hard enough." And as soon as people were settling down, he opened his part of *Anna Karenina*, and read. When people looked his way, curiously or not, he confided in them. "No, it really is the only way to travel." He knew the novel, liked it, and this original mode of reading did add spice to what was after all a well-known book.

When he reached the end of a section of the book, he called the air hostess, and sent the chapters back to his secretary, travelling in the cheaper seats. This caused much interest, condemnation, certainly curiosity, every time a section of the great Russian novel arrived, mutilated but readable, in the back part of the plane. Altogether, this clever way of reading *Anna Karenina* makes an impression, and probably no one there would forget it.

Meanwhile, in the Indian store, the young woman is holding on to the counter, her little children clinging to her skirts. She wears jeans, since she is a modern woman, but over them she has put on the heavy woollen skirt, part of the traditional dress of her people: her children can easily cling onto its thick folds.

She sends a thankful look to the Indian, whom she knew liked her and was sorry for her, and she steps out into the blowing clouds. The children are past crying, and their throats are full of dust. This was hard, oh yes, it was hard, this stepping, one foot after another, through the dust that lay in soft deceiving mounds under her feet. Hard, but she was used to hardship, was she not? Her mind was on the story she had been reading. She was thinking, She is just like me, in her white headscarf, and she is looking after children, too. I could be her, that Russian girl. And the man there, he loves her and will ask her to marry him. She had not finished more than that one paragraph. Yes, she thinks, a man will come for me, and take me away from all this, take me and the children, yes, he will love me and look after me.

She steps on. The can of water is heavy on her shoulders. On she goes. The children can hear the water slopping about. Half way she stops, sets down the can. Her children are whimpering and touching it. She thinks that she cannot open it, because dust would blow in. There is no way she can open the can until she gets home.

"Wait," she tells her children, "wait." She has to pull herself together and go on.

She thinks, My teacher said there is a library, bigger than the supermarket, a big building and it is full of books. The young woman is smiling as she moves on, the dust blowing in her face. I am clever, she thinks. Teacher said I am clever. The cleverest in the school—she said I was. My children will be clever, like me. I will take them to the library, the place full of books, and they will go to school, and they will be teachers—my teacher told me I could be a teacher. My children will live far from here, earning money. They will live near the big library and enjoy a good life.

You may ask how that piece of the Russian novel ever ended up on that counter in the Indian store?

'The can of water is heavy on her shoulders. On she goes. The children can hear the water slopping about. Half way she stops, sets down the can. Her children are whimpering and touching it. She thinks that she cannot open it, because dust would blow in. There is no way she can open the can until she gets home.'

'That poor girl trudging through the dust, dreaming of an education for her children, do we think that we are better than she is—we, stuffed full of food, our cupboards full of clothes, stifling in our superfluities?'

It would make a pretty story. Perhaps someone will tell it. On goes that poor girl, held upright by thoughts of the water she will give her children once home, and drink a little of herself. On she goes, through the dreaded dusts of an African drought.

We are a jaded lot, we in our threatened world. We are good for irony and even cynicism. Some words and ideas we hardly use, so worn out have they become. But we may want to restore some words that have lost their potency.

We have a treasure-house of literature, going back to the Egyptians, the Greeks, the Romans. It is all there, this wealth of literature, to be discovered again and again by whoever is lucky enough to come upon it. A treasure. Suppose it did not exist. How impoverished, how empty we would be.

We own a legacy of languages, poems, histories, and it is not one that will ever be exhausted. It is there, always.

We have a bequest of stories, tales from the old storytellers, some of whose names we know, but some not. The storytellers go back and back, to a clearing in the forest where a great fire burns, and the old shamans dance and sing, for our heritage of stories began in fire, magic, the spirit world. And that is where it is held, today.

Ask any modern storyteller and they will say there is always a moment when they are touched with fire, with what we like to call inspiration, and this goes back and back to the beginning of our race, to the great winds that shaped us and our world.

The storyteller is deep inside every one of us. The story-maker is always with us. Let us suppose our world is ravaged by war, by the horrors that we all of us easily imagine. Let us suppose floods wash through our cities, the seas rise. But the storyteller will be there, for it is our imaginations which shape us, keep us, create us—for good and for ill. It is our stories that will recreate us, when we are torn, hurt, even destroyed. It is the storyteller, the dream-maker, the myth-maker, that is our phoenix, that represents us at our best, and at our most creative.

That poor girl trudging through the dust, dreaming of an education for her children, do we think that we are better than she is—we, stuffed full of food, our cupboards full of clothes, stifling in our superfluities?

I think it is that girl, and the women who were talking about books and an education when they had not eaten for three days, that may yet define us.'

Barack Obama

'Our Spirit Is Stronger and Cannot Be Broken'

**Presidential inauguration speech,
Washington, DC, 20 January 2009.**

US President Barack Obama delivers his inaugural address in Washington, 20 January 2009.

The speeches in this book opened with an impassioned plea by British philanthropist William Wilberforce in 1789 for an end to the African slave trade. It is fitting, then, to end it with words spoken 230 years later by the son of an African man who became president of the United States of America.

The year 1789 is a major one in the calendar of history. It was the year of the French Revolution, when, to paraphrase Barack Obama 'change came to the world'. In 1789, the United States was a very new nation, fresh from its triumphant War of Independence with Britain, and fired, like the French who followed them to revolution, with fervid ideas about human freedom and equality.

Nonetheless there were many who were certainly not free and not equal in the United States of 1789. Its African population remained enslaved, and its women could not vote and lacked a great number of other liberties now considered basic human rights.

The election of the Democratic Party candidate Barack Obama to the presidency on 4 November 2008, and his inauguration as the US republic's 44th president on 20 January 2009, not only installed a black man in the White House. It showed to the world that profound change can be achieved through peaceful means when it is pursued with deep resolve and enormous persistence, in the spirit of great thinkers and leaders such as Mahatma Gandhi, Kwame Nkrumah, Martin Luther King, Jr, Corazon Aquino and Aung San Suu Kyi.

'My fellow citizens:

I stand here today humbled by the task before us, grateful for the trust you have bestowed, mindful of the sacrifices borne by our ancestors. I thank President Bush for his service to our nation, as well as the generosity and co-operation he has shown throughout this transition.

Forty-four Americans have now taken the presidential oath.

The words have been spoken during rising tides of prosperity and the still waters of peace. Yet, every so often the oath is taken amidst gathering clouds and raging storms. At these moments, America has carried on not simply because of the skill or vision of those in high office, but because We the People have remained faithful to the ideals of our forebears, and true to our founding documents.

So it has been. So it must be with this generation of Americans. That we are in the midst of crisis is now well understood. Our nation is at war against a far-reaching network of violence and hatred. Our economy is badly weakened, a consequence of greed and irresponsibility on the part of some but also our collective failure to make hard choices and prepare the nation for a new age.

Homes have been lost, jobs shed, businesses shuttered. Our healthcare is too costly, our schools fail too many, and each day brings further evidence that the ways we use energy strengthen our adversaries and threaten our planet.

These are the indicators of crisis, subject to data and statistics. Less measurable, but no less profound, is a sapping of confidence across our land; a nagging fear that America's decline is inevitable, that the next generation must lower its sights.

Today I say to you that the challenges we face are real, they are serious and they are many. They will not be met easily or in a short span of time. But know this America: They will be met.

On this day, we gather because we have chosen hope over fear, unity of purpose over conflict and discord. On this day, we come to proclaim an end to the petty grievances and false promises, the recriminations and worn-out dogmas that for far too long have strangled our politics.

We remain a young nation, but in the words of Scripture, the time has come to set aside childish things. The time has come to reaffirm our enduring spirit; to choose our better history; to carry forward that precious gift, that noble idea, passed on from generation to generation: the God-given promise that all are equal, all are free, and all deserve a chance to pursue their full measure of happiness.

In reaffirming the greatness of our nation, we understand that greatness is never a given. It must be earned. Our journey has never been one of shortcuts or settling for less. It has not been the path for the faint-hearted, for those who prefer leisure over work, or seek only the pleasures of riches and fame. Rather, it has been the risk-takers, the doers, the makers of things—some celebrated, but more often men and women obscure in their labor—who have carried us up the long, rugged path towards prosperity and freedom.

For us, they packed up their few worldly possessions and travelled across oceans in search of a new life. For us, they toiled in sweatshops and settled the West, endured the lash of the whip and ploughed the hard earth. For us, they fought and died in places such as Concord and Gettysburg; Normandy and Khe Sanh.

Time and again these men and women struggled and sacrificed and worked till their hands were raw so that we might live a better life. They saw America as bigger than the sum of our individual ambitions; greater than all the differences of birth or wealth or faction.

This is the journey we continue today. We remain the most prosperous, powerful nation on Earth. Our workers are no less productive than when this crisis began. Our minds are no less inventive, our goods and services no less needed than they were last week or last month or last year. Our capacity remains undiminished. But our time of standing pat, of protecting narrow interests and putting off unpleasant decisions—that time has surely passed.

Starting today, we must pick ourselves up, dust ourselves off, and begin again the work of remaking America. For everywhere we look, there is work to be done. The state of our economy calls for action: bold and swift. And we will act not only to create new jobs but to lay a new foundation for growth. We will build the roads and bridges, the electric grids and digital lines that feed our commerce and bind us together.

We will restore science to its rightful place and wield technol-

'Starting today, we must pick ourselves up, dust ourselves off, and begin again the work of remaking America. For everywhere we look, there is work to be done. The state of our economy calls for action: bold and swift.'

ogy's wonders to raise health care's quality, and lower its costs. We will harness the sun and the winds and the soil to fuel our cars and run our factories. And we will transform our schools and colleges and universities to meet the demands of a new age.

All this we can do. All this we will do.

Now, there are some who question the scale of our ambitions, who suggest that our system cannot tolerate too many big plans. Their memories are short, for they have forgotten what this country has already done, what free men and women can achieve when imagination is joined to common purpose and necessity to courage. What the cynics fail to understand is that the ground has shifted beneath them, that the stale political arguments that have consumed us for so long, no longer apply.

The question we ask today is not whether our government is too big or too small, but whether it works, whether it helps families find jobs at a decent wage, care they can afford, a retirement that is dignified. Where the answer is yes, we intend to move forward. Where the answer is no, programs will end.

And those of us who manage the public's dollars will be held to account, to spend wisely, reform bad habits, and do our business in the light of day, because only then can we restore the vital trust between a people and their government. Nor is the question before us whether the market is a force for good or ill. Its power to generate wealth and expand freedom is unmatched.

But this crisis has reminded us that without a watchful eye, the market can spin out of control. The nation cannot prosper long when it favours only the prosperous. The success of our economy has always depended not just on the size of our gross domestic product, but on the reach of our prosperity; on the ability to extend opportunity to every willing heart—not out of charity, but because it is the surest route to our common good.

As for our common defence, we reject as false the choice between our safety and our ideals. Our Founding Fathers faced with perils that we can scarcely imagine, drafted a charter to assure the rule of law and the rights of man, a charter expanded by the blood of generations. Those ideals still light the world, and we will not give them up for expedience's sake.

'We will restore science to its rightful place and wield technology's wonders to raise health care's quality, and lower its costs. We will harness the sun and the winds and the soil to fuel our cars and run our factories. And we will transform our schools and colleges and universities to meet the demands of a new age.'

And so, to all other peoples and governments who are watching today, from the grandest capitals to the small village where my father was born: know that America is a friend of each nation and every man, woman and child who seeks a future of peace and dignity, and we are ready to lead once more.

Recall that earlier generations faced down fascism and communism not just with missiles and tanks, but with the sturdy alliances and enduring convictions. They understood that our power alone cannot protect us, nor does it entitle us to do as we please. Instead, they knew that our power grows through its prudent use. Our security emanates from the justness of our cause;

the force of our example; the tempering qualities of humility and restraint.

We are the keepers of this legacy, guided by these principles once more, we can meet those new threats that demand even greater effort, even greater co-operation and understanding between nations. We'll begin to responsibly leave Iraq to its people and forge a hard-earned peace in Afghanistan.

With old friends and former foes, we'll work tirelessly to lessen the nuclear threat and roll back the spectre of a warming planet.

We will not apologize for our way of life nor will we waver in its defence. And for those who seek to advance their aims by inducing terror and slaughtering innocents, we say to you now that, "Our spirit is stronger and cannot be broken. You cannot outlast us, and we will defeat you."

'For we know that our patchwork heritage is a strength, not a weakness. We are a nation of Christians and Muslims, Jews and Hindus, and non-believers. We are shaped by every language and culture, drawn from every end of this Earth.'

For we know that our patchwork heritage is a strength, not a weakness. We are a nation of Christians and Muslims, Jews and Hindus, and non-believers. We are shaped by every language and culture, drawn from every end of this Earth. And because we have tasted the bitter swill of civil war and segregation and emerged from that dark chapter stronger and more united, we cannot help but believe that the old hatreds shall someday pass; that the lines of tribe shall soon dissolve; that as the world grows smaller, our common humanity shall reveal itself; and that America must play its role in ushering in a new era of peace.

To the Muslim world, we seek a new way forward, based on mutual interest and mutual respect.

To those leaders around the globe who seek to sow conflict or blame their society's ills on the West, know that your people will judge you on what you can build, not what you destroy.

To those who cling to power through corruption and deceit and the silencing of dissent, know that you are on the wrong side of history, but that we will extend a hand if you are willing to unclench your fist.

To the people of poor nations, we pledge to work alongside you to make your farms flourish and let clean waters flow; to nourish starved bodies and feed hungry minds. And to those nations like ours that enjoy relative plenty, we say we can no longer afford indifference to the suffering outside our borders, nor can we consume the world's resources without regard to effect. For the world has changed, and we must change with it.

As we consider the road that unfolds before us, we remember with humble gratitude those brave Americans who, at this very hour, patrol far-off deserts and distant mountains. They have something to tell us, just as the fallen heroes who lie in Arlington whisper through the ages. We honour them not only because they are guardians of our liberty, but because they embody the spirit of service: a willingness to find meaning in something greater than themselves.

And yet, at this moment, a moment that will define a generation, it is precisely this spirit that must inhabit us all. For as much as government can do and must do, it is ultimately the faith and determination of the American people upon which this nation relies.

It is the kindness to take in a stranger when the levees break; the selflessness of workers who would rather cut their hours than see a friend lose their job which sees us through our darkest hours. It is the firefighter's courage to storm a stairway filled with smoke, but also a parent's willingness to nurture a child, that finally decides our fate.

Our challenges may be new, the instruments with which we meet them may be new, but those values upon which our success depends, honesty and hard work, courage and fair play, tolerance and curiosity, loyalty and patriotism—these things are old.

These things are true. They have been the quiet force of progress throughout our history.

What is demanded then is a return to these truths. What is required of us now is a new era of responsibility—a recognition, on the part of every American, that we have duties to ourselves, our nation and the world, duties that we do not grudgingly accept but rather seize gladly, firm in the knowledge that there is nothing so satisfying to the spirit, so defining of our character than giving our all to a difficult task.

This is the price and the promise of citizenship. This is the source of our confidence: the knowledge that God calls on us to shape an uncertain destiny. This is the meaning of our liberty and our creed, why men and women and children of every race and every faith can join in celebration across this magnificent mall. And why a man whose father less than 60 years ago might not have been served at a local restaurant can now stand before you to take a most sacred oath. So let us mark this day in remembrance of who we are and how far we have travelled.

In the year of America's birth, in the coldest of months, a small band of patriots huddled by dying campfires on the shores of an icy river. The capital was abandoned. The enemy was advancing. The snow was stained with blood. At a moment when the outcome of our revolution was most in doubt, the father of our nation ordered these words be read to the people: "Let it be told to the future world that in the depth of winter, when nothing but hope and virtue could survive, that the city and the country, alarmed at one common danger, came forth to meet it."

America, in the face of our common dangers, in this winter of our hardship, let us remember these timeless words; with hope and virtue, let us brave once more the icy currents, and endure what storms may come; let it be said by our children's children that when we were tested we refused to let this journey end, that we did not turn back nor did we falter; and with eyes fixed on the horizon and God's grace upon us, we carried forth that great gift of freedom and delivered it safely to future generations.'

Afterword

What constitutes a good speech? What are the hallmarks of a speech that connect directly with us as listeners?—And, in book form, as readers, perhaps centuries later? I hope that having read the speeches in this book, the reader has emerged with a new conception about these questions. I certainly feel that I have, after compiling them.

To me, there are three key elements that mark the finest and most memorable of speeches: they must have the commitment of belief, they must be truthful and they must be candid.

The first, commitment or belief, we tend to take for granted. It is a fundamental requirement of any speech on an important matter that the audience at least believe in the commitment of the speaker to their cause. It is obviously there in Nehru's 'Tryst with Destiny', in Emmeline Pankhurst's 'Our Civil War', and in Helen Caldicott's chilling reminder that decades after the Cold War supposedly ended, the nuclear threat hangs yet above us all.

Commitment is there too, though, or at least so it would seem, in the speech of Adolf Hitler. But compare the truthfulness in Hitler's speech with that of Bob Brown in 'This Finite, Fragile Living Planet', and it becomes obvious who is speaking what they really believe to be the truth—as opposed to merely feigning it for the audience. As such, Hitler's speech falls into the category of historical record, and it was to give the reader another angle on wartime Nazi Germany that it was included.

What then of candour? Surely that falls into the same category as truth. Not so, in my view. Candour is the openness of the speaker about themselves, the speaker's own personal truth which helps to inform and confirm the wider truth they are trying to convey in their words. It often takes the form of self-criticism, humour, personal reflection, and it is what makes us most open to a speech, and what will give it lasting resonance. For what is a speaker but one of our own speaking of things that are of concern to us all: that is why, after all, we are listening in the first place. The more human they are then, the more like one of us—flawed, worried, vexed, yet somehow still singularly able to stir us to their vision of a better world—the more closely we will listen, and take to heart.

This is exemplified in speeches like Paul Keating's 'We Brought the Disasters', in which in very simple terms the then Australian prime minister shoulders blame with all of white Australia for the crimes of the past against the nation's indigenous population; Jane Fonda's reflections upon marriages and men, and how she felt sheltering in a hole in the ground with a Vietnamese schoolgirl to escape bombs being dropped by American planes; and Virginia Woolf's 'You Have Won Rooms of Your Own', in which she muses with captivating frankness and wit on her career and her privileged life, in which she still faces, as the young women she is addressing will do, the internalized blocks of sexist society.

As for 'vision' and 'soaring rhetoric'—the stuff that newspaper leader writers sometimes praise in a major speech—for these to be associated with any speech I believe the three key elements of commitment of belief, truth and candour must be there first; otherwise they may be little more than cadences of empty visionary fancies, grating rhetorical cant. Some noted 'soaring rhetoric' as missing in Barack Obama's presidential inauguration speech, but it resounded because it had the three fundamentals of a memorable speech, though as a speech of his it is to my mind eclipsed by his remarkable and moving 'A More Perfect Union" speech.

My personal favourites, for what it is worth, are the Virginia Woolf speech mentioned above, Bertrand Russell's 'The Road Towards the Abyss' and Martin Luther King Jr's 'Always Fight With Love'. Though a lesser-known speech of Dr King's, in it the 20th century's finest orator illuminates the fundamental concerns of his time with his signature clarity, immediacy and intimacy.

SOURCES

English Historical Documents 1906-1939, J.H.Bettey (ed.), Routledge and Kegan Paul, London, 1967
Documents of American History, Volume II since 1898, Henry Steele
Commager (ed.), Appleton-Century-Crofts, New York, 1968
Barry Jones Dictionary of World Biography, Information Australia, Melbourne, 1996

Speeches

William Wilberforce
http://www.famous-speeches-and-speech-topics.info/famous-speeches/william-wilberforce-speech-horrors-of-the-slave-trade.htm

Thomas Jefferson
http://www.princeton.edu/~tjpapers/inaugural/infinal.html

Napoleon Bonaparte
http://www.napoleonguide.com/farewell.htm

Abraham Lincoln
http://avalon.law.yale.edu/19th_century/gettyb.asp

Lord Asquith
http://www.bbc.co.uk/history/worldwars/wwone/mirror01_02.shtml

Woodrow Wilson
http://wwi.lib.byu.edu/index.php/Wilson's_War_Message_to_Congress

Emma Goldman
http://sunsite3.berkeley.edu/Goldman/Writings/Speeches/170614.html

David Lloyd George speech
English Historical Documents 1906-1939, p68

Neville Chamberlain
http://news.bbc.co.uk/2/hi/special_report/1999/08/99/world_war_ii/430071.stm

Winston Churchill
http://www.winstonchurchill.org/i4a/pages/index.cfm?pageid=420

Benito Mussolini
http://www.ibiblio.org/pha/policy/1941/410223a.html

Afolf Hitler
http://www.hitler.org/speeches/05-04-41.html

Joseph Goebbels
http://www.calvin.edu/academic/cas/gpa/goeb36.htm

Franklin D. Roosevelt
http://millercenter.org/scripps/archive/speeches/detail/3338

Harry S. Truman
http://www.classbrain.com/artteenst/publish/article_99.shtml

William Faulkner
http://nobelprize.org/nobel_prizes/literature/laureates/1949/faulkner-speech.html
© The Nobel Foundation 1949

Bertrand Russell
http://nobelprize.org/nobel_prizes/literature/laureates/1950/russell-lecture.html
© The Nobel Foundation 1950

Dwight D. Eisenhower
http://millercenter.org/scripps/archive/speeches/detail/3358

John Foster Dulles
http://everything2.com/index.pl?node_id=638924

Albert Schweitzer
http://nobelprize.org/nobel_prizes/peace/laureates/1952/schweitzer-lecture-e.html

John F. Kennedy
http://www.jfklibrary.org/Historical+Resources/Archives/Reference+Desk/Speeches/JFK/003POF03UnitedNations09251961.htm

Helen Caldicott
http://radio4all.net/index.php/program/29868

Susan B. Anthony
http://www.law.umkc.edu/faculty/projects/ftrials/anthony/anthonyaddress.html

Emmeline Pankhurst
http://www.guardian.co.uk/theguardian/2007/apr/27/greatspeeches

Virginia Woolf
http://s.spachman.tripod.com/Woolf/professions.htm

Jessie Street
http://www.boardofstudies.nsw.edu.au/syllabus_hsc/pdf_doc/english-standard-speeches-2009-2012.pdf

Claudia (Lady Bird) Johnson
http://gos.sbc.edu/j/johnson1.html

Betty Friedan
http://gos.sbc.edu/f/friedan.html

Jane Fonda
http://www.feminist.com/resources/artspeech/genwom/newfeminism.html

Luisa Dias Diogo
http://www.womenspeecharchive.org/women/profile/speech/index.cfm?ProfileID=141&SpeechID=552

Hi Chi Minh
http://facultystaff.richmond.edu/~ebolt/history398/DeclarationOfIndependence-DRV.html

Nehru
http://www.fordham.edu/halsall/mod/1947nehru1.html

Martin Luther King
http://www.mlkonline.net/nation.html

Lyndon Baines Johnson
http://www.lbjlib.utexas.edu/johnson/archives.hom/speeches.hom/650315.asp

Vaclav Havel
http://old.hrad.cz/president/Havel/speeches/1990/0101_uk.html

Aung Sun Suu Kyi
http://nobelprize.org/nobel_prizes/peace/laureates/1991/kyi-acceptance.html

Paul Keating
http://www.austlii.edu.au/au/journals/ILB/2001/57.html

Yitzhak Rabin
http://www.mideastweb.org/rabin1995.htm

Bob Brown
http://www.aph.gov.au/senate/senators/homepages/first_speech/sfs-QD4.htm

Corazon Aquino
http://gos.sbc.edu/a/aquino.html

Julius Nyerere
http://www.uneca.org/eca_resources/Speeches/amoako/98/julis.htm

Desmond Tutu
http://www.southafrica-newyork.net/consulate/speeches/tutuspeech.htm

Michelle Bachelet
http://www.leadershipreview.org/2008fall/article2.pdf

Barack Obama "A More Perfect Union" speech
http://www.npr.org/templates/story/story.php?storyId=88478467

Margaret Thatcher
http://www.margaretthatcher.org/archive/displaydocument.asp?docid=110946

Ronald Reagan
http://www.fordham.edu/halsall/mod/1982reagan1.html

George Bush Sr
http://www.scribd.com/doc/18673 5/1990-09-11-George-H-W-Bush-speach-Toward-a-New-World-Order

George W. Bush "Bullhorn speech"
http://video.aol.com/video-detail/bush-bullhorn-speech/2142620394

George W. Bush Speech to Congress
http://www.washingtonpost.com/wp-srv/nation/specials/attacked/transcripts/bushaddress_092001.html

Queen Elizabeth II
http://news.bbc.co.uk/2/hi/uk_news/1728216.stm

Kofi Annan
http://nobelprize.org/nobel_prizes/peace/laureates/2001/presentation-speech.html

Yoko Ono
http://www.a-i-u.net/yo_oct02.html

Benazir Bhutto
http://www.ppp.org.pk/mbb/speeches/speeche57.html

Nelson Mandela
http://news.bbc.co.uk/2/hi/uk_news/politics/4232603.stm

Muhammad Yunus
http://news.bbc.co.uk/2/hi/uk_news/politics/4232603.stm

The Dalai Lama
http://www.dalailama.com/news.171.htm

Al Gore
http://nobelprize.org/nobel_prizes/peace/laureates/2007/gore-lecture_en.html

Doris Lessing
http://nobelprize.org/nobel_prizes/literature/laureates/2007/lessing-lecture_en.html

Barack Obama Inauguration Speech
http://www.nytimes.com/2009/01/20/us/politics/20text-obama.html National Library of Australia
Cataloguing-in-Publication entry

First published in Australia in 2009 by
New Holland Publishers (Australia) Pty Ltd
Sydney • Auckland • London • Cape Town
www.newholland.com.au

1/66 Gibbes Street Chatswood NSW 2067 Australia
218 Lake Road Northcote Auckland New Zealand
86 Edgware Road London W2 2EA United Kingdom
80 McKenzie Street Cape Town 8001 South Africa

National Library of Australia Cataloguing-in-Publication Data:
Buttrose, Larry.
Speeches of War and Peace / Larry Buttrose.
ISBN: 9781741108361 (hbk.)
Speeches, addresses etc.
War, peace.
Other Authors/Contributors
Buttrose Larry

303.66

Publisher: Fiona Schultz
Publishing Manager: Lliane Clarke
Project Editor: Helen McGarry
Editor: Aruna Vasudevan
Proofreader: Victoria Fisher
Designer: Domenika Fairy
Production Manager: Olga Dementiev
Printer: KHL Printing, Singapore